For
Jim Lawler and Dick and Bob Shanahan,
True Brothers in Communion

Church
A Spirited Communion

Church
A Spirited Communion

Michael G. Lawler
and
Thomas J. Shanahan, S.J.

A Michael Glazier Book
THE LITURGICAL PRESS
Collegeville, Minnesota

THEOLOGY AND LIFE SERIES
Volume 40

A Michael Glazier Book published by The Liturgical Press

Cover design by David Manahan, O.S.B. Photo by Gene Plaisted, O.S.C.

1	2	3	4	5	6	7	8

Library of Congress Cataloging-in-Publication Data

Lawler, Michael G.
    Church : a spirited communion / Michael G. Lawler and Thomas J. Shanahan.
        p.   c.m. — (Theology and life series ; v. 40)
    "A Michael Glazier Book."
    Includes bibliographical references.
    ISBN 0-8146-5821-0
    1. Communion of saints.   2. Catholic Church—Doctrines.
   3. Postmodernism—Religious aspects—Catholic Church.   I. Shanahan, Thomas J., 1936– . II. Title. III. Series.
BX1746.L34   1995
262'.73—dc20   94-41758
                                                          CIP

Contents

Abbreviations

AAS   Acta Apostolicae Sedis: Commentarium Officiale (Roma: Typis Polyglottis Vaticanis)

AG   *Ad gentes,* Decree on the Missionary Activity of the Church

BEM   *Baptism, Eucharist and Ministry* (Geneva: World Council of Churches, 1982)

CD   *Christus Dominus,* Decree on the Bishops' Pastoral Office in the Church

CL   John Paul II, *Christifideles laici,* Apostolic Exhortation on the Laity

DS   *Enchiridion symbolorum definitionum et declarationum de rebus fidei et morum,* ed. Henricus Denzinger and Adolphus Schönmetzer (Freiburg: Herder, 1965)

DV   *Dei Verbum,* Dogmatic Constitution on Divine Revelation

GS   *Gaudium et spes,* Pastoral Constitution on the Church in the Modern World

LG   *Lumen gentium,* Dogmatic Constitution on the Church

MAN   *Sacrorum Conciliorum nova et amplissima collectio,* ed. J. D. Mansi (Paris: Welter, 1903-1927)

PG   *Patrologiae cursus completus: Series Graeca,* ed. J. P. Migne

PL   *Patrologiae cursus completus: Series Latina,* ed. J. P. Migne

PO   *Presbyterorum ordinis,* Decree on the Ministry and Life of Priests

SC   *Sacrosanctum Concilium,* Constitution on the Sacred Liturgy

ST   *Summa Theologiae Sancti Thomae de Aquino*
UR   *Unitatis redintegratio,* Decree on Ecumenism

All abbreviations in the Endnotes are listed without any italicized emphasis. All translations from languages other than English are the authors'. All the documents abbreviated are from the Second Vatican Council unless otherwise noted.

Foreword

We agree with Walter Kasper: "There is no doubt that the out-standing event in the Catholic theology of our century is the sur-mounting of neo-scholasticism."[1] Neo-Scholasticism sought to construct a systematic theology that would provide a timeless norm for a timeless Church, a thesis-theology in which theological posi-tions were boldly stated, logically explicated, and sweepingly de-fended against all adversaries, real and imaginary. The problem with this systematic approach was that it turned out to be not historically, and therefore not theologically, systematic enough. Though grandly conceived and grandly presented, and in its ahistorical grandeur im-pressive, the timeless norm turned out to be just too timeless. It could not stand as the theology of a Church which, far from being timeless, is inescapably time-conditioned;[2] it could not stand in the light of the real time of real Christian history.

It could not stand in the light of the fundamental Christian norm, sacred Scripture, interpreted not timelessly but according to "what meaning the sacred writer intended to express and actually expressed in particular circumstances as he used contemporary literary forms *in accordance with the situation of his own time and culture*" (DV 11). It could not stand in the light of the variegated, time-conditioned riches of the Fathers of the Church, East and West. It could not stand in the light of liturgical history, East and West, never before known or, perhaps, simply ignored. It could not stand in the light of a twenti-eth-century ecumenical openness which valued open and honest dia-logue not only between Christians, East and West, but also between

Christians and non-Christians. It could not stand timelessly aloof, finally, as religion and theology became more and more compart- mentalized in post-Holocaust Europe, postcolonial Third World, and a postmodern America. For followers of Christ, the twentieth century demanded an urgent "scrutinizing the signs of the times and inter- preting them in the light of the gospel" (GS 4). That scrutinizing and interpreting was initiated by theologians of all Christian traditions and, for the Roman Catholic tradition, was canonized by the Second Vatican Council.

In the twentieth century, the official theology of Church bodies has centered largely on ecclesiology, the theology of Church. For almost the entire century, Orthodox, Anglican, and Protestant Christians in the World Council of Churches, and especially in the Faith and Order Commission, have been studying the nature and the structure of the Church. The impetus for this work has been doubly rooted. It is rooted, first, in the desire to discover and describe in contemporary terms what the one Church established by Christ is in the plan of the God confessed as Father, Son, and Spirit. It is rooted, secondly, in the painful desire to embrace all the Churches that have arisen in history in that communion for which Christ so fervently prayed: "that they may all be one, even as thou, Father, are in me and I in thee; that they also may be in us" (John 17:21).

In the Roman Catholic Church, which initially remained aloof from this ecumenical movement, a preparatory commission for the First Vatican Council in 1870 drew up a lengthy document on the Church. It consisted of fifteen chapters to be discussed at the council, but the outbreak of the Franco-Prussian War and the invasion of the Papal States by the armies of Piedmont cut short the deliberations of the Council and permitted the discussion of only four chapters on the papacy. The result was an unbalanced theology which cast Church in hierarchical terms and as an almost absolute monarchy.

Though Pope Leo XIII in *Satis Cognitum* (1896) and Pope Pius XII in *Mystici Corporis* (1943) sought to emphasize the Church's connection to the triune God, much remained to be done to right the ecclesiological imbalance. It was no surprise therefore that, in prepa- ration for the Second Vatican Council and for the *aggiornamento*- updating called for by Pope John XXIII, a theological commission prepared a draft document on the Church. There was a surprise, how- ever, at least for those wedded to the Neo-Scholastic theology in which the document was articulated, when it was discussed at the opening of the council. The draft was roundly rejected by the council fathers and was returned to the theological commission with Pope John's words ringing in its ears. "This deposit of faith, or truths which are contained in our time-honored teaching, is one thing; the manner in which these truths are set forth with an unchanged meaning is another."[3] We believe it is fair to say that Neo-Scholasticism was rejected as the exclusive way to articulate Catholic doctrine in the rejection of this preparatory document on the Church and the preparatory document on revelation.

The Dogmatic Constitution on the Church has been almost unanimously advanced as the principal achievement of the Second Vatican Council. We agree, for two reasons: first, because of the importance of its content to the Church and the Church's mission in the world and, second, because of its central position in the entire conciliar *corpus*. In one way or another, the work of the council focused on the Church. As Pope Paul VI put it in his first encyclical, *Ecclesiam Suam* (1964), the Church was the principal object of attention of the Second Vatican Ecumenical Council.[4] The foundation of this central document, in again almost unanimous judgment, as we shall see, is the theological notion of *koinonia*, "communion." This book grows out of the ecclesiology of the council, as a systematic treatment of the Church as communion.

Though we are aware and make use of the data of disciplines other than theology (history, the social sciences, philosophy especially), this book intends to be a thoroughly *theo-logical* work. As Catholic theologians, we intend to do here not only a theology *of* the Church but also a theology *in* the Church and *from* the Church. It cannot be otherwise for Catholic theologians who are also believers. The Nicene-Constantinopolitan Creed (381), which the Church continues to pray as its Creed, states our faith here. "We believe in the Holy Spirit, the Lord, the giver of life . . . who has spoken through the prophets, and in [*eis*] the one, holy, catholic and apostolic church."

Yves Congar comments: "The preposition *eis* or *in* has usually been omitted before *ecclesiam* (church) and this fact has often been accorded a religious or theological significance. It is, in other words, possible to believe *in* God, to accept him as the end of one's life, but it is not possible to believe in the same way *in* the church."[5] Aquinas articulates the medieval tradition: "The phrase 'the holy catholic church' is to be understood to mean that our faith is in the Holy Spirit who sanctifies the church. The meaning is, therefore, I believe in the

Holy Spirit sanctifying the church."[6] It is also "I believe in the Holy Spirit who refashions life in baptism, who forgives sins, who raises from the dead and gives life everlasting."

In the Church, we receive with thanksgiving *(eucharistia)* and praise *(exomologesis)*[7] the creation, the word, the love, and the truth of God; without the Church, we would not have this sure truth. But the object of our faith is not the Church, nor is the object of our theology, Anselm's faith seeking understanding, the Church. The object of both our theology and our faith, our "comprehensive 'Yes' to God's revealing himself as [our] savior in Christ,"[8] is God and God's revelation. Our theology is truly *theou-logos,* the study of God.

This book, therefore, though it is *in* and *from* the Church, is not directly *about* the Church. It is a book about the God who is Father, Son, and Spirit, and about this God's word and truth which summons the Church in every age to hear, to serve, and to explain faithfully with the help of the Holy Spirit (DV 1, 10). It is a book about the Church only indirectly, to the extent that the Church is in communion with God. It is a book about the faith of the Church only to the extent that faith is in the God revealed and remembered in the Church. It is a book about the ministry of the Church only to the extent that the Church ministers to the people of the world the communion-life, the word, and the truth of God. It is a book about the life of the Church only to the extent that life is with and from the triune God. Because it is primarily a theo-logy, and only secondarily an ecclesio-logy, some may see it as a theology critical of present structures and practices in the Church, in the most negative meaning of the word *critical.* To them we respond, with Kasper: "A theological theology is a critical theology. In fact, it is the most critical theology of all."[9] To the extent that it values and seeks to "obey God rather than men" (Acts 5:29), it is also prophetic theology.

The fact that Pope John XXIII summoned a "pastoral" council has led to some confusion. It has even been abused by some who have argued that, since it was a *pastoral* council, it made no *doctrinal* decisions. That argument completely misunderstands the nature of the pastoral and its relationship to doctrine. There is no separation between them. The pastoral *is* the doctrinal expressing itself in practice; it *is* abstract doctrinal theory expressing itself in concrete time and history. Doctrine is not some timeless, absolute reality to be gazed at or to be chanted as a mantra. Doctrine is to be lived (cf. Matt 7:21) in every here and now, and when it is lived, it is translated into pastoral theology. There is no effective doctrinal theology without pastoral theology; there is no genuine pastoral theology unless it is firmly rooted in orthodox doctrine. Paraphrasing the opening "Message to Humanity" of the Second Vatican Council, we declare that we wish to suggest how the Church may renew itself, so that it may be found "increasingly faithful to the gospel of Christ." We seek to present to the men and women of our age God's truth for the Church "that they may understand it and gladly assent to it"[10] and be drawn to live it in both the Church and the world.

We rejoice in the freedom we enjoy as Catholic theologians. Not that it could, or should, be otherwise in a Church instituted by Christ and constituted, as we shall see, by his Spirit, for "the Lord is the Spirit and, where the Spirit of the Lord is, there is freedom" (2 Cor 3:17; cf. Gal 5:1). We embrace fully the teaching of the Second Vatican Council that "all the faithful, clerical and lay, possess a lawful freedom of inquiry and thought, and the freedom to express their minds humbly about those matters in which they enjoy competence" (GS 62). Since we embrace also, and hold as sacred, the council's central notion of communion which we shall explicate in this book, we acknowledge that our freedom is not unlimited, that it is bound at once to divine truth and ecclesial responsibility. Our book does not seek only to analyze Church as communion. It seeks also to promote communion and to avoid anything that would endanger it.

We confess that it is not for theologians to formulate the doctrine or the practice of their Church. That is for the Church-communion itself. The theologian's task, however, is critical, in every sense of that word. It is the task of "interpreting the documents of the past and present magisterium, of putting them in the context of the whole of revealed truth, and of finding a better understanding of them by the use of hermeneutics."[11] That is the task we seek to fulfill critically, but positively and not destructively, in this book. Since we do not dare, in a pilgrim Church (LG 48), to suggest that the Lord Spirit has breathed the final word about the Church-communion, we invite the reader also to be critical. Let that criticism, however, be positive and not negative, and certainly not destructive of the communion that is the Church instituted by Christ and constituted by the Spirit that is at once the Spirit of Christ, the Spirit of God, the Spirit of "righteousness and peace and joy" (Rom 14:17; cf. Eph 4:3).

1

Church as Graced Communion

Preamble

The years that followed the two world wars were characterized by
calls for renewed human community to replace impersonal institutions. Totalitarian and communist systems developed in response to
those calls, but so too did basic human communities emphasizing
common ownership, solidarity, and coresponsibility. In the Catholic
Church, this desire for genuine community provided a sociohistorical
precondition for the Second Vatican Council's vision of Church. The
guiding idea of this vision is the notion of Church as communion.
This, at least, is the opinion of the secretary of the council's central
commission, Monsignor Philips,[12] of the 1985 Roman Synod, which
judged that the council's vision of Church as *koinonia*-communion
was its most important teaching,[13] and of Pope John Paul II, who
taught in his important letter on the laity that "communion is the very
mystery of the Church" (CL 18). Cardinal Ratzinger and his Congregation for the Doctrine of the Faith agree, citing with approval in a recent letter the words of John Paul II to the bishops of the United
States: "the concept of communion lies 'at the heart of the church's
self-understanding.' "[14]

There should be today no theological doubt about the correctness
of Jerome Hamer's judgment: *The Church Is a Communion.*[15] But
there is doubt; there is still suspicion in the Church that there is something doubtfully new and nontraditional about the claim that the
Church is communion; there is still the effort, as in Ratzinger's letter,
to sustain an overly juridical vision of Church. A brief analysis of the
genesis of Vatican II's Dogmatic Constitution on the Church, *Lumen*

1

gentium, will clarify both the root of that suspicion and the fact that it is unfounded. It will show that the conception of Church as communion is not a *new*, but a *renewed*, vision in the Catholic traditions.

In preparation for the council, a central theological commission had prepared a then-traditional, post-Tridentine, Neo-Scholastic document on the Church. It was organized in four chapters, entitled "Nature of the Church," "Hierarchy in the Church," "Laity in the Church," and "States of Perfection in the Church." In 1962, during the opening session, that document was roundly rejected by the council fathers and returned to the commission to be, not just cosmetically touched up, but radically reworked to bring it in line with Pope John XXIII's call for the *aggiornamento* of doctrinal language. By the end of the second session in 1963, the document had been suggestively rearranged in eight chapters entitled "The Mystery of the Church," "The People of God," "The Hierarchical Structure of the Church," "The Laity," "The Call of the Whole Church to Holiness," "Religious," "The Eschatological Nature of the Church," "The Role of the Blessed Virgin Mary in the Mystery of Christ and the Church." This rearranged document became the Dogmatic Constitution on the Church, *Lumen gentium*, approved overwhelmingly at the council's third session on 21 November 1964 by a vote of 2151 to 5. This document became the Magna Carta for any subsequent reflection on Church in the Roman Catholic tradition.

Congar describes the transition from the preparatory document to *Lumen gentium* as a transition from the priority of "organizational structures and hierarchical positions" to "the priority and even the primacy of the ontology of grace."[16] Edward Schillebeeckx describes it as a twofold decentralization: first, a vertical decentralization from triumphalist Church to glorified Christ; second, a threefold horizontal decentralization from an exclusive focus on Roman primacy, hierarchical ministry, and Roman Catholic Church to an inclusive focus on universal episcopacy, the people of God, and other Christian Churches respectively.[17] However, a different description seems more fitting.

The transition from the preparatory document to *Lumen gentium* is a transition from a juridical vision that sees Church as institution and structure to a theological one that sees it as mystery and graced communion. It is a transition from a fixation on hierarchical office and power to an appreciation of coresponsibility and service, from an exclusive focus on Roman primacy to an inclusive ecclesial communion. It is a transition from a focus on the external reality of institu-tion to a focus on the internal reality of grace. The suggestive re-arrangement of the four chapters of the preparatory document into the final eight, and especially the emphasis intended by placing chapters on mystery and the people of God before one on hierarchy, provide ample evidence of the council's conviction that the Church is a mysterious vertical communion between God and believers, and a horizontal communion between believers, before it is a hierarchical institution.

Lumen gentium affirms that the Church is a mystery (LG 1), "a communion of faith, hope and love" (LG 8), "a kind of sacrament or sign of intimate union with God" (LG 1), a pilgrim people of God (LG 48; 9), before it has an external and hierarchical structure (LG 18). The constitution speaks at length, of course, and necessarily, of those structures. But it speaks of them only as the external sign and instrument of what really counts, namely, a people of faith and hope and love called into communion-being by the Trinitarian God to whom it is on its pilgrim way. However *renewed* that vision may be for post-Tridentine Catholics, it can hardly be considered *new*, since its themes are recovered from the early apostolic Church. Old or new, we need to consider it at some length.

Church as Trinitarian

Schillebeeckx notes correctly the vertical decentralization from Church to Christ, which *Lumen gentium* highlights in its opening sentence. "Christ is the light of the nations" (LG 1). The Church exists only since Christ, only in Christ through his Spirit, only by Christ, and only for Christ and the God he reveals. If it is ever separated from Christ, absolutized in itself, considered only in its institutional aspects, it ceases to be Christian Church and becomes just one more human institution among many in the world. The Church is not only an institution which Christ established; it is also, and mysteriously, his body in the world (LG 7; cf. Eph 1:23; Col 1:18). As his humanity provided a body for the historical Jesus, so now does the Church provide a body for the glorified Christ to continue his saving presence and action in the world. Hence it is "the universal sacrament of salvation" (LG 48), the outward sign in the world of the grace who is God's Christ. Where this Church acts for the salvation of humankind, it is Christ who acts. Where this Church preaches the gospel, baptizes, cares for the afflicted, in Augustine's words, it is Christ who preaches, baptizes, and cares.[18]

"Christ is the light of the nations." Any light in the Church is but a reflection of the light of Christ. Christ is the sun and the Church but a moon reflecting the sun's light to the world.[19] To accomplish his work of salvation, "Christ is always present in his Church, especially in her liturgical celebrations" (SC 7). He is present in his body in the Eucharist; he is present in his word. "Where two or three are gathered together for my sake," he is present with them (Matt 18:20). Christ is at the heart of the Church, indeed, at the heart of all that is Christian. "The heart of Christianity," Schillebeeckx asserts, "is not just the abiding message of Jesus and its definitive relevance, but the persisting eschatological relevance of his person."[20] There is no Church without Christ. After his resurrection, he is the head of an *ekklesia-koinonia,*[21] a fact frequently obscured by the post-Tridentine, institutional vision that dominated Roman Catholicism prior to the council. If the Church cannot be conceived without reference to Christ, neither can it be conceived without reference to the Spirit whom the Father sends in Christ's name (John 14:16, 26). It is only because, and to the extent that, it is rooted in both Christ and his Spirit that the Church can be the sacrament of salvation leading to communion with God. The Old Testament has sometimes been described as the revelation of God, the New Testament as the revelation of the Son who makes God known as Father. If that is true, then the Church is both the time and the place of the revelation of the Spirit, who makes God known as Trinity and makes it possible for women and men to share in God's Trinitarian life. *Lumen gentium* teaches, therefore, that "when the work which the Father had given the Son to do on earth was accomplished, the Holy Spirit was sent on the day of Pentecost in order that he might forever sanctify the Church, and thus all believers would have access to the Father through the Christ in one Spirit" (LG 4).

The Spirit of God is always creative. In the beginning he moved over the waters to create the world and *'ad'am,* man and woman in the world (Gen 1:2, 27). He moved over Mary to make Jesus her son (Matthew and Luke) and over Jesus to make him also Son of God (Mark), to constitute him as the Son of God for us, the Christ and the new *'ad'am* (1 Cor 15:45). In our day, he continues to create and to recreate, moving over the waters of baptism to fashion the body of the new *'ad'am,* the body of Christ, "a people made one with the unity of the Father, the Son and the Holy Spirit" (LG 4). He anoints this people to make it mysteriously *christos*, the very body of Christ,[22] and for the building up of this body "he distributes special graces to the faithful of every rank" (LG 12). These gifts are "given to everyone for profit" (1 Cor 12:45), but for the profit of the body, not for personal profit (Eph 4:12). Charism is never for personal profit. It is gift from the Spirit of God for the good of the body and all its members.

In the theology of the Latin Church, until recently, the Holy Spirit was rightly described as the forgotten God;[23] however, Orthodox theology has consistently emphasized the central role of the Spirit in constituting the Church. Orthodox theologian Olivier Clement laments the fact that "the role of the Holy Spirit—the Spirit of communion—is not more strongly underlined" in Cardinal Ratzinger's letter mentioned earlier.[24] John Zizioulas asserts that, though Christ *instituted* the Church, it is the Spirit that constantly *constitutes* it. "Institution is something presented to us as a fact, more or less a *fait-accompli*. Constitution is something that involves us in its very being, something we accept freely, because we take part in its very emergence."[25] In an ecclesiology in which a constitutive role is assigned to the Spirit, the Church is never an absolute *fait accompli*, an institution. It is always an eschatological reality, a people-to-be-constituted in communion, as we shall see, and on its pilgrim way to the triune God.

As Christ and the Spirit are at the core of the Church, so also is the eternal Father who sent and sends them both. God created "the whole world" (LG 2), planned to renew it in Christ (Eph 1:10), and to that end sent the Son into the world (John 3:17), raised him from the dead and made him manifest to Peter and to the other apostles (cf. 1 Cor 15:4; Acts 2:24). The raising of Jesus, which was accompanied by the sending of the Spirit (John 7:39), was also the creation of the Church. Without God, there would be no Church, for there would be no men and women to be gathered into a people, no Christ to fashion the people as his own, no sending of the Spirit to constitute the people-in-communion and to shower them with gifts. Everything that is Church is from this God who wishes all men and women "to be saved and to come to the knowledge of the truth" (1 Tim 2:4). It is only to the degree that the Church acknowledges and acts upon this radical theocentric character, this gracious mystery which is at and which *is* its heart, that it can claim to be Church at all.

These theocentric, Christocentric, and pneumatocentric dimensions of the Church give ecclesiology a quite different focus from the juridical and triumphalist focus of the post-Tridentine era. *Lumen gentium* declares that the primordial elements of the Church are not structures, laws, doctrines, sacraments, or hierarchical ministers, but the mysterious presence at its core of the God who is triune communion and who calls men and women to communion with one another and with God. The human desire for communion we noted at the outset is not satisfied ultimately by merely human communion. It is satisfied only by communion with God, the council teaches, echoing Augustine's ancient confession, "thou hast made us for thyself, and our hearts are restless until they rest in thee."[26]

The Church and its structures are not ultimate but only a means to communion. If the Church is to be faithful and thus survive the gates of death (Matt 16:18), it will not be because of infallible doctrine, unchanging structure, or magical sacraments. It will be because of the indefectible presence and saving action of the God confessed as Father, Son, and Holy Spirit (Matt 28:28). The novelty of *Lumen gentium* is not that it teaches new doctrine, but that it recalls the Church to a renewed contemplation of the presence of God within it and asserts that it is communion with this God that constitutes its very essence as a communion of salvation.

There are two common usages of the word *communion* in the Church. The first, holy communion, an expression for receiving the Eucharistic body of Christ, is of the utmost significance for the communion the Church is. Paul already enunciates the significance. "The cup of blessing which we bless, is it not a communion in the blood of Christ? The bread which we break, is it not a communion in the body of Christ? Because there is one bread, we who are many are one body, for we all partake of the one bread" (1 Cor 10:16-17). The council adds its judgment. "Truly partaking of the body of the Lord in the breaking of the Eucharistic bread, we are taken up into communion with him and with one another" (LG 7). The reality of communion is an essentially Eucharistic reality, in both a weak and a strong sense. The weak sense is holy communion in the sacramental body of Christ. The strong sense is that Eucharist is the sacrament, that is, both the sign and the instrument, of the communion of believers with one another and with their God in the ecclesial body of Christ. It is this ecclesial communion that leads surely to the second use of *communion* in the Church, namely, the communion of saints. The communion of believers in the body of Christ with one another and with God in Christ through the Spirit is but a guarantee (2 Cor 1:22; 5:5;

Eph 1:14) of the eternal communion with the same body and God in heaven.

Church as Mystery

As already noted, an opening chapter on the mystery of the Church was added to *Lumen gentium* in the reworking that followed the rejection of the preparatory document in 1962. The word *mystery* is used in the first chapter and four other times in the document (LG 5, 39, 44, 63), but nowhere is it defined. In 1964, however, after insistent questions, an official interpretation was provided. The word *mystery* "points to a transcendent, divine reality that has to do with salvation and that is in some sensible way revealed and manifested. The term, therefore, which is found in the Bible, is very suitable as a designation for the church."[27]

According to the council, therefore, to say that the Church is a mystery is to say, first, that in and through it a divine, salvific reality is made visible in the world. It is to say, secondly, that because this mystery is a reality in the human world it conceals as much as reveals the presence of the divine. Paul VI underscored this dimension. "The Church is a mystery," he taught, "that is, a reality imbued with the presence of God and, therefore, of such a nature that there are ever-new and deeper explorations of it possible."[28] John Paul II echoes this position: "The Church is a great mystery, and how do we communicate mystery?"[29]

The council's insistence on locating the Church in the category of mystery rather than in the category of nature was intended to direct attention to the grace at the interior of the Church rather than to its all-too-human outerness. "The Council's *aggiornamento* [updating]," Kasper notes, "consisted in the fact that it again moved into the foreground the mystery of the church, which can only be grasped in faith, over against the one-sided concentration on the visible and hierarchical form of the church, which had held sway during the previous three centuries."[30] When we look more closely at that mystery, we shall discover that it is a mystery of communion.

Church as Communion

Webster derives *communion* from the Latin *communis*, "common," itself deriving from *cum munus*, common duty, common task, common undertaking. Etymology, however, seldom tells the whole story of religious language and by itself is not an adequate guide to the Church's faith. "Communion" translates the Greek word *koinonia*, which connotes common possession, solidarity, and coresponsibility.[31] Its Latin equivalents are manifold: *congregatio, societas, coetus, adunatio, corpus, communio, populus, ecclesia,* each with a specification such as *fidelium* or *christianorum,* as in *communio fidelium,* the "communion of the faithful." The fundamental Christian meaning of communion designates the communion of the faithful with God in Christ through the Spirit, and hence their common participation in Christian goods. In that each is in communion with God, all are also in communion with one another (see 1 John 1:3, 6).

Communion in the Church is, first, with the triune God: the Creator who created men and women for participation in the divine communion (LG 2), the Son who was sent "to establish peace or communion between sinful human beings" and the Creator (AG 3), the Holy Spirit who unites the Church in "communion and service" (LG 4). It is, secondly, and as the fruit of communion with God, a communion of historical men and women with one another. The Orthodox have long honored this twofold communion as *sobornost,* communion animated by the Spirit of God.[32]

There is, therefore, ancient warrant for the official note from the Vatican Council in November 1964. *"Communion* is an idea which was held in high honor in the ancient church. . . . It is understood, however, not of a certain feeling, but of an *organic reality* which demands a juridical form."[33] This explanation makes clear that communion is not only internal, invisible, sacramental communion with God but also external communion instituted by Christ and constituted by the Spirit of Christ, and "composed of all those who receive him in faith and in love" (GS 32). It is a historical "communion of life, love and truth" (LG 9; cf. AG 19), the life, love, and truth of God in Christ through the Spirit actively shared in the communion of believers that confesses the three as one God.

This *koinonia* (communion) is already clearly exemplified in the earliest Jerusalem Church, which devoted itself to "the apostles' teaching and communion *[koinonia]"* (Acts 2:42) and "had everything in common *[panta koina]"* (Acts 4:32). Paul lets us know that the sharing in communion is not limited to a local Church but reaches out to all the Churches: the Churches in Macedonia and Achaia "have been pleased to make *koinonian"* for the Church at Jerusalem (Rom 15:26; cf. 2 Cor 8:4). He indicates the personal cost of such sharing when he praises "the generosity of your *koinonias* for them and for all others" (2 Cor 9:13).

John Paul II characterizes this *sobornost*-communion as "the incorporation of Christians into the life of Christ and the communication of that life of love to the entire body of the faithful" (CL 19). Hamer characterizes it as external communion in the *means* of grace, word, faith, doctrine, sacrament, and internal communion in the *life* of grace, loving union with the triune God.[34] We characterize it differently, distinguishing three levels of ecclesial communion.

There is a first level on which all confess the same truth, participate in the same sacraments, worship the same God. There is a second level on which all live the same Spirit-filled life, shepherded by the same Spirit-gifted authority. There is a third level on which all love and act as members of one people and one body in communion with one another and with the God who called them into, and sustains them in, communion-being as the people of God and the body of Christ. It is only this third level that gives to Churches as far apart as Scotland and Singapore more than an agreement in faith and obedience, ultimately, to the same visible head. It is on this third level that all are genuinely united in the one Spirit-constituted communion for, as we shall see in our final chapter, it is only in and through the love of the neighbor-in-communion that we can genuinely love and be in communion with God.

That is why we choose throughout the active word *communion* over the passive word *community*. History teaches us that there are many human and ecclesial groups that arrogate to themselves the name of community while they give no evidence of genuine human communication, communing, or communion. There is no genuine community without active communion, without the active and mutual sharing of life, love, and truth. "We give one another life," Jürgen Moltmann comments, "and come alive from one another. In mutual participation in life, individuals become free beyond the boundaries of their individuality."[35] We normally call this solidarity, even love. Communion always produces a community of love, but community does not always produce communion. In the people "made one with the unity of the Father, the Son and the Holy Spirit" (LG 4), communion is not optional. A consideration of that people will illuminate also the communion that is Church.

People of God and Communion

The communion that is the Church is a communion of individuals-in-relation, that is, of persons, and *Lumen gentium* selects an interpersonal people-image as its preferred image for Church (LG 9). We note this fact because it is theologically significant and, to some extent, unexpected, for prior to the council the preferred image had been that of the body of Christ, highlighted in Pius XII's encyclical *Mystici Corporis*. We must avoid an easy error here. It is easy to deal with *people of God* and *body of Christ* as if they presented us with an either-or situation, wherein one of the two is thought to be the best and even the only image for Church.[36] Nothing could be further from the truth. The two images are not in competition but are, rather, complementary"Both attempt to highlight certain dimensions of the disciples of Jesus Christ in their communion with the triune God, Jesus and one another."[37] We shall deal with each image in turn.

Since the council, there have been two misplaced emphases related to *people of God*. The first underscores *people,* whereas the emphasis should fall on *God.* The specific characteristic of the people that is Church is not just that it is a people but that it is *God's* people. Such was the Deuteronomist's message to Israel: "The Lord your God has chosen you to be a People for his own possession, out of all the peoples that are on the face of the earth" (Deut 7:6). Such also was Peter's message to the new people of God, the Church: "You are a chosen race, a royal priesthood, a holy nation, God's own People" (1 Pet 2:9). Such too was Vatican II's message: "It has pleased God to make men holy and save them not merely as individuals without any mutual bonds, but by making them into a single People" (LG 9). God calls this people into, and sustains it in, being as people-in-communion, with God and with one another. The people have no meaning, not as people, not as Church, apart from the God who is their origin and goal, their Alpha and Omega (Rev 1:8).

We must note here a theological debate over the extension of the term *people of God*. Some theologians argue that *people of God* refers to the whole of humanity, others that it refers only to the Church. There are valid arguments on both sides of this issue. Karl Rahner puts his position this way: "Based on the two coinciding facts of the natural unity of the human race and of the real incarnation of the word of God," there is a people of God long before either Israel or the Church.[38] The Church, instituted by Christ and constituted by the Spirit, is a sacrament, that is, both a sign and an instrument, of the fact that the entire human race is the consecrated, graced, and saved people of God. Yves Congar, on the other hand, while admitting that "this People of God is *de iure* [that is, by right] coextensive with humanity," suggests that there is more to being a people than simply belonging to humankind. There is required a certain structure and, in the case of the People of God, that structure results from a further initiative of God.[39]

That post-creation initiative is God's election. God was pleased "to make men holy and save them not merely as individuals without any mutual bonds, but by making them into a single people" (LG 9). God "gathered together as one all those who in faith look upon Jesus as the author of salvation and the source of unity and peace, and has established them as the Church" (LG 10). This people-Church is "the new people of God." It is "a messianic people" whose head is Christ, whose law is "the new commandment to love as Christ loved us," whose goal is "the kingdom of God" (LG 9).

Congar is right. All of humanity, created and saved by God in Christ, is *de iure* the people of God in communion. The original fall, however, detailed in Genesis, is a falling out of communion with God and with one another (Gen 3; 11:1-9). *De facto,* the people of God is the Church. That people is in the world as a "wondrous sacrament" (SC 5), that is, as both a sign and an instrument, of the reconciliation, communion, and peace to which all of humankind is called. When *Lumen gentium* uses the term *people of God,* and when we use it in this book, it is to be understood in the *de facto* sense as referring to Church and not to humankind in general.

The second misplaced emphasis related to *people of God* also falls on *people,* this time as if it referred to lay people distinct from ordained people, laity distinct from hierarchy. This misinterpretation has led to the further misunderstanding of the people of God in political categories, as a *democracy* rather than as a *communio,* and led to a call for the democratization of the Church. Nothing could be further from the meaning of the biblical and conciliar image *people of God.*

It is true that the English word *laity* derives ultimately from the Greek word *laos,* people. But, again, etymology does not tell the whole story. Theologically, *laos tou theou,* "people of God," distinguishes between those who are and those who are not God's people *de facto.* It does not distinguish between groups within the people, between laity and clergy. It denotes not parts but the whole, not distinction but communion, not individuals but persons, that is, individuals-in-relation. It denotes the whole people of God in communion. The Church is not a political democracy, which emphasizes equal *individuals.* Neither is it a political monarchy, which emphasizes unequal *individuals.* It is a *koinonia,* a communion of persons, individuals in relationship, sharing equally in the good things of the one people of God, "life, love and truth" (LG 9).

Body of Christ and Communion

Neils Dahl asserts that the difference between *people of God* and *body of Christ* lies in the fact that "the Church in the Old Testament was exhaustively expressed by the term people of God, while the Church of the New Testament is the people of God only in that it is simultaneously the body of Christ."[40] *Qahal,* the Hebrew assembly brought together by God's call (Deut 4:10; 9:10; 10:4; 18:16; 23:2-9), becomes in the Septuagint *ekklesia,* the word used also for the assembly of Christians in the New Testament (Acts 5:11; 8:3; 1 Cor 4:17; Phil 4:15). In the Old Testament, the assembly of Israel is God's people; in the New Testament, the assembly of Christians, *ekklesia* (Church), is God's people too, but only in Christ, only to the extent that they are also Christ's people. The Church of Christ is also the Church of God (cf. 1 Thess 1:1; Rom 16:16; 1 Cor 1:2; 10:32; 11:16, 22; 15:9; 2 Cor 1:1; Gal 1:13; 1 Thess 2:14; 2 Thess 1:4). *People of God* and *body of Christ* do not describe two different realities, but one reality from two different perspectives, the one people that is simultaneously Christ's and God's.

There are two different, but again complementary, themes in the development of the term *body of Christ* in the Pauline literature.[41] In the letters to the Romans and Corinthians, "the chief interest," as Heinrich Schlier notes, "is that the local Church is one body from many members, that is, it is a charismatic organism."[42] That communion of all in the ecclesial body of Christ is made visible in, and is nourished by, the communion of all in the Eucharistic body of Christ. "Truly partaking of the body of the Lord in the breaking of the Eucharistic bread," *Lumen gentium* explains, "we are taken up into communion with him and with one another" (LG 7; cf. 1 Cor 10:17).

In the Catholic traditions, sacraments do not merely manifest some reality, they also realize it, they make it concretely real. Eucharist, therefore, does not merely manifest communion in the body of

Christ, it also makes communion. In Eucharist the Holy Spirit moves believers to communion, thus constituting the *koinonia*-communion that is the Church of Christ and of God. Where Eucharist is celebrated in communion, there is wholly Church. When we say in this book that the Church of Christ is essentially Eucharistic,[43] we mean that it is in the Eucharistic meal, above all, that the Spirit of God makes believers-in-communion, thus constituting the Church.

Lumen gentium cites with approval the words of the Byzantine prayer of episcopal consecration: a bishop is "the steward of the grace of the supreme priesthood, especially in the eucharist . . . by which the church constantly lives and grows." It adds that "this church of Christ is truly present in all local congregations of the faithful which, united with their pastors, are themselves called churches in the New Testament" (LG 26). What this means theologically, as a recent letter from the Congregation for the Doctrine of the Faith explains, is that the communion that is Church "is rooted not only in the same faith and in the common baptism, but above all in the eucharist and in the episcopate."[44] While acknowledging this teaching, however, along with the further conciliar teaching that this Church is formed in and out of the Churches, *ecclesia in et ex ecclesiis* (LG 23; cf. can. 386), the letter proceeds to read this formula in John Paul II's new and inverted version, the Churches in and out of the Church, *ecclesiae in et ex ecclesia*.[45] Since this latter teaching appears to qualify that of the council, we must consider it briefly.

The congregation's letter confronts the question of unity and diversity in ecclesial communion (2), a question which, in reality, is the question of the relationship between the one catholic Church of Christ and the diverse local Churches. It develops this relationship along the lines of John Paul II's new formulation. The universal Church has priority, both temporal and ontological, over all local Churches, which develop in and from it (9), and the bishop of the universal Church, who exercises the Petrine ministry, has ontological priority over all other bishops. This line of argument permits the conclusion that a Church or ecclesial community not in full communion with the Church of Rome and its bishop is "wounded" (17). It would appear also to lead to the conclusion that local Churches are merely "parts" of the universal Church, which is then no more than a federation of local Churches, a conclusion that the letter explicitly rejects (10).

It seems to us sounder, both theologically and ecumenically, to say with the Joint Working Group of the Roman Catholic Church and the

World Council of Churches that "the universal church is not the sum, federation or juxtaposition of the local churches, but all together are the same church of God present and acting in this world."[46] The universal Church and the local Churches exist simultaneously, with no precedence of one over the other, as the very birth at Pentecost of what was at once the first local and universal Church demonstrates. The universal Church is not the sum of all the local Churches; but neither are the local Churches simply parts of a pre-existing universal Church.

Each local Church, as the ecumenical pioneer Jean Jacques von Allmen once expressed it, "is wholly Church, but it is not the whole Church."[47] That is, of course, what *Lumen gentium* also taught, though in other words. "The Church of Christ is truly present in all legitimate congregations of the faithful. . . . Christ is present [in them]. By virtue of him, the one, holy, catholic and apostolic Church gathers." The council's clinching argument is the ancient Pauline one about the body of Christ. "The partaking of the body and blood of Christ does nothing other than transform us into that which we consume" (LG 26). A local Church, gathered for Eucharist with its bishop, and because it is so gathered, is wholly the body of Christ.

A second Pauline theme touching the body of Christ emerges in the letters to the Ephesians and Colossians. While retaining the formula that "we are members of his body" (Eph 5:30; Col 3:15), a new theme is introduced, namely, that the body which is the Church has a "head," a leader, who is Christ (Eph 1:22-23; Col 1:18; 2:19). Since Christ is now risen, "the body of Christ is more clearly the risen body become the fullness of divinity, that is, the bodily instrument through which divine blessings come to the world."[48] We must, however, grasp the import of the word *body*. In Hebrew usage, "*basar* does not signify a principle or element of a human being, but rather the entire human being in its concrete individuality."[49] For Hebrews, like Jesus and Paul, the body is the person made accessible and visible, the person acting in the world. Augustine's articulation still expresses it best: "the whole Christ is head and body . . . the head the Savior himself . . . the body the Church throughout the whole world."[50]

To say, then, that the Church is the body of Christ is to say that the people in communion with Christ incarnate him, make him visible, accessible, and active in the world. After his resurrection, Christ in that body is active in the human world as a "life-giving spirit" (1 Cor 15:45), showering the members of his body with gifts "as he [and his

Spirit] wills" (1 Cor 12:11; Eph 4:11-16). "By these gifts he makes them fit and ready to undertake the various tasks and offices advantageous for the renewal and upbuilding of the Church" (LG 12). The *charismata* of the Spirit fit the body of Christ for communional[51] ministry in the fallen world. They also ensure that the body's ministry is in continuity with the ministry of Christ, for there is no ministry in the body other than Christ's ministry.[52]

Vatican II Ecclesiology

We have described the transition from the preparatory document on the Church to *Lumen gentium* as a transition from a vision of Church as structure and hierarchical institution to a vision of it as communion and grace. In the post-Reformation period, the structural emphasis was necessary to affirm, against Protestant claims, the historical visibility of Christ's Church. It was not an incorrect affirmation, but it did become an overly exclusive one. Reading nineteenth-century Roman manuals on ecclesiology, one could be forgiven for assuming that the Church was only a visible, hierarchical institution, even only pope, bishops, and priests, and nothing more. *Lumen gentium* eliminated the exclusivity of that juridical emphasis, and replaced it with a communional and sacramental emphasis. As Congar comments, "the first value is not organization, mediatorial functions or authority, but the Christian life itself and being a disciple." He adds, correctly, that "all this was evident to one who reads the holy scriptures, the Fathers of the church, even the great medieval and scholastic theologians."[53]

The modern treatment of the Church as the body of Christ emphasizes the presence of God within it, calling attention to the life of the Spirit and grace which is, therefore, available to all the members. The treatment of the Church as people of God complements this by focusing on the Church as a historical reality composed of human beings. The official theological instruction introducing the chapter on the people of God in *Lumen gentium* indicated that one of the purposes of the chapter was to show the Church as a reality being formed in history. Christ's Church is a divine-human communion, composed of a divine head and a human body. As a communion embracing historical women and men, as well as the eternal God, the Church is necessarily situated in history. At each succeeding moment of that history, it behoves it to remember its origin and its goal in God. It behoves it also to heed the council's call: "embracing sinners in her bosom, [the Church] is at the same time holy and always in need of being purified, and incessantly pursues the path of penance and renewal" (LG 8).

Lumen gentium sketches the history of God's *de facto* people, from Israel's election to the Church's election to be God's people (LG 9). This notion of election highlights the graced character of the people. It is a priestly people, "participating in the one priesthood of Christ" (LG 10); it is a prophetic people, sharing in "Christ's prophetic office" (LG 12); it is a royal people, sharing in the royal office (can. 204) of Christ the King. It is a people made priest and prophet and king by the constituting action of the Holy Spirit. Since Church leaders have not always known how to resist misreading and abusing their kingly office, it is necessary to state that this office is a sharing, not in the autocratic power of Roman emperors and seventeenth-century European kings, but in the service of the shepherd-king Christ. It is *diakonia* (service), not *dominium* (rule). The Church is called more to shepherd God's people and to nurture Christ's body than to rule over either as a divine-right monarch (cf. Acts 20:28). As Zizioulas remarks, in institution authority is imposed upon us, in constitution it springs from amongst us.[54]

For these communional priestly, prophetic, and kingly shepherd functions, the Spirit "distributes special graces among the faithful of every rank," fitting them "to undertake the various tasks or offices advantageous for the renewal and upbuilding of the Church" (LG 12). These graces or charisms are not restricted to any group in the people. They are distributed to everyone. This is what communion, people of God, and body of Christ all emphasize, that it is the people and all its members, and not only some exclusive group within the people, that is gifted and summoned to tasks commensurate to its gifts. The Church is neither a democracy nor a monarchy; it is a communion of equal believers in one people and one body.

Since the people confess God as the God of all, the *people of God* implies catholicity or universality. The people is catholic, in the general sense that "all men are called to belong to it" (LG 13); no one is excluded *de iure*. It is catholic also in the *de facto* sense that "there belong to it or are related to it in various ways the [Roman] Catholic faithful as well as all those who believe in Christ, and indeed the whole of mankind" (LG 13). The catholicity of election to the people of God *de iure* specifies the tasks of the people *de facto*. It is a "messianic people . . . a lasting and sure seed of unity, hope and salvation for the whole human race" (LG 9).

The communion-Church is, as we have seen, a "universal sacrament of salvation" (LG 48), both a sign and an instrument, of the forgiveness, reconciliation, communion, and peace between women, men, and the God who created them as *'ad'am.* Eucharist, of course, is the sacrament of salvation *par excellence,* for it is in Eucharist that the hoped-for reconciliation, communion, and peace is not only manifested but also realized. It is in Eucharist also, therefore, that the catholicity of the Church is manifested and realized.

The connection between Eucharistic reconciliation and communion and what is hoped for in the *parousia* calls attention to a final, and necessary, characteristic of the people of God in history. It is an eschatological people, a pilgrim people on its way to a land of promise not yet reached. It will attain its full perfection not in this present age but "only in the glory of heaven" (LG 48). The Church, as we have noted, is but a moon revolving around the sun who is Christ. The sun shines constantly, while the moon waxes and wanes. Because this church-moon waxes and wanes in history, because it sometimes is near to Christ and sometimes far from him, it is *ecclesia semper reformanda,* a Church always in need of renewal. It is a pilgrim people, "genuinely but imperfectly holy" (LG 48), constantly summoned by Christ "to that continual reformation of which she always has need, in so far as she is an institution of men here on earth" (UR 6).

"Faith," the people and the body confess, "is the assurance of things hoped for, the conviction of things not seen" (Heb 11:1). When faith gives way to vision, when we see face to face what we see now in a mirror dimly (1 Cor 12:12), the Church that perdures in faithful communion will be transformed by that vision. Until that moment of glory, when God will become all in all (1 Cor 15:28), the doctrine that the Church is a communion is more than a dogma to be contemplated and defended against all comers. It is a summons to all God's people to enter into reconciliation, communion, and peace, with God and with one another. It is a promise that the human desire for communion has its best hope for realization in the people who are God's people because they are the body of Christ.

Karl Rahner once said of the Chalcedonian formulation of the mystery of Jesus that it is both an end and a beginning. "We shall never stop trying to release ourselves from it," he said, "not so as to abandon it but to understand it . . . so that through it we might draw near to the ineffable, unapproachable, nameless God, whose will it was that we should find him in Jesus Christ."[55] So we say also of the Second Vatican Council's doctrine of the Church as mystery and communion. It is but a beginning in the search for the real thing, communion with God in Christ through the Holy Spirit whose desire it is to be found in the human communion that is the Church, the body of Christ and the people of God.

Summary

In this chapter, we sought to call attention to and to underscore a crucial change of focus introduced into Roman Catholic ecclesiology by the Second Vatican Council's *Lumen gentium*. That change is from a focus on Church as institution to a focus on Church as communion, from a focus on hierarchical structure and authority to a focus on the indwelling presence and grace of God. We sought to illuminate divine presence as the life-source of the Church as communion, the body of Christ and the people of God. We highlighted that people as being in communion with God and with one another, in faith, in sacrament, in discipleship, in service, and in love. Everything that follows in this book is built on this foundation.

Questions for Reflection

1. What implications result from the discussions that led the Second Vatican Council to reject its prepared document on Church and replace it with *Lumen gentium*? Do those implications affect your life as a member of the Church?

2. How do you understand the word *mystery,* and what does that understanding imply for your life as a member of the Church?

3. Reflect on the difference, if any, between the statements that the Church is a *communion* and that it is a *community.*

4. How do you differentiate the images *body of Christ* and *people of God?*

5. How do you understand Pope John Paul's teaching that the Church is "a communion of disciples, each of whom in some way is following Christ"? Reflect on the implications for your Christian life.

2

Church as Prophetic Communion

Holy Spirit

In chapter 1, we hinted at the role of the Holy Spirit in both creation and the Church, the new creation (2 Cor 5:17). In this chapter, in which we inquire into the prophetic function of the Church, we return to speak again, and in some detail, of that Spirit, for prophecy is a gift of the Spirit. "No one can say 'Jesus is Lord' except by the Holy Spirit" (1 Cor 12:10). Before we speak of the Holy Spirit, however, or before we ever speak of God, there is a religious caveat we must heed. Fully understanding God or God's Spirit lies beyond all created beings.

In various creeds, Christians confess "I believe in the Holy Spirit," but when asked to explain what that means they are at a loss. Part of the problem is that the Holy Spirit cannot be imaged or pictured as easily as Father and Son. We all know fathers and mothers and their children and, therefore, we can easily image the Father-Mother and Son we confess in the Trinity. Our image of Spirit, on the other hand, if we have one, is a faceless, formless, vaguely immaterial and, therefore, not concretely helpful image. Facelessness, however, is the least of our problems when thinking of the Holy Spirit.

The Christian tradition is united in teaching that we can easily be deceived in our imaging of God, for father, mother, son, and spirit are human images and are applicable to the divine Trinity only analogically. Theological language is not literal language, describing the way God is or was or will be. It is analogical language, simultaneously suggesting what God *is like* in image but literally *is not*. God is like a person, but is not a person in the human meaning of the word. God is like a father and a mother, but is neither a father nor a mother in the human meanings of the words.

All the great religions of the world agree on this teaching. The ancient Hindu Upanishads declare: "Who says the Spirit is not known, knows; who claims he knows, knows nothing." In the ancient Hebrew Torah God declares: "You cannot see my face, for man shall not see me and live" (Exod 33:20). The ancient Christian gospel affirms this same teaching: "No man has ever seen God" (John 1:18). Bernard speaks for the entire Western theological tradition. "I know what God is for me, but what he is for himself he knows."[56] Aquinas agrees. "Anything about God is completely unknown to men in this life; it is unknown what God is."[57] The exact nature of God, including, perhaps especially, God's Trinitarian nature, defies full human categorization, explanation, and understanding. In our effort to understand the theology of the Holy Spirit, therefore, we shall have to be attentive to the function of the theological images in which the Spirit has been presented in both the Jewish and the Christian traditions.

Aquinas is again our guide here. The article of faith is, he teaches, *perceptio divinae veritatis tendens in ipsam,* a glimpse of divine truth *tending* toward that truth.[58] Our search for an understanding of God and of God's Spirit is a search which allows us to tend toward understanding without ever being able to embrace it fully. The Second Vatican Council expresses magisterial teaching here. "As the centuries succeed one another, the Church constantly moves forward towards the fullness of divine truth until the words of God reach their complete fulfillment in her" (DV 8). That fulfillment is inescapably eschatological. "Beloved, we are God's children now . . . when he appears, we shall be like him, for we shall see him as he is (1 John 3:2; cf. 1 Cor 13:12). Rahner's exegesis of this passage is simple and succinct: "and God *is* mystery." Nothing needs to be added.

One thing is taken to be certain about the Holy Spirit in the Christian traditions, the connection between the Spirit and the Church. The Church, as we noted in the opening chapter, is said to be the time of the Spirit, as the Old Testament is said to be the time of the Father and the New Testament the time of the Son. The Acts of the Apostles portrays the Holy Spirit as the major actor in the wondrous deeds that take place within the communion of those who confess Jesus as their Christ and Lord. Prior to Pentecost, only Jesus is described as "full of the Holy Spirit" (Luke 4:1). After Pentecost, the disciples are also "filled with the Holy Spirit" (Acts 2:4; 4:8, 31; 6:5; 11:24; 13:9, 52), and they act in the power of the Spirit.[59]

In his earliest letter, the First Letter to the Thessalonians, Paul insists that the Spirit accompanies his word and makes it effective. "Our gospel came to you not only in word, but also in power and in the Holy Spirit" (1 Thess 1:5; cf. 1 Cor 2:4-5; 2 Cor 3:3-6; Rom 15:18-19). Whoever disregards his gospel-word "disregards not man but God, who gives his Holy Spirit to you" (1 Thess 4:8). In this chapter, we seek to make explicit the connection between the Spirit and the Church, between the Spirit's gift of prophecy and the prophetic giftedness of the people-in-communion. To this end, we sketch the biblical notion of the Spirit, and trace the theology of the Holy Spirit and its contribution to an understanding of the prophetic Church.

Given the rich and varied history of God's activity in the world, as we learn of it from both Old and New Testaments, it might seem presumptuous to seek to categorize that activity in a single phrase. That, however, is precisely what we propose to do. The power and the essential role of the Holy Spirit in God's creation, and in particular in God's human creation, is to move to action. Where the Spirit of God is, there is action; where the Spirit is, things happen, things get done. Where the Spirit is, in John Wesley's poetic phrase, people "feel their hearts strangely warmed." That should not come as a great surprise, for God's word is always effective. When we speak, our word is not effective; what we say does not happen without additional action. When God speaks, however, his word is effective; his word, *dabar* in biblical Hebrew, *logos* or *rhema* in biblical Greek, includes action.

We see this verified at the very dawn of creation, when "the Spirit of God was moving over the waters" and "God said 'let there be light' and there was light" (Gen 1:1-2). We see it verified in the call of every prophet, from Moses (Exod 3:1-12) to Jesus (Mark 1:9-14). We see it verified in the events surrounding the birth of Jesus, at least in Luke's original Greek, which English translations obscure: "Let us go over to Bethlehem and see this word *[rhema]* that has happened" (Luke 2:15; cf. 2:19, 51). We see it verified, again in the original Greek obscured by the English translation, in the almost boundless activity of the post-Pentecost Church (Acts 5:32). It is to be verified also in the contemporary Church-communion.

This communion of believers, in the word and power of the indwelling Spirit, is summoned as were Isaiah (6:1-13), Jeremiah (1:4-12), Ezekiel (2:1–3:11), and Jesus (Mark 1:9-15) to be "a prophet to the nations" (Jer 1:5). It is useless to counter with the obvious protest that we are unworthy or too young or too old, for the Spirit replies, "Do not say 'I am only a youth,' for to all to whom I send you you shall go, and whatever I command you you shall speak." He adds also words of consolation. "Do not be afraid of them, for I am with you to deliver you" (Jer 1:7-8; cf. Exod 3:2). The communion-Church is gathered by God's Holy Spirit to speak God's words and to do God's deeds in a rebellious world (Ezek 2:3). It is summoned, that is, to be God's prophet.

The Hebrew word *ruah,* which occurs some 378 times in the Old Testament, means "wind" or "breath" (Gen 2:7; 8:1; Acts 2:2; Rev 1:11). It is usually translated in Greek by *pneuma,* in Latin by *spiritus,* and in English by "spirit," even "Spirit of God." The wind is mysterious and wonderful; it "blows where it wills" (John 3:8). It cannot be seen or grasped, it can only be experienced in its effects; it induces wonder and awe. Gentiles honored it as a deity of nature; Israelites saw it as effecting God's saving actions in history. Wind, which moves things, warms them into life, drives them to action, is an apt metaphor for the Spirit of God. As does the wind, so also does the Spirit.

Torah never uses the expression "Holy Spirit." It speaks only of the Spirit, but it presumes that the origin of the Spirit is God. The Spirit is the power of God experienced. Since God is essentially holy (Lev 11:44; 19:2; 20:26; Isa 1:4; 6:3; Jer 50:29; Ezek 39:7), the Spirit of God cannot but be a *Holy* Spirit (Ps 51:11; Isa 63:10). There is no systematic theology of the Spirit in the Old Testament. The Spirit of God is simply the power and the action of God in history, especially in the history of Israel, in nature, and in humanity. The Spirit is God powerfully making things happen in history for the good and the salvation of God's people.[60] The presence of the Spirit can be detected in actions like the heroic feats of the Judges (Judg 6:34; 1 Sam 11:6), in ecstatic speech (1 Sam 10:10; 19:23), and in the artistic talents of artisans (Exod 35:31). It can be detected most compellingly in the words and actions of the Prophets, ancestor-figures of the prophetic Church. To understand the prophetic Church, we turn our attention first to these prophets.

Prophet

We must first dispel a common misconception, lest all that follows be misconception. Prophets are not seers. They do not *foretell* the fu-

ture; they *forthtell* the word of God. A prophet is one who speaks for
God, one to whom God's covenantal word has been entrusted to be
spoken authoritatively when men and women are driven to ask what
God intends in a historical situation. The Hebrew word for prophet,
nabi', names a person who is an intermediary between God and the
human world. Rooted faithfully in the covenant tradition (Exod 19:5;
Deut 4:13; 5:12), a prophet speaks God's word to and translates it
into concrete action for God's covenanted people.

The prophet's authority resides in his claim to be possessed by the
Spirit of God and, therefore, to be assured of speaking God's word.
The inaugural visions reported in the Bible attest to this. Isaiah's is,
perhaps, the most famous. "Then flew one of the seraphim to me,
having in his hands a burning coal. . . . He touched my mouth and
said: 'Behold, this has touched your lips; your wickedness is taken
away. . . . And I heard the voice of the Lord saying, 'Whom shall I
send and who will go for us?' Then I said: 'Here I am, send me!' And
he replied: 'Go and say to the people . . .'" (Isa 6:6-9). Jesus' baptismal vision is equally well known. "He saw the heavens opened and
the Spirit descending upon him like a dove, and a voice came from
heaven: 'Thou art my beloved Son, with thee I am well pleased.' And
the Spirit immediately drove him out into the wilderness" (Mark
1:10-11). Through such charismatic experiences, prophets were convinced of their anointing by the Spirit of God, moving them to speak
God's word to God's people.

When prophets and prophecy are referred to in the New Testament,
nothing new is intended. The New Testament authors saw the classical prophets as part of the process of God's revelation. "In many and
various ways God spoke of old to our fathers by the prophets" (Heb
1:1). They saw John the Baptist as the last in the line of the Old Testament prophets, the immediate precursor of the great prophet, Jesus of
Nazareth (Matt 21:11; Luke 7:16; John 6:14; 7:40). Though Jesus
was ultimately a puzzlement for his contemporaries (Mark 8:27-30),
he was most easily understood in the line of the great prophets of the
Old Testament.

Luke refers several times to prophets in the Church of the Acts.
Prophets come from Jerusalem to Antioch (11:27); the prophets Judas
and Silas "exhorted the brethren with many words" (15:32); the
prophet Agabus came to Caesarea from Judea and prophesied, that is,
spoke God's effective word, concerning Paul's life (21:10-11). Paul
himself values highly the charism of prophecy, always listing it second

after that of the apostle, that is, one sent to preach the gospel. "God has appointed in the church first apostles, second prophets, third teachers, then workers of miracles, then healers, helpers, administrators, speakers in various kinds of tongues" (1 Cor 12:28; Eph 2:20; 3:5; 4:11-12).

In the earliest Church, there is an order of believers called apostles; there is also an order called prophets. The title of *prophet,* as C. Perrot argues, "seems to be attached not to an individual as such, but to the order within which the individual who prophesies is situated."[61] It is a title for an order in the Church, and only to the extent that an individual belongs to that order is she or he to be called prophet. We shall see in chapter 6 that it is the same with bishops, priests, and deacons. The nature of the Church is always symbolized by orders which the Church recognizes. If there is an order of apostles in the Church, those sent to make disciples of all nations, it is only because the Church itself is apostolic. If there is an order of priests, those designated for pastor-al and cultic ministry, it is only because the Church itself is priestly. If there is an order of prophets, those gifted to forthtell the word of God in concrete circumstances, it is only because the Church itself is prophetic, sent to tell and to live the word of God to and in an errant world.

Prophets continued to arise and to be recognized in the early Church. The *Didache* establishes rules for the reception of visiting prophets and for distinguishing genuine prophets from false. "Not everyone who speaks in the Spirit is a prophet, but only if he follows the conduct of the Lord . . . every prophet who teaches the truth and fails to do what he teaches is a false prophet."[62] Polycarp is described as "an apostolic and prophetic teacher,"[63] and Justin informs the Jew Trypho that the gift of prophecy, once found in Judaism, is now found "among us" in the Christian Church.[64] At the end of the second century, Irenaeus writes that "many brethren in the Church have the prophetic charism and, in the power of the Spirit, speak in many tongues . . . revealing the mysteries of God."[65]

In the middle of the second century, the heretical movement led by Montanus, who claimed the gift of prophecy exclusively for himself and his followers, gave prophecy a bad name. Origen was led to argue that, though there was a preliminary time when prophets were necessary, they are no longer needed in a Church that possesses the clarity of Christ.[66] Miltiades, on the other hand, though equally opposed to Montanism, takes the opposite tack, on the basis that Paul teaches that "the gift of prophecy must continue in the whole Church until the coming of the Lord."[67]

Prophecy did, however, lapse in the later Christian Church, as it lapsed in later Judaism after the post-exilic restoration of Jerusalem and its Temple. In Judaism, the written word of Torah replaced the spoken word of the prophet as vehicle for the revelation of God; the prophet gave way to the scribe. In Christianity, the prophet gave way to the priest; the authoritarian word of the magisterium, the teaching Church, replaced the discomfitting word of the prophet. Avery Dulles comments that "the frequency with which prophetic spirits in the later Middle Ages ended up as heretics or martyrs (St. Joan, Savonarola) seems to indicate that the institutional church was becoming less receptive to prophetic criticism."[68] John Henry Newman and Charles Journet, at the end of the nineteenth century and in the days immediately preceding the Second Vatican Council respectively, raised the prophetic activity of the magisterium to the status of quasi-doctrine.[69] The council sought to rectify this situation and to verify the gift of prophecy in the entire contemporary Church.

In the Old Testament, prophets were anointed for their roles, ritually establishing the authenticity of their gift from God. In the New Testament, Jesus, anointed by the Spirit in his baptism and therefore Christ, *the* anointed one, is presented in this line of prophets (Matt 21:11; Luke 7:16; John 6:14; 7:40; 13:13). In his life and work, he recapitulates their life and work; their life and work of speaking and doing the word of God serves as figure of his. At Pentecost, and at each succeeding sacrament of Christian initiation, the Church is also anointed by the out-poured Spirit to continue Christ's work in history. It is within this biblical context that we are to understand what *Lumen gentium* says of the Church.

"The holy People of God shares in Christ's prophetic office" (LG 12). "Christ, the great prophet, who proclaimed the Kingdom of his Father by the testimony of his life and the power of his words," continually fulfills his prophetic office in the Church. He does this "not only through the hierarchy who teach in his name and with his authority, but also through the laity," who are to let the power of the gospel "shine forth in their daily social and family life" (LG 35). The Church and each one of its members has been called, after the model of Jesus, to be *nabi'*-prophet, to be God's spokesperson in history, to be the forthteller of God's word to the men and women of every age. Planted as firmly in its gospel root as were the Hebrew prophets in the covenant, and as anointed as they, the Church is called to speak and to act out of its tradition as God's prophet in the world.

The nature of this speaking and acting is never explicitly specified in *Lumen gentium*. It is, however, specified implicitly in *Gaudium et spes*, which describes the prophetic function of the Church without mentioning it by name. "The Church has always had the duty of scrutinizing the signs of the times and of interpreting them in the light of the gospel" (GS 4). The function of a prophet could not be more clearly delineated: to scrutinize the times, the circumstances of the times, the behaviors of the times, and to proclaim the gospel message to them. To fulfill its prophetic function, the people "is led by the Spirit of the Lord . . . to decipher the authentic signs of God's presence and purpose in the happenings, the needs and desires . . . of our age" (GS 11). The council was not as timid in speaking of prophets and prophecy as Congar believes.[70] Though it rarely speaks of them by name, it boldly speaks of what prophets traditionally do.

The council also confesses that what prophets traditionally do, forthtell what is required by the covenant or the gospel in this or that circumstance, is needed not only in the contemporary world but also in the contemporary Church. Christ "summons the Church, as she goes her pilgrim way, to that continual reformation of which she always has need" (UR 6). He summons it "to make an honest and careful appraisal of whatever needs to be renewed and achieved in the Catholic household itself, in order that its life may bear witness more loyally and luminously to the teachings and ordinances which have been handed down from Christ through the apostles" (UR 4). What the council confesses here, without ever mentioning the words *prophet* or *prophecy*, is the need for prophets to speak God's word not only to the world but also to the Church.

Even today, long after the biblical experience of the prophets, the communion-Church continues to need prophets, women and men who, afire in the Spirit, tell forth and show forth God's gospel word of communion, justice, reconciliation, and peace. God's prophets do not need to be Church hierarchs; they seldom have been. We list Ghandi, Martin Luther King, Dorothy Day, Thomas Merton, Dietrich Bonhoeffer, and Mother Teresa of Calcutta, along with countless more obscure of our contemporaries. These prophets summon us to look at ourselves and our world in the light of the God in whom we say we believe. They point out to us our failings with respect to God and urge us to move beyond them. They not only *tell forth* the word of God, they also *show forth* in their lives its implications in our world. Prophets are men and women so possessed by the Spirit-power of God that, in their words and actions, we discern the word of God spoken in the circumstances of our times. Prophets are never comfortable people to be around. Their sayings are as hard as the sayings of Jesus (John 6:60; Matt 19:10), and who can hear them save those "to whom it is given" (Matt 13:11)? It is always the breath of the Spirit that gives life (John 6:63).

It is not enough, of course, simply to name someone a prophet; a prophet, like a priest, must be called by God. "One does not take the honor upon himself, but he is called by God" (Heb 5:4). A prophet is also to be tested (1 Cor 14:29-33), for not every spirit is the Spirit of God (1 John 4:1). The rules for testing prophets laid down in the *Didache* continue to be operative (cf. Matt 7:21). These rules apply to the prophetic Church, including the magisterium. The "teaching office is not above the word of God, but serves it, teaching only what has been handed on, listening to it devoutly" (DV 10).

Newman was attracted to a Catholic Church which spoke with authority, which was ever the same, which was decisive in its statements, and which could elicit faith. His image of Church was the monolithic image rejected by the Second Vatican Council. Christ's Spirit of truth and of prophecy is given not just to the magisterium but to the whole Church. The Spirit gives gifts, including the gift of prophecy, to the faithful of every rank "for the renewal and upbuilding of the Church" (LG 12). Though the prophetic Church includes the magisterium of Newman's vision, it is not confined to the magisterium. When it comes to prophecy, there is no institutional division between those who speak God's word and those to whom they speak. The prophetic Church is the whole Church, the entire people of God and the total body of Christ in communion. That entire Church is summoned to be in communion both prophet and tester of prophets according to the established rules.

The Rule of God

Just as the Hebrew prophets called and recalled their people to covenant with God, so too the prophetic Church calls and recalls its people to covenant with God in Christ through the Spirit. It looks beyond itself to the kingdom or rule of God proclaimed by Jesus (Mark

1:15; Matt 4:17) and sees its mission as the continuation of that of Jesus, to work for the coming of that rule (LG 3; GS 45; AG 1). "Kingdom of God" *(basileia tou theou)* or, in Matthew's pious Jewish equivalent, "Kingdom of heaven" *(basileia ton ouranon)* occurs 104 times in the Synoptic Gospels. "This distribution is high and, along with the content, justifies considering the formula a theological theme."[71] To illuminate the prophetic nature of the Church, we must make a brief excursus on the kingdom-rule of God.

The Torah never uses the phrase "kingdom of God." Again, however, linguistic analysis alone does not lead to useful conclusions for, though the Torah does not use the phrase, the conviction that the God of Israel is also the king of Israel is absolutely fundamental to it. The Jewish scholar Martin Buber states it as beyond debate: "The realization of the all-embracing rulership of God is the Proton and the Eschaton of Israel."[72] The God of Israel is also the Lord and King of Israel. God rules over creation, especially over the people who are called the people of God because God has chosen them and has covenanted with them. When that people, in their piety, sought translations or *targums* from their original Hebrew, they also sought ways to avoid anthropomorphic images of God. One common way was to avoid making the word *God* the subject of an active verb. Instead of saying, for example, "God rules," they said, "the kingdom of God is here." That is the first thing we must learn. The kingdom of God is not a geographical place, either in heaven or on earth; it is not a regime, even a theocratic regime. The kingdom of God is simply the rule of God. It is, more simply still, the presence and action of God in history.

A common Christian misconception identifies the kingdom of God with heaven, and identifies it further as the goal of all earthly endeavor. There are two sources for this misconception. The first is Matthew's alternative version of "kingdom of God," "kingdom of the heavens." Pious Jewish readers of his time understood that this meant the active rule of God, but later Gentile readers have tended to understand it as simply heaven, the place where God rules eternally and where the just go after death. This understanding is reinforced by a second biblical misreading, this time of Jesus' answer to Pilate.

"My kingship is not of this world" (John 18:36), Jesus replies to Pilate in the common translation. This version, however, does not do justice to the Greek text, because it ignores the preposition *ek*, meaning "from." "My kingship is not *from* this world," Jesus says in the original Greek. The kingdom is *from* God, or *from* heaven as Matthew would have it, but it comes down to and is to be achieved ultimately on earth. Jesus teaches his disciples to pray specifically that "thy Kingdom come" (Matt 7:10). There is no place for it to come other than to earth, and this was the common Jewish teaching of the time (cf. Dan 7:13-14). The rule of God originates with God or in heaven, but its final achievement is on earth where God the Creator and Lord rules his people. *Cool!*

It is not enough, however, simply to state that the kingdom or the rule of God comes. We must also explain what comes when the kingdom comes. Again, there is no explicit, linguistic statement in the Old Testament, but there is in the New and it is supported by the entire thrust of the Old. "The Kingdom of God is not food and drink but justice/righteousness *[dikaiosune]* and peace and joy in the Holy Spirit" (Rom 14:17). It could not be stated more clearly. When the kingdom comes, when God rules, there is justice, for God is a God of justice (Deut 10:17-18; 32:4; Isa 5:16; 30:18; Jer 9:24) and God's people are summoned to justice and righteousness (Deut 16:19-20; 24:17; Isa 1:17; 16:3; 33:5; 56:1; Jer 7:5; 22:3; Hos 2:19; Amos 5:24).

When the kingdom comes, there is also peace and communion between nations and peoples and between people and God (Isa 9:5-6; 32:17; 54:10; 59:8; Jer 31:1-14; Ezek 37:26-28; Zech 8:11-12, 19). Jewish Matthew has no doubt about these characteristics. He exhorts the followers of Jesus to "seek first his kingdom and his justice and all these things shall be yours as well" (6:33); he declares blessed those who are peacemakers (5:9) and those who are persecuted for justice (5:10). The kingdom of God is, indeed, a rule of peace and justice and consequent joy.

Jesus' proclamation which introduced this section, "the kingdom of God is at hand, repent and believe in the gospel" (Mark 1:15), specifically the meaning of "is at hand," has been the subject of great debate. C. H. Dodd argued that it means that the kingdom is already come and is having its effect in the present.[73] Johannes Weiss argued that it means that the kingdom is coming, that it is near but not yet arrived, in other words that it is in the future.[74] Weiss is correct that the Greek verb *eggizo* has this future sense. Besides, Jesus taught his disciples to pray "thy kingdom come" (Matt 6:10). He taught them and us, that is, to pray in the future for the gift already present in him. The kingdom-rule of God is in Christ, it is proleptically here, but it is not yet definitively here.

When the kingdom comes, how does it come? The Lord's prayer provides us with a first answer to that question. "Thy kingdom come" insinuates a teaching in agreement with a universal Catholic teaching that everything is gift of God or grace (DS 397). The rule of God is a gift of God like everything else. It is not something that any man or woman, or any collection of men or women, including that collection we have named Church, the body of Christ, the people of God, controls to the extent of making it happen. This is important for us to understand, for all through Christian history there has been a tendency to identify the kingdom of God with this or that pet political, social, or ecclesiastical project. No human program, no matter how exalted, can be so identified. The kingdom is God's gift, not the result of human endeavor.

There is, however, a second answer to our question, deriving from the biblical milieu in which the notion of the kingdom of God arose. The members of Christ's Body and of God's people are to pray for the kingdom: "Thy kingdom come." They are to seek the kingdom and its justice and its peace (Matt 6:33; 5:9). They are to "hasten" its coming (2 Pet 3:12). This hastening, at least according to the rabbinic tradition understandable and congenial to Matthew and Peter, is brought about by the good deeds of God's people-in-communion. "If the Israelites observed one Sabbath as it should be observed," taught the Rabbi Levi, "the Son of David would come immediately."[75] The same thing can be asserted of the prophetic Church.

The Church, like Jesus, is the servant of the kingdom of God; the rule of God is what it seeks in and for human history. Schillebeeckx points out that the rule provides a central foundation for humanizing action in our world. Humanizing the world in which we live, establishing structures of love and justice, communion and peace, is not optional action. It is action which is at the core of both human history and the hastening of the kingdom of God. It is made possible, Christians confess, by the fact that the communion-Church proclaims and makes explicit the saving word of God in the midst of the human struggle to discover and to create meaning in history, which will not be complete until the kingdom of God is finally come.[76]

It is because it exists in the world, because it *is* the world in communion with God, and because, in imitation of Christ, it is to be *lumen gentium*, "light for the nations," that the Church of necessity is summoned to a prophetic role. Like the prophets, the Church is immersed in human history; it is not an outsider alien to it. We recall that the prophet does not foretell the future but forthtells the word of God in the present. That is what the Church in communion is summoned to do always, to scrutinize the signs of the times and to interpret them in light of the word of God (GS 4), to forthtell the word of God as it speaks out against injustice (GS 66), poverty (GS 70), war (GS 79), and inhumanity in all its forms.

It is more correct to say of the Second Vatican Council, not that it called the Church to a prophetic role in the world, but that it *recalled* the Church to a prophetic role it had forgotten. We hear this recall most clearly, as we have already said, in *Gaudium et spes,* where it is evident that the Church functions within and not outside the world, and equally evident that it functions not as lord but as servant of the world. How could it be otherwise for the people who are the body of the servant Christ? "Inspired by no earthly ambition, the Church seeks but a solitary goal: to carry forward the work of Christ himself under the lead of the befriending Spirit. And Christ entered this world to give witness to the truth, to rescue and not to sit in judgment, to serve and not to be served" (GS 3). Although the Church is not simply a human institution alongside other institutions, it is deeply immersed in human history where it "believes it can contribute greatly toward making the family of humankind and its history more human" (GS 40).

The fact that it is called to be a humanizing influence within human existence underscores the provisional character of the Christian Church, for everything that is human is subject to death. Along with every other reality in the human world, the Church stands under, and is judged by, the rule of God. Christ, transformed in the Spirit from death to life with God, and the Christian hope of resurrection like Christ in the Spirit, portray a wholly new conception of the Church and the world not yet finished and awaiting transformation. Jürgen Moltmann, and others who espouse a political theology for the Church, remind us of this unfinished quality of the world. The Church's prophetic mission is to proclaim in words and deeds God's word, and with them to enliven faith and hope and love in a faithless, despairing, and uncaring world. It is to effect the very transformation of all that is human from death to life in the kingdom of God. The prophetic task of the people-Church, Moltmann argues, is "to disclose to [the unfinished world] the horizon of the future of the crucified Christ."[77]

The Holy Spirit and the Contemporary Church

The source of speaking and acting for God, as we have said, is the Spirit of God. The Spirit who empowered the prophets of the Old Testament continues to empower the Church. The Spirit who is the power in the life, death, and resurrection of Jesus is the power in the Church. For the New Testament, Jesus and the Spirit are in inseparable communion. The Synoptics present Jesus as the *bearer* of the Spirit, who comes upon him in his baptism (Mark 1:10; Matt 3:16) and drives him into the wilderness and prophetic life (Mark 1:12; Matt 4:1). John presents Jesus as the *sender* of the Spirit (16:7). For Paul, the communion between the risen Jesus and the Spirit is so intimate that, after the resurrection, believers experience the Lord as the Spirit (2 Cor 3:17). The Spirit who caused the apostles to speak fearlessly, Novatian argues prior to his schism (251), "causes prophets to appear in the Church, instructs the Church's teachers, works wonders in the Church, brings about the discernment of spirits . . . and dispenses other gifts of grace."[78] Among those other gifts is the constitution of Jesus as the never-to-be-surpassed model for the Church, including the Church summoned to prophetic witness in the world.

"The holy People of God shares in Christ's prophetic office" (LG 12). It shares also the Spirit's demand that it authenticate its prophetic call with the same proof that authenticated Jesus' call and mission. "The blind receive their sight and the lame walk, lepers are cleansed and the deaf hear, and the dead are raised up, and the poor have good news preached to them" (Matt 11:5). There is much talk in our day about the Church's preferential option for the poor and unprivileged. The council declared that, with special concern, bishops "should attend upon the poor and the lower classes to whom the Lord sent them to preach the gospel" (CD 13), that "a priest has the poor and the lowly entrusted to him in a special way" (PO 6). Both the order of bishops and the order of priests, however, each of which symbolizes the communion-Church, are challenged to a special care for the poor only because the prophetic Church itself is summoned to a special care for those the world holds cheaply. Prophets, be they named Isaiah, Jesus, or Church, are always summoned to comfort the challenged as much as to challenge the comforted.

In his farewell address in the supper room, Jesus promises to send the Holy Spirit to his disciples, those to whom he speaks and those who will come after them forever. He is about to leave them, but he does not leave them orphans. "I will ask the Father, and he will give you another *parakleton* [Counselor-Advocate] to be with you forever, even the Spirit of truth, whom the world cannot receive, because it neither sees him nor knows him; you know him, because he dwells with you, and will be in you" (John 14:15-18). As he senses his end Jesus, the one in whom the divine and the human intersect, promises that the end of his life will not be the end of his Spirit-empowered work. It will continue in his disciples in the power of the same Spirit, a second Counselor-Advocate with Jesus (1 John 2:1), who will empower their work for God's rule. They will not be left alone.

A new point of intersection between the divine and the human is established after the death and resurrection of Jesus. A new body, the communion of the disciples of Christ, is overshadowed by Christ's life-giving breath, to make it the body of Christ. A new sacramentality is foreshadowed in Jesus' promise of sending the Spirit. The Spirit of God, who overshadowed Mary to make Jesus her son (Luke 1:35) and anointed him to be also the Son of God (Mark 1:10-11), will now indwell and be the life-principle of the body of believers in communion with God. God's saving work will continue in history in the work of the Church, the communion or fellowship of the Holy Spirit (2 Cor 13:14).

The Acts of the Apostles records the fulfillment of Jesus' promise to send the Holy Spirit to his disciples. "Suddenly a sound came from heaven like the rush of a mighty wind . . . there appeared to them tongues as of fire, distributed and resting on each one of them. And they were all filled with the Holy Spirit" (Acts 2:1-4). Peter interprets this event as the outpouring of the Spirit celebrated by Joel, as a result of which "your sons and daughters shall prophesy" (Acts 2:17). Now, like Jesus, the disciples will be "led by the Spirit" (Matt 4:1) to speak and act for God in the world. In the power of the Spirit, they have moved from the relative security of the closed supper room to the insecurity and challenge of life in a world open to everything except the word of God. The Pentecost experience was not only the beginning of the Church; it was also the beginning for the Church. It was the beginning of the task of incarnating Christ in the world, a task that continues to challenge the security and comfort of the Church-communion today.

The presence and action of the free Spirit of God in the world is, of course, never to be restricted to the Church. As we saw in the opening chapter, the Spirit of the new creation, the Church, is equally the

Spirit of all creation. The life-giving power of Pentecost, none the less, continues to enliven the Church, and through the Church the world. The communion-Church, the temple of the Spirit (1 Cor 3:16; 6:19), is not just the example but also the sacrament of the re-creation of all things. When it gathers for Eucharist, it prays that communion be established in the Spirit. "Grant that we, who are nourished by his body and blood, may be filled with the Holy Spirit, and become one body, one spirit in Christ." When the disciples of Christ gather to keep memory of him sacramentally, the Spirit-power of God makes them sacramentally communion, Church, body of Christ, people of God, prophet "to love and serve the Lord."

The Church is in communion with God through the breath of the Holy Spirit of communion. Through the rituals of Christian initiation, the believer is incorporated into the communion of the Trinity, an incorporation which the earliest Church, especially in the East, named *divinization*. This divinization, however, is, paradoxically, equally humanization. It does not make either the individual believer or the communion of believers divine, for only God is divine. It does make both fully human. The Spirit "fully reveals man to man himself" (GS 24) and, by making men and women fully human, introduces them into the very life of God.

The Holy Spirit, promised in Jesus' last will and testament, was given to his disciples on the first Pentecost. They were transformed from a group of people locked in fear in a closed supper room to a communion of disciples afire with God's Spirit. Having received the promised Spirit, like the prophets of the Old Testament, they were driven to share God's word and actions with others. They were set aflame by the breath of God and driven to speak and to act out of the Spirit's fire. There was no assurance of ease or of success in preaching and living the good news of God in Christ. In a world in which God respects human freedom, there were and there are as many failures as successes.

The disciples were assured, however, of the continuing presence of the Holy Spirit in the Church until the end of time. "I will be with you" (Exod 3:12; John 14:17) is almost a divine name; the Christian God is God with us, Emmanuel (Matt 1:23). The Church-communions that followed the Spirit-powered, and therefore prophetic, work of the apostolic Churches shared in the inheritance of the Spirit's prophetic breath. The very same Spirit who "spoke of old to our fathers by the prophets" (Heb 1:1), and who made the Church one, holy, catholic, and apostolic in the past, continues to speak through the Church today, distributing gifts to believers of every rank, fitting them for the task of "the renewal and upbuilding of the church" (LG 12). The challenge for the Church-communion today is the same challenge it received yesterday, the challenge to be the Holy Spirit's prophetic voice and action within human history. It is also Christ's missionary challenge to "make disciples of all nations, baptizing them in the name of the Father, and of the Son and of the Holy Spirit" (Matt 28:19).

Summary

This chapter focused on two theological realities, the Spirit of God, who is also the Spirit of Christ and the Spirit of prophecy, and the Church-communion which this Spirit indwells as life-principle and calls to be God's prophet in the world. From the example of Old Testament prophets and the New Testament prophet, Jesus, it is clear that prophets do not foretell the future. Authentic prophets, according to the rules laid down by the *Didache,* forthtell the word of God in this or that circumstance and live according to that word. The gospel story sees Jesus in the line of the great Jewish prophets, proclaiming the word and the rule of God in both word and action. It sees him as possessed by the Spirit of God in his Jordan-baptism, and anointed for his prophetic office. The same Spirit possesses believers and the communion of believers in the sacraments of Christian initiation, and anoints them for their prophetic office in the footsteps of Jesus.

We considered the prophetic office of the Church in relation to the kingdom of God proclaimed by Jesus. The kingdom of God is not a place; it is the rule of God in the world. It "is not food and drink," Paul insists, "but justice and peace and joy in the Holy Spirit" (Rom 14:17). The prophet Jesus spoke words and did deeds of justice and peace, of reconciliation and communion, and the prophet Church is called to do the same, to hasten the rule of God in the world. The Spirit who indwells believers and the Church incorporates them into the life of God, not to make them divine but to make them fully human in the mold of Jesus. Fully humanized, they are then to be in the world as a prophetic *lumen gentium*, a light to the peoples of the world.

The short opening excursus on theological language, which does not exhaustively grasp the truth of God but only tends toward it, tempers everything we say in this chapter and in this book.

Questions for Reflection

1. How do you understand theological language? What are the implications of this understanding? Can you distinguish the kind of information given in theological language from that given in other academic disciplines?

2. Reflect on the images in which the Holy Spirit is spoken of in the Old and New Testaments. What do you learn from these images?

3. What does it mean to you to say that someone is a prophet? Besides those named in the text, whom do you consider a modern prophet? By what criteria?

4. Reflect on the Church and the kingdom of God. Are they identical? How can the relationship between the two be best expressed?

5. What does it mean to you when you hear that the Holy Spirit is the life-principle of the communion-Church? What are the signs that the Church is responding authentically to the presence of the Spirit within it?

3

Church as Sacramental Communion

Sacrament

In the opening chapter, we dealt with the Church as mystery, a reality imbued with the presence of God. *Mystery* was not originally a theological word. It derives ultimately from the Greek *muein,* to close or to shut, to close one's lips, for instance, and therefore to keep a secret. It derives proximately from *mysterion,* which itself derives from *muein* and which came to mean a secret, something hidden, something not fully manifest and, therefore, not fully intelligible. We find this meaning of mystery used theologically in both Old and New Testaments.

In Daniel, *mysterion* denotes God's secret plan for the end times and the revelation of this plan (2:18-19, 27-30, 44-47). It means the same in Paul, who specifies that the plan revealed through the prophets and the apostles (1 Cor 2:7-10; Rom 16:25-26; Col 1:26-27; 2:3; 4:3; Eph 1:9-10; 3:3-12; 1 Tim 3:16) is to save humankind in Christ. The mystery is revealed to those of mature faith (1 Cor 2:6) and to spiritual persons (1 Cor 3:1), because only those who are Spirit-filled receive the knowledge that the Spirit gives. In Ephesians, marriage is called a secret symbol *(mysterion)* of the union between Christ and the Church, a secret originally hidden but now revealed (5:32). Neither in this nor in any other biblical text does *mysterion* ever refer to those rituals which today are called sacraments.

This brief excursus on the Christian meaning of *mystery* was necessary because the Latin word *sacramentum,* which is at the heart of this chapter, translates the earlier Greek *mysterion. Sacrament,* therefore, is to be understood as *mysterion,* a secret revealed in part, leaving "ever-new and deeper explorations of it possible."[79] It is in this biblical sense of a mystery-secret revealed in Christ, and not in the precise, technical sense of the later, theological definition, that the Church is said to be sacrament. This meaning of mystery and sacrament, and the dimension of both that requires ever-new and deeper exploration, must be kept in the forefront as this chapter progresses.

Like *mysterion, sacramentum* was not originally a theological word. It was in common use in classical Rome, with two meanings. It meant the oath of loyalty taken by soldiers, both the oath and the soldier being considered as consecrated to the gods. It also meant a deposit of money pledged by each party in a civil lawsuit and forfeited to the state by the loser. This money was deposited in the temple and was also, therefore, regarded as consecrated to the gods.[80]

 Tertullian, a third-century African (d. ca. 225), is the first theologian to use *sacramentum* in reference to the Christian rituals of baptism and Eucharist. Baptism, he argues, is a sacrament analogous to the soldier's oath. As a soldier pledges allegiance to his leader and is thereby consecrated, so a Christian pledges allegiance to Christ in baptism and is thereby consecrated to Christ and to his God.[81] Eucharist is also a sacrament, but in a different way; it is a sign of something, better of someone, who sanctifies Christians.[82] This double meaning of sacrament as both a signifying and a sanctifying reality was developed in North Africa by Cyprian of Carthage (d. 258) and Augustine of Hippo (d. 430), and was eventually enshrined in the Western tradition in Peter Lombard's definition. A sacrament is "a sign of the grace of God and the form of invisible grace in such a way that it is its image and its cause."[83]

In Lombard's definition, *mysterion* became definitively *sacramentum,* a reality imbued with grace, "God himself in his forgiving and divinizing love,"[84] and both a sign and an instrument of that grace in the world. To characterize any reality as a sacrament is to assert two things: first, it is a reality imbued with grace, and second, it is both a sign and an instrument of that grace. To characterize the Church as a sacrament is to say, therefore, that it is a mystery, a reality imbued with the grace of God and both a sign and an instrument of that grace in the world.

Church as Sacrament

Thomas Aquinas has no doubt about the validity of the tradition initiated by Tertullian and Augustine. "Sacraments belong in the category of sign."[85] Not every sign, however, is a sacrament, but only that sign "which is a sign of the sacred in so far as it [the sacred] sancti-fies man."[86] Sacraments are not only signs of grace, they are also causes of graces; they doubly contain grace, as Trent would later teach, by both signifying and causing it.[87] Sacraments, indeed, cause by signifying, they effect what they signify; they are not only signs of grace but also *efficacious* signs. In such aphorisms, we must under-stand, the Catholic Church is asserting that it is the sacred reality sig-nified that causes grace, not the sign itself. Though the sign is an instrument of God in Christ,[88] the principal cause of the sanctification of men and women is always God in Christ through the Spirit, not the sign or sacrament. So it is with the sacrament named Church, whose sacramentality derives from everything we said in the opening chapter.

The Second Vatican Council insisted on the mystery of the Church, and we have established the linguistic connection between mystery and sacrament. The linguistic connection, however, does not consti-tute the Church as sacrament. Epistemology derives from ontology, knowledge and language from being. The Church is a mystery, the council teaches; "a reality imbued with the presence of God," Paul VI explains. There is a mysterious divine innerness to the Church as well as an obvious human outerness, and the former is ontologically prior to the latter. The relationship of these inner and outer dimensions constitutes the Church as sacrament.

Kasper argues that "the definition of church as universal sacrament of salvation is one definition among others."[89] While we acknowledge the element of truth in that judgment, and have indeed argued a sim-ilar position in the preceding chapter, we align here more with Otto Semmelroth. The designation of Church as sacrament is not just one more image of Church among many, not just one more model in Dulles's sense.[90] Rather it "is the meaning and ontological sense of the mystery expressed in the statements found in revelation about the church." The essence of sacrament "is to bind together a complex of realities, interior and exterior, human and divine, in the relation of sign to signified, of cause to effect."[91] The characterization of Church as a sacrament makes explicit the connection between its divine inner and human outer dimensions. The human dimension of the Church, the women and the men who comprise it and the Christ-like life they live in communion, is the efficacious sign of God's saving presence in the world. It is, in the traditional words, the visible or outward form of invisible grace.

We note two false approaches to the understanding of Church in modern ecclesiology. One approach, which views the Church as *only* a social institution, is exemplified in Bellarmine's definition. "The Church is a body of men who, bound together by the confession of a Christian faith and the partaking of the same sacraments, stand under the direction of their lawful pastors."[92] This approach emphasizes institution and what institution does, which in the case of Christ's Church usually means teaching, sanctifying, and governing. It divides the Church into those who teach and those who are taught, those who sanctify and those who are sanctified, those who govern and those who are governed. The preparatory document on the Church for the First Vatican Council enshrined this view, teaching that "the church of Christ is not a society of equals as if all the faithful in it had the same rights. It is a society of unequals . . . because in the church there is a power from God whereby some are authorized to sanctify, teach and govern, and others do not have this authority."[93]

Though it would be an injustice to suggest that Bellarmine did not understand the inner dimension of the Church, his definition took no account of it, and led to a seemingly exclusive emphasis on the outer dimension. It led to the conception of the Church as a "perfect society," a replication of the society in which he lived, in which it was taken for granted that the power of hierarchs derived directly from God and was exercised over common people by divine right. This vision dominated Catholic manuals on ecclesiology and the preparatory document rejected by the Second Vatican Council as clericalist and juridicist.[94] The council's demand for an approach to Church as mystery was a demand to move away from this one-sided view, and we must keep this fact in mind if we would understand the council's teaching on the Church as sacrament. The sacramental approach assigns an important place to external structures, but it insists that these are neither primary nor ultimate, that they are but the outward sign of the inner, divine core of the Church, the triune God indwelling it.

The sacramental approach is firmly embedded in the basic Christological claim that Christ, not the Church, is the *primal* sacrament of grace. Indeed "it was from the side of Christ as he slept the sleep of death upon the cross that there came forth the wondrous sacrament which is the whole Church" (SC 5). Christ is "the author of salvation and the source of communion and peace," the Church only "the visible sacrament of this saving communion" (LG 9). The claim that the Church is a sacrament does not dispute, but rather highlights, Christ's pre-eminence. Christ, as we argued earlier, is the sun that lights the world, the Church but a moon reflecting the light of this sun.

The treatment of Church as a perfect society was a Catholic overemphasis. The Protestant corrective was an overemphasis on the true Church as an invisible communion of believers in Christ, in Paul Tillich's phrase, a spiritual community.[95] This facilitated an erroneous distinction between the invisible, true Church and the visible, errant Churches, which were regarded as merely human institutions. The invisible, spiritual community is one; the visible Churches are not and need not be one.

In *Mystici Corporis,* Pius XII explicitly rejected this notion of an invisible Church separate from the visible Catholic Church. "They err in a matter of divine truth," he taught, "who imagine the Church to be invisible, intangible, a something merely pneumatological."[96] The notion of sacrament gives ontological validity to his argument. Though there is an invisible dimension to the Church, the indwelling presence of the Christ, the Father who sent him, and the Spirit who is sent by both, this is not simply the Church. The true Church is a mysterious communion of this invisible God and the visible believers who embody God in the world. The Church is simultaneously, as the biblical notion of body of Christ suggests (cf. 1 Cor 6:12-20; 10:17; 12:12-27; Rom 12:4-5; Eph 1:22; 2:14-16; 3:6; 4:4-16; 5:22-30; Col 1:18, 24; 2:19; 3:15), outward sign and inner divine presence or grace. As such it is, as Vatican II taught, a mystery and a sacrament.

We recall here the explanation of *communion* given by the Second Vatican Council: "It is an *organic reality* which demands a juridical form, and is simultaneously animated by love."[97] The theological notion of sacrament underscores this organic reality. The Church is not a human institution and a divine presence at work side by side in the world, but a communion in which the divine and the human so interpenetrate that the result is an organic unity. One Church, one people, one body, in which the divine and the human intersect and interpenetrate as Cause and effect, as Grace and graced, as Reconciler and reconciled, as Communion and communion.

As sacrament, the Church, the people in communion with God in Christ through the Spirit, proclaims, makes explicit, and celebrates the presence in its depth of the God who is Love and loves (1 John 4:16). Little wonder that the people are in loving communion also with one another and with the world in which they live. Little wonder that they comprise a communion of faith and life and love (LG 9;

AG 19). As sacrament, the Church proclaims, makes explicit, and celebrates the presence in its depth of the God who is Salvation and saves. Little wonder that the people in communion with this saving God comprise a communion of salvation, a true "sacrament of salvation" (LG 48; AG 5). As sacrament, the Church proclaims, makes explicit, and celebrates the presence in its depth of the God who is Grace and graces. Little wonder that the people comprise a communion with Grace and a communion of graces, common faith, common sacrament, common discipleship, common service, and common love. We shall have to ask in detail how those goods relate to sacrament. Before we do, however, we must first inquire into a general sacramental principle that has implications for any claim, including that of the Church, to valid sacramentality.

Sacrament and Personal Disposition

Since the Council of Orange, in 529, the Catholic tradition has doctrinally recognized that sanctification and salvation are both always graces, always gifts from God, but also always gifts which believers must themselves realize in free cooperation (DS 397). Every saving event has these two dimensions: the self-gift of God through Christ in the Spirit and the free acceptance of this gift by believers and their self-gift in return through Christ in the Spirit to the Father. The saving event that is a sacrament is no exception, not even that sacrament called Church. Church is not simply a thing that believers might receive, nor simply a social institution to which they might belong or in which they might gather. It is, rather, an interpersonal and graced communion in which they reveal, make explicit, and celebrate the gift of God, their acceptance of the gift, and the gift of themselves in return. It is only thus that it can be sacrament.

As divine-human interactions, sacraments necessarily encompass three components: God, believers, and the actions in which they interact. By definition, believers' actions are sensible and immediately accessible; God's actions are nonsensible and, therefore, not immediately accessible. In sacrament, the two are essentially related as sign and signified; believers' solemn actions in the Church are "a sign of the grace of God and the form of invisible grace."[98]

There are three, complementary, theological theses to be considered in relation to the claim that the Church is a sacrament. The first thesis is that personal faith is required for salvation. One cannot read the New Testament without being impressed by its emphasis on the necessity of faith for salvation. The Gospels record that Jesus complained about the absence of faith and just as insistently praised its presence (Matt 8:5-13, 23-27; 9:2, 20-22; 17:19-21; 21:18-22; Mark 5:25-34; 6:1-6). Paul vehemently defended the necessity of personal faith for salvation (Rom 1:16-17; 3:26-30; 5:1; Gal 3:6-9). The tradition of the necessity of faith continued in the Church and flowered on both sides of the Reformation controversies.

Martin Luther (d. 1546) made his stand on *sola fides,* teaching that faith alone is required for salvation. Though wishing to combat this Lutheran teaching, the Council of Trent left no doubt about the necessity of faith. "We may be said to be justified through faith, in the sense that 'faith is the beginning of man's salvation,' the foundation and source of all justification, 'without which it is impossible to please God' (Heb 11:6) and to be counted as his sons" (DS 1532). The same teaching is repeated in the important chapter on justification where baptism is described as "the sacrament of faith, without which no man has ever been justified" (DS 1529). The Latin text leaves no doubt that the phrase "without which," *sine qua,* qualifies faith and not sacrament or baptism, both of which would require *sine quo.*[99] There can be no doubt that the fathers of Trent wished to affirm the necessity of active, personal faith for salvation.

This firm Tridentine position notwithstanding, the polemical context of the times created an uneasiness in Catholic assertions about faith and its place in the process of salvation and sanctification. Following Trent's lead of isolating and highlighting, in order to condemn, the error in the assertions of the Reformers, Counter-Reformation theologians advanced their theologies as counterpoint to those of the Reformation. This strategy created a narrow approach to theological questions, but nowhere is this approach more evident or more harmful than in sacramental theology, specifically in the role of personal faith in sacramental activity. We can detect that harm crystallized most clearly in a restricted understanding of the nature of the sacramental rite, the Scholastic *opus operatum.*[100]

Our second thesis is that the faith of the participant is required for the validity of any sacrament. In the years immediately preceding the convocations at Trent, nominalism was rampant in the theological disciplines. Nominalist theologians taught that all a person receiving a sacrament need do was to place no obstacle to grace. This meant simply being free from mortal sin; grace was then conferred by the mere physical positing of the rite. It was such a mechanical, quasi-magical[101] understanding of sacrament that provided the basis for the objections of the Reformers about automatic grace, and led to their rejection of the efficacy of sacraments. Since nominalist theologians were in the majority at Trent, it was the nominalist definition that became *"the* exhaustive definition of the *opus operatum* of the efficacy of any sacrament."[102]

No real dichotomy between the rite and the contribution of the recipient to the rite, *opus operatum* and *opus operantis* respectively, can be found in the theological thinking of the great Scholastics. Aquinas frequently uses the concept *opus operatum* in his early *Commentary on the Sentences,* but never in his final work, the *Summa Theologiae.* This may indicate that he did not consider the term necessary to the presentation of a mature sacramental theology. "The truth that this terminology was intended to bring out was presented satisfactorily, and even in finer detail, in his Christological appreciation of the sacraments."[103] A valid sacrament is an action of God in Christ.[104]

It is true that Aquinas distinguishes two separate effects of sacraments. There is, first, the *perceptio sacramenti,* the reception of a valid sacrament, which he teaches is quite unrelated to the faith of the participant. There is, second, the *perceptio rei sacramenti,* the fruitful reception of sacramental grace.[105] Insofar as he teaches the validity of a sacrament without any contribution on the part of the participant, this must be understood in its own context and not in that of a later, more juridical theology. The latter views sacrament as simply a thing, which owes its reality to the fact that it is an action of God in Christ and, therefore, valid *qua* sanctifying thing irrespective of any contribution from the participant or the minister.

Though he subscribes to the established view, Aquinas also has no doubt about the abnormal character of a one-sided hypothesis. "Every sacrament for him remains a sign and a proclamation of personal faith. Whoever receives it without believing in his heart places himself in a violent state of 'fiction' and deprives himself of sacramental grace."[106] *Opus operatum* and *opus operantis* were not dichotomized for Aquinas as they were to be later in the Counter-Reformation Church. They were essentially related. The latter was regarded as the "personal aspect in the justifying process of any sacrament, that aspect by which a responsible person accepted God's grace" offered in the former.[107] A sacrament is a sign, not only of the grace of God in Christ but also of the participant's faith-filled desire for that grace.

The doctrinal fact that opened this discussion is that men and women are free persons and are graced, not against their will, but according to their free cooperation (DS 373-97). If they have no intention of personally participating in a sanctifying interaction, then no mere physical submission to a physical rite will constitute for them a saving sacrament. In such a case, though we have no doubt that a sacramental *opus operatum* is objectively offered by God in Christ in the Church, we equally have no doubt that it is not participated in by the subject. The sacrament offered in the Church still signifies the saving action of God in Christ, but not as *concretely* significative, and therefore effective and sacramental, for this subject. The cooperating participation of the subject transforms an objective sign into an efficacious sign of the action of God in Christ. It transforms it into a valid sacrament.[108]

It is for valid signification and, therefore, valid sacramentality that the faith of the participant is required. The participant "must signify genuine acceptance of what the church offers. Otherwise the sacrament is not a *concrete, practical* sign of the divine will to save all men."[109] Since the Catholic tradition of the past millennium universally accepts that sacraments cause by signifying, when they do not signify neither do they cause, and when they do not cause, they are not valid sacraments. It is not just, as Thomas and the Counter-Reformation theology that claimed to follow him argued, that they are valid but fruitless. They are fruitless precisely because they are not valid sacraments, that is, efficacious signs. The personal disposition of the participant is required to make a sacrament fruitful because it is first required to make a sacrament a concrete and *valid sign.*[110]

A sacrament that is fully a sacrament is a sign, not only of the gracing action of God in Christ but also of the free action of the participant cooperating with grace. A true sacrament requires the conjunction of both, and only in such conjunction is there free, and therefore valid and fruitful, encounter between human beings and God. As Aquinas taught long ago: the passion of Christ, the saving activity of God, "achieves its effect in those to whom it is applied through faith and love and the sacraments of faith."[111]

Our third thesis is that the personal faith of the participants is necessary for the genuine sacramentality of the Church. If what we argued in the preceding sections is valid, then this thesis is already demonstrated. The active faith of the participants is an essential prerequisite not just for the fruitfulness of a sacrament but also for its very validity. Today, the faith-situation of those who claim to belong to the Church is anything but clear, and the Church and its theologians recognize two kinds of baptized, believers and nonbelievers.[112] The two are easily distinguished theologically on the basis of the presence or absence of active personal faith.

In any given case, of course, the active faith or nonfaith of a baptized person, and the various shades in between, will not be easy to ascertain. No amount of legal presumption, however, will ever supply for lack of active faith and consequent lack of sacramentality. Convinced of the necessity of faith for valid baptism, Augustine sought to make good the evident lack of the infant's faith in baptism by arguing that the faith of others, at root the faith of the Church, made good the infant's lack.[113] That argument cannot be applied in the case of adults, who are required to have an active faith to participate in any sacrament, even in baptism, as the scrutinies at the baptism of adults show.

Human communion becomes Christian communion and sacrament, not because of some juridical effect of baptism, but because of the active Christian faith of the communers. Those who claim to be in the Church without active Christian faith, be they ever so baptized, cannot be in the Church as *Christian* sacrament. The validity of this assertion follows from a brief consideration of the adjective *Christian*. *Christian* embraces explicit reference to Jesus, confessed as the Christ; to the Holy Spirit, confessed as the Spirit of God (Rom 8:9; 1 Cor 2:11, 14; 12:3; 1 Pet 4:14; 1 John 4:2) and the Spirit of Christ (Rom 8:9; Phil 1:19; 1 Pet 1:11); to the Father who sent and sends them both; and to that communion-people called Church, which is actively confessed as Christ's body enlivened by the Spirit.

In his magisterial *Jesus,* Schillebeeckx argues that "the heart of Christianity is not just the abiding message of Jesus and its definitive relevance, but the persisting eschatological relevance of his person."[114] The person of Jesus the Christ, not just his memory or his message, is at the heart of everything that is Christian, including Christian sacraments, including the sacrament that is Christian Church. The adjective *Christian* links Church to Christ; it specifies Church as a Christ-event like any other sacrament. The intention to participate in any sacrament is the intention to participate in such a Christ-event. The intention to participate in the sacrament of the Church is the intention to participate in, not merely human communion, but specifically Christian communion confessed as a Christ-event. In J.-M.R. Tillard's words, "The request for a sacrament can never be the request for a purely external ritual that has no connection with the mystery of salvation. The request for a sacrament is a request for a 'rite that gives salvation.' "[115]

"Lumen gentium Christus est," proclaimed the Second Vatican Council. Christ is the light of nations, Christ is the sun and the Church but a moon reflecting that sun's light (LG 1). All of this, Christ-sun and Church-moon, and not just human communion, must be embraced in the intention to create Christian sacramental communion. Human communion becomes sacramental Church only when the members freely consent to commune "by passing through Christ into whom they were incorporated in baptism."[116] The key that opens the door to sacramentality is not just the intention of men and women to be in communion with one another, but rather their intention informed by faith to be rooted in, to represent, and to live their life in Christ and in his Church. Consent to commune together may make social institution, but it is only Christian faith, a "comprehensive 'yes' to God's revealing himself as man's savior in Christ,"[117] that makes Christian communion and sacrament.

Ladislas Örsy states broadly the relationship of faith and sacramental validity. If the baptized person "has never accepted the Christian mysteries as real gifts from God, or never accepted God as revealing himself in human history, how can he responsibly and freely give and take the sacrament?"[118] If he has not, in faith, accepted the mysteries of God in Christ in the Church, how can he ever accept human communion as a Christ-event, a salvation event, a "sign of the grace of God and the form of invisible grace"? Tillard states the relationship more precisely. "The request for a sacrament is always the request for a 'rite that gives salvation.'" If it is not the request for a salvation rite, then it is "not a request for a sacrament in the strict sense" and what the Church offers "will not be 'sacramental' for him."[119] The personal disposition of the baptized, minimally believing in, loving, and living in the Spirit like Christ, is required for the mystery-Church to be Christian sacrament.

There is no theological debate about whether or not personal faith is necessary for sacramental validity. It is taken as a given that it is. The debate is about what qualifies as faith. Some judge that faith cannot be reduced to "an explicit and conscious act of faith," and that a person "can possess the habit of faith . . . most especially through baptism."[120] This habit seals the new Christian's condition as "believer." That judgment, we believe, rests on a classic Scholastic distinction which opens the word *fides,* "faith," to serious ambiguity and misunderstanding.

In the tradition derived from Scholasticism, *faith* is used both analogically, *virtus fidei,* the power of faith, and univocally, *actus fidei,* the explicit and conscious act of faith. A *virtus* is a habit,[121] a quality[122] ordered to an act;[123] it is a power to act. A virtue is a necessary prerequisite to the corresponding act, but it is not the act nor does the act ineluctably follow from the virtue. The Catholic tradition holds that it is the virtue of faith that is bestowed in baptism.[124] For that virtue to become a personal act of faith, it must be activated, freely, explicitly, consciously, and however minimally. It is a personal act of faith, always under the grace of God, that transforms the human being from a potential believer into an actual believer. It is in such active personal faith, and not just in the virtue of faith, that a believer cooperates with God-in-Christ, Christ-in-the-Church, and the Spirit-in-Christ-and-in-the-Church in the transformation of secular realities, including human communion, into Christian sacraments. It is such active personal faith, again however minimal, Aquinas insists, that is required for right sacramental intention.[125]

To conclude this section, we return, as promised, to the communional goods already highlighted as shared by the members of the Church. We need to explicate them further in the light of the preceding discussion of personal disposition and its place in sacramentality.

The first good is communional faith, not the virtue of faith received in baptism but an act of faith, an active yes to the triune God revealed in Christ and to the communion that is people of God and body of Christ in the world. That yes is to be not only intellectual but also personal assent. It is an assent, that is, that makes on the one giving it the kinds of practical demands discussed in the preceding chapter. It is only in fulfilling these practical demands, in performing faith-filled actions, that the Church is the sacrament of Christ in the world. If all it offers is talk, however beautiful, then there is no sacrament.

The second good, communional sacrament, is one of those practical demands. When we say "communional sacrament," we mean two different, but related, things. We mean, first, that believers are called to participate actively in the sacramental life of the communion. Incorporated in baptism into the Church, and also into the life of God, they are "sealed with the gift of the Holy Spirit"[126] in confirmation, built up in communion in Eucharist, and sent forth from each as disciples, servants, and prophets to love and serve the Lord and one another. Cut off from communion by sin, they are restored to ecclesial, and therefore also divine, communion in reconciliation. They are prepared for the eternal communion of saints in the anointing of the sick and viaticum. They proclaim and ritually make real their free choice of a state of life or order in the Church in the sacraments of marriage and holy orders. We mean, second, that all these ritual sacraments, signs and instruments of God's grace though they be, are not ultimate. They are to fit believers for communion in the Church, with God and with neighbors, so that the whole Church and each individual believer may be in the world communional sacraments, signs and instruments, of the God who is Life, Love, and Truth and who calls men and women to share life, love, and truth in communion.

The third good, the communional life of disciples, which requires the living of a Christ-like life in the world, is yet another practical demand that Christian faith makes upon believers. That claim can be, and frequently is, misunderstood and needs, therefore, to be explicated. The members of the Christian communion are called to live a Christ-like life, not only in the Church but especially in the world. The Church is the sacrament of Christ, not merely an institution which offers sacraments to believers but a communion which is itself the basic sacrament of Christ in the world. *Lumen gentium* emphasizes that a secular quality is proper and special to lay people and that it is the lay person's task "to illumine and organize" worldly affairs "in such a way that they may always start out, develop and persist according to Christ's mind" (LG 31). John Paul II confirms that the world is "the place and the means for the lay faithful to fulfill their Christian vocation" (CL 15). The communion-Church is the sacrament of Christ *in the world*; it is only by living and acting like Christ in the world that the Church can truly be that sacrament.

The fourth good believers share in the Church, communional *diakonia,* service of God and of the world in which God is mysteriously present, is another demand of Christian faith. The Church is called to be *diakonos,* "servant," for it is the body of the Christ who came not to be served but to serve (Mark 10:45). The Gospels record Christ's pluriform service, but here we note only one of its characteristics: it is in the world. We shall return to this characteristic in detail in chapter 5, where we deal with laity. For the moment, we note only that sacramental service is as much of the world as of the Church, for it is in the world that Christ is to be the sacrament of God and the Church is to be the sacrament of Christ.

Given the Lord's great commandment to "love your neighbor as yourself" (Mark 12:31), the fifth and final ecclesial good is too obvious to require any detailed elaboration. Faith, sacramental activity, discipleship, and diaconal service in the world are all to be informed by that love of God and of neighbor declared to be the great commandment (Mark 12:30-31) and the fulfillment of the Law (Rom 13:8).

Matthew succinctly summarizes this section on personal disposition. "Not everyone who *says* to me, 'Lord, Lord,' shall enter the kingdom of heaven, but the one who *does* the will of my Father who is in heaven" (7:21). The *Didache*'s rules for discerning authentic prophets, as we learned in the preceding chapter, agree. It is clear that, from the beginning, the Church that is the sacrament of Christ in the world is perceived not as a crowd of passive spectators but as a communion of active participants. That is all this chapter has argued. To claim that the Church is sacrament is to claim two things: first, that it is a communion of men and women with the triune God and with one another, and second, that this communion is active in the world as the visible sign of the graceful presence of this invisible God.

Sacramentality

We recall Semmelroth's claim that sacrament is not just one image of Church among many but is "the meaning and ontological sense of the mystery expressed in the statements found in revelation about the church."[127] That claim specifies the more general claim that sacramentality, the mediation of God and God's grace through created reality, is the very foundation of the Catholic traditions. "Grace does not come like a bolt out of the blue but rather passes through the corporality of this world in order for God to encounter humanity."[128] The God who is Presence and Grace is always mediated to human creatures in and through some sacrament. That mediation is achieved most notably, Christians confess, in the man Christ Jesus, "the one mediator between God and men" (1 Tim 2:5), who "is for us, in his humanity, the sacrament of God."[129] Those who judge that formulation to be new, twentieth-century theology need only consult Augustine: "There is no other mystery [sacrament] of God besides Christ."[130] This chapter has added only that neither is there any other mystery-sacrament of Christ besides the Church.

Catholicism has long lived with the Tridentine judgment that there are no more nor less than seven sacraments (DS 1601). Does the claim that both Christ and the Church are sacraments, outward signs and instruments of the presence of the gracious God, deny this solemn teaching? Does it raise up an eighth and a ninth sacrament to stand side by side with the traditional seven? It does not. It does something at once more radical and more traditional. It recalls Catholics to a forgotten tradition of incarnation, that God is incarnate in all of creation which is, therefore, sacramental for all who have faith-filled eyes to see.

In the decree *Dei Verbum*, the Second Vatican Council taught that God's plan of revelation is realized by "deeds and words having an inner unity" (DV 2). That formulation is explicitly an assertion of the sacramental character of revelation. It may be taken, however, also as an assertion of the sacramental character of the whole economy of salvation. We specify three moments in the Christian phase of that economy: *incarnation,* in which the Son of God is incarnated in the man Jesus; *Church,* in which the glorified Christ is incarnated in the communion of those who believe in him; *sacraments,* in which the Church, the Christ, and the God he makes known are proclaimed, made explicit, and celebrated in representation in ritual actions. All three of these phases are essentially sacramental, in the sense that all three are both signs and instrumental causes in the world of the Presence, Grace, and Salvation of God.

To protect the Tridentine teaching of no more nor less than seven sacraments, Semmelroth draws a distinction between the traditional seven sacraments and the Church as sacrament. "The seven sacraments are actions which, carried out in a moment, are soon done with and gone, persisting only in their effects, whereas the Church is not a passing action but an enduring institution."[131] The distinction is doubtfully defensible, and quite unnecessary in contemporary Catholic theology.[132] The Second Vatican Council, however, shared the reluctance to name the Church "sacrament," and so judged it to be only "a kind of sacrament" (LG 1).

In the beginning of this chapter, we established the theological equivalence of *mysterion* and *sacramentum,* mystery and sacrament, and the root meaning of both as a secret now revealed, at least in part. We noted also that nowhere in the biblical corpus does *mysterion* mean sacrament in its twelfth-century, technical sense. When *Lumen gentium* speaks of the Church as sacrament, it is in the context of this biblical sense of mystery, a reality imbued with the presence of God, a secret now revealed in Christ. In terms of the twelfth-century definition, it is only analogically "a kind of sacrament." It might be time, however, to acknowledge once again that sacramentality is a characteristic not only of seven symbolic actions, but of the whole of God's creation. As Robert Kress notes, correctly if awkwardly, sacramentality describes "the ontology (the way being 'bes') implicit in the Judaeo-Christian revelation, history and tradition."[133]

Prior to the technical definition of sacrament in the twelfth century, a wide range of created reality was acknowledged as sacramental of God.[134] As the definition took root, the idea of the sacramentality of all created reality became more narrowly focused into either the seven sacraments acknowledged in the Catholic traditions or the two acknowledged in the Protestant traditions. It is time to abandon the theological fixation on these two or seven and to acknowledge again the sacramentality of all created reality. We agree with Kasper. Only when we do this will the sacramentality of the two or the seven sacraments become genuinely meaningful.[135]

Karl Rahner took this integrated view of sacramentality as the basis of his explanation of Christ's institution of sacraments. By being himself the incarnation, the mystery-sacrament, of God, Christ set a pattern for sacramentality. Paul's treatment of the Church as the body of Christ, the mystery-sacrament of Christ, continued that pattern. Christ is the root mystery, the primal sacrament of God. The Church is the derived mystery, the fundamental sacrament of Christ. Formal, solemn actions of the Church are, therefore, signs and instruments of mystery; they are sacraments of the gracing action of God and of Christ. Each time the Church, the sacramental body of Christ, acts formally and solemnly as the body of Christ in the Spirit its action is sacramental of Christ and of God. In the explicit institution of Church as sacrament is the implicit institution of solemn sacramental action as sacrament.[136]

There is no slight to the two or seven sacraments in naming the Church "sacrament." More crucially for Christians, there is no slight to Christ, as the council makes clear in the words of Augustine: "It was from the side of Christ as he slept the sleep of death upon the cross that there came forth the wondrous sacrament which is the whole Church" (SC 5). As Eve was created to be a fit helper for Adam as he slept a deep sleep, so also the Church was created to be a fit helper for Christ, the new Adam (1 Cor 15:45), as he slept the sleep of death.[137] Christ, Church, and ritual sacraments share, in descending and derived order of importance, in the same pattern of mystery and sacramentality. *Lumen gentium*'s extension of sacramentality to the Church was an effort to restore that pattern to the breadth it had before the medieval definition restricted it so narrowly to the seven sacraments.

Summary

This chapter began with a treatment of mystery and sacrament in general and progressed to a consideration of the Christian Church as mystery and sacrament in particular. The Church is a communion between believers and the God who is at once mysteriously present and seeking to become explicitly present in the world. The external structures of that Church, necessary though they are for a historical people, are neither primary nor ultimate but merely the sign and instrument of the gracious presence of God. Active faith, an active yes to God, is absolutely necessary for both grace and salvation in general and for sacramentally mediated grace and salvation in particular. Active Christian faith is a prerequisite for the genuine sacramentality of the Church, for the life of discipleship and for the service of God in the world. We can now proceed to a consideration of the ministry to which all Christian believers are called.

Questions for Reflection

1. What do you understand by the claim that a sacrament is a mystery, a reality imbued with the presence of God? What implications do you see for your life as a member of the Church?

2. Reflect on the claim that the outer structures of the Church are related to the inner presence of God as sign and signified. Do you see any implications for you?

3. Is a sacrament an automatic means of grace or must each participant contribute something personal to be graced? What is the Catholic teaching about this?

4. Reflect on the claim that a sacrament is a sign, not only of the grace of God but also of the participant's desire for that grace. What are the implications, if any, of this claim?

5. What, in your opinion, must the Church do to be really and truly the sacrament of God in the world?

4

Church as Ministerial Communion

Christian Initiation, Communion, and Mission

In his *Theology of Ministry*, Thomas O'Meara points out that "thinking about ministry is theology reflecting upon the church."[138] We submit that the reverse is also true: thinking about Church is also, and necessarily, thinking about ministry. We ought not to think of the communion as, first, being fully constituted by the Holy Spirit and, then, doing ministry. Ministry is not something the Church-communion *does;* it is something it *is.* Christ's Church is essentially ministerial. The Spirit's abundant charisms of ministry are not given to an already-constituted body of Christ and people of God. They are not given because a Church-communion already exists in history to receive them. They are given, rather, to constitute the body and the people, to bring the Church into existence at each historical here and now as not only communion but also mission. In this chapter, we shall argue that they bring the Church into existence as necessarily a missionary communion.

Earlier, when explaining the term *kingdom of God,* we noted that Mark and Matthew open their account of the preaching of Jesus with the same proclamation: "The Kingdom of God is at hand; repent and believe in the gospel" (Mark 1:15; Matt 4:17). The message *of* Jesus, they realized, was centered on the kingdom or the rule of God, and so too therefore were their Gospels. The New Testament message *about* Jesus was also centered on the rule of God, specifically on the fact that God ruled in the death of Jesus as much as in his life. Jesus the preacher of the kingdom, much of whose preaching had sounded blasphemous in pious Jewish ears, gave way to Jesus preached as the one raised from the dead and confirmed by the God of Israel (cf. 1 Cor 15:4; Acts 2:24). This belief that the crucified preacher had been raised by God gave rise to a theology which saw in him the righteous one (Acts 3:14; 7:52; 22:14), the Lord and Christ established in power (Acts 2:36), who calls and sends disciples to carry on his proclamation of the kingdom of God (Matt 28:16-20).

The New Testament remembers the existential confusion that surrounded the identity of Jesus. "Who do they say that I am?" he asks. "John the Baptizer," they respond, "or Elijah or one of the prophets" (Mark 8:27; Matt 16:13-14). The post-resurrection preaching sets this confusion straight: "You are the Christ, the Son of the living God" (Matt 16:16). That answer, as Paul realized, hinges on belief in his resurrection, for "if Christ has not been raised, then our preaching is in vain and your faith is in vain" (1 Cor 15:14). God's raising of Jesus from the dead, that is, in the Jewish understanding of the times, God's transforming him from death and accepting him in glorified life, is a definitive clue which dispels confusion about the identity of both Jesus and the God whose kingdom he proclaimed.

The resurrection of Jesus is an act that reveals and makes explicit the ultimate meaning of his person, his words, and his deeds. That meaning, at the mysterious and sacramental intersection of humanity and divinity, is twofold. On the one hand, Jesus can be trusted, for he has been declared righteous by the God of Israel. On the other hand, the God to whose rule the person, the words, and the deeds of Jesus point can also be trusted, for that God raised him from the dead. To a superficial reading of the trial and execution of Jesus, it appears that God did not protect him. To confess, however, with the New Testament that Jesus died according to the "deliberate plan and foreknowledge of God" (Acts 2:23) is to confess that, in his death, God transcended all previous human conceptions of deity. When Jesus died, the Protector-God of every human desire died with him. When Jesus was raised from the dead, the God who raised him was revealed as the One who makes new.[139]

Such is the vision and the hope of humanity, divinity, and their sacramental intersection that Christianity holds out. Beyond past and present sin, the God who is in Jesus can make all things new, even death. John's Church glimpsed this message of transformation and salvation at the beginning of the Christian movement. "We are God's children now," he says; but "it does not yet appear what we shall be." Only one thing is clear: "We shall be like him" (1 John 3:2), that is, made new, as was Jesus. To believe in Jesus, and in the God he reveals, is to anticipate that future now and to be drawn forward to see the entwined mystery of the human and the divine as it will be. It is to such a vision and a hope, and to a ministry founded in both, that the Church-communion is called.

Not only was Jesus raised from the dead by God, but also "he was made manifest to Cephas, then to the twelve" (1 Cor 15:5). This being "made manifest," "appeared" as it is in earlier translations, has an incontrovertible source. As the God of Israel raised Jesus from the dead, so also God made him manifest to selected witnesses. These witnesses were called to believe Jesus' resurrection on the basis of this divine manifestation, or revelation as Paul chose to call it (Gal 1:15-16). Everyone else is called to believe it on the testimony of the witnesses and declared blessed, not if they have seen, but if they have believed (John 20:29). Those who did believe felt themselves called in the Spirit to be Christ's people, *ekklesia,* Church.

Ekklesia was an established Greek word denoting a public assembly called together by a herald for political purposes. It is used in this sense, for instance, in Acts 19:39-40. Because, however, the Jewish followers of Jesus made no distinction between their political and religious selves, the word took on religious overtones. It was used in the Septuagint, the Greek version of the Hebrew Bible, to render the Hebrew *qahal,* the assembly of the people of God. It was used in the New Testament to designate the gathering of those who believed in Jesus, the assembly or the Church of God (1 Cor 1:2; 10:32; 11:22; 15:9; 2 Cor 1:1; Gal 1:13; 1 Tim 3:5, 15). As Alfred Loisy once said, with more positive intent than is usually ascribed to him, "Jesus announced the kingdom of God, and what arrived was the Church."[140]

The New Testament is the record of the Church's understanding, not only of Jesus and of the God he preached, but also of itself. Its central kerygma, to repeat, is that God raised Jesus from the dead (1 Cor 15:3-4; Rom 8:34; Gal 1:1; Eph 1:20; Acts 2:24), and made him head of a body, which is the Church (1 Cor 6:12-20; 10:17; 12:12-27; Rom 12:4-5; Eph 1:22-23; 2:14-16; 3:6; 4:4-16; 5:22-30; Col 1:18, 24; 2:19; 3:15). The record not only declares that members of the Church are "in Christ" but it also explains how they got to be in Christ and to be, therefore, one body. "As many of you as were baptized into Christ have put on Christ. There is neither Jew nor Greek, there is neither slave nor free, there is neither male nor female; for

you are all one person in Christ Jesus" (Gal 3:27-28). Believers somehow are grafted onto the body of Christ and into communion in the
ritual of Christian initiation. For most Christians this needs careful
elaboration.

For the ancient Semite, both Arab and Jew, water was an element
to the whim of which men and women were constantly subject. Because of this subjection, water was celebrated in their most revered
mythologies. The Babylonian *Enuma Elish,* in which creation is described as the god of Babylon, Marduk, overcoming and putting in
order the chaos that is Tiamat-Sea, is the most detailed of such
mythological accounts. But elements of the chaotic water motif are
found also in the Jewish account of creation in Genesis. In the beginning, we read, "the earth was without form and void, and darkness
was upon the face of *tehom"* (1:2). If *tehom,* the watery deep, is not
exactly identical to Tiamat-Sea, it is at least a remnant of that mythical personification of sea.

An even clearer remnant is found in the Book of Job, where we
learn that "with his power [God] stilled Sea, with his skill he smote
Rahab [a mythical seamonster], with his wind he bagged Sea"
(26:12-13). Yahweh, the God of Israel, like Marduk, the god of Babylon, creates by putting chaotic water in its place. God creates, not out
of nothingness, but out of primordial water. Nor does creation ex-
haust God's activity with water. There are other mythological narra-
tives, the Babylonian *Gilgamesh Epic* and the Jewish account of the
great flood, which present God as letting water rage forth again to
bring death. The same water is the source of those two primal realities in human existence, life and death. It is not surprising that water
became a primordial symbol representing both life and death.

If water is such an omnipresent symbol in mythology, it is pre-
dictable that it will be a prominent symbol also in ritual. And, of
course, it is, in both Judaism and Christianity. The occasion for the
Jewish water rite of passage, *tebilah,* is the conversion of Gentiles to
Judaism, the passage from one cultural condition (being a Gentile) to
another (being a Jew).[141] Before they can become Jews, Gentiles must
be separated from their Gentile state. What better way to do this than
to return them, at least in ritual, to the water of chaotic non-being? So
they were immersed in water to become again, as in the beginning,
"without form and void." Then the Spirit of God, again, as in the beginning, swept over the water and from it again brought new life. The
once and former Gentiles were returned, ritually, to their original

nothingness, to be brought forth again by God to new life as now and future Jews.

The occasion for Christian baptism is conversion to belief in Jesus the Christ. When faced with the question of how to become like Christ, who died and was raised from the dead, the first Semitic believers reached back into their water symbolisms. To become like Christ, they would have to do what he did, namely, die and be raised again to new life. What better way to effect this and to celebrate this death and resurrection than to be immersed in the waters of ritual death and from there be raised to new life by God? What better way, in short, than to be baptized? So baptized they were.

In the early Syrian Church, the emphasis in this ritual fell on being born again "of water and the Spirit" (John 3:5). In the earlier Palestinian Church, it fell on death and resurrection: "We were buried with him by baptism into death, so that as Christ was raised from the dead by the glory of the Father, we too might walk in newness of life" (Rom 6:4). That these two interpretations coalesced is clear from the baptismal catecheses of Cyril of Jerusalem (d. 387), who explains to the newly baptized that "in the very same moment you were both dead and born, and that saving water became both tomb and mother [womb] to you."[142]

In initiation, then, Christians are ritually born to new life, communional life in the body of Christ. As God raised Jesus from death to new life and anointed him as *Christos*, so also God raises to new life those who are baptized in Christ and anoints them as *christos*. But, for all its wonder, baptismal rebirth is not enough. Too much weight can be and, in recent centuries has been, placed on baptism, as if immersion in water is all that is necessary to become Christian. But baptism is only a beginning. Becoming Christian requires also a Christlike life of service in the world. Initiation effects not only incorporation into communion but also ordination to mission. "Every disciple of Christ has the obligation to do his part in spreading the faith" (AG 23; cf. LG 17, 33; AA 2). Paul Bernier puts it directly. "Since the church is mission, the Christian is essentially a missionary."[143]

Cyprian, the third-century bishop of Carthage, always concerned with baptismal life, is in no doubt. Putting on Christ in baptism is quite meaningless unless baptism is followed by a Christ-like life. "To put on the name of Christ and not continue along the way of Christ, what is that but a lie?"[144] "The Church must walk the same road which Christ walked: a road of poverty and obedience, of service and self-sacrifice to the death" (AG 5). John Paul II asserts the same thing in contemporary theological language when he says that "communion and mission are profoundly connected with one another, they interpenetrate and mutually imply each other. Communion gives rise to mission, and mission is accomplished in communion" (CL 32). One cannot be genuinely in communion with the Church, with Christ and with God without actively responding to the mission charge to "make disciples of all nations" (Matt 28:19).

Both the Spirit's call to be not only passively in the communion-Church but also actively engaged in communional mission, and the believer's acceptance of the call, are symbolized in the sacraments of Christian initiation. The prayer for the consecration of the chrism used for anointing highlights the sacramental meanings of anointing. "Confirm this creature, chrism . . . in order that, when the corruption of the first birth shall have been swallowed up, the pure perfume of a life pleasing to you may yield fragrance in each one's temple." As baptism proclaims, makes real, and celebrates the swallowing up of the corruption of the first, biological birth by the second, ritual birth in Christ, so also confirmation proclaims, makes explicit, and celebrates that the new life in Christ is to be not only cherished but also lived in active mission. As Jesus was anointed as *christos* by the Holy Spirit in both his baptism and his resurrection, so also are those in Christ anointed as *christos* in their baptism and confirmation. Through baptism and confirmation, they are also commissioned to ministry "by the Lord himself" (LG 33).

Thomas Aquinas views the relationship between baptism and confirmation as analogous to relationships in human life. There is a moment of origin in life, and for life in Christ that is the moment of baptism. There are also moments of growth, and for life in Christ that is the moment of confirmation (and of Eucharist). The situation of the believer after baptism and after confirmation is illumined by analogy with the situation of the disciples before and after Pentecost. Before Pentecost, the Spirit of God dwelt with each disciple for his own life in Christ; after Pentecost, the same Spirit dwelt with them, moving them to preach Christ to others.[145] So also in baptism, the Spirit of Christ indwells believers for their life in Christ and, in confirmation, for the preaching of that life to others. Aquinas argues that confirmation "makes a believer fervent in heart and well known by confession."[146] We add that it ritualizes the believer's call to public ministry and the public acceptance of that call.

Aquinas describes the grace of confirmation as, not the gift of the Spirit, who is already given in baptism,[147] but the courage publicly to live the life in Christ embraced in baptism. Jean Latreille describes it well. "The person confirmed is designated to a spiritual combat, which is distinguished from the spiritual combat of the baptized person as an external combat is distinguished from an internal combat, or as a public testimony is distinguished from a private."[148] It is Thomas's theological version of Matthew's gospel statement. "Not everyone who *says* to me 'Lord, Lord' shall enter the kingdom of heaven, but the one who *does* the will of my Father who is in heaven" (Matt 7:21). Not everyone who claims to have received the Spirit of God in baptism is to be believed, but only those who do Spirit-gifted, Christ-like deeds (cf. Matt 7:16-20).

This discussion of the effects of baptism and confirmation, especially given their place in the present ecclesiastical order, could easily give the impression that the two sacraments are quite unrelated to one another. Nothing could be further from the truth. They are intimately related, not only to one another but also to Eucharist, with which they comprise one symbol-dense ritual of Christian initiation. To complete our present discussion, we must say something here about Eucharist.

The communion-Church is born in the waters of baptism. It is revealed and built up as communion of the members with Christ and with one another in the ritual meal called Eucharist. Though it is clear historically that sacraments were made by the Church, it is equally clear theologically that the Church is made by sacraments. Eucharist is the great sacrament, the sign and instrument, of communion. It is holy communion, in the sense that it reveals, makes real, and builds up the communion that is holy, namely, communion with God and with one another. Communion in the Eucharistic body of Christ both signifies and builds up communion in the ecclesial body of Christ which is the Church. Hence *Lumen gentium* teaches that "truly partaking of the body of the Lord in the breaking of the Eucharistic bread, we are taken up into communion with him and with one another" (LG 7). And this is but an echo of Paul's "we who are many are one body, for we all partake of the one bread" (1 Cor 10:17).

Ignatius of Antioch (d. ca. 110) so valued the "one bread" that he exhorted the Philadelphians "to observe *one* eucharist. For there is one flesh of our Lord, Jesus Christ, and one cup of his blood that makes us one."[149] This understanding of the central role of Eucharist as symbol of the Church's communion was continued at Rome. There, for centuries, fragments of the bread consecrated at the bishop's Eucharist were sent to be placed in the cups at all other Eucharists, joining all together in one Eucharist and one communion-Church.[150] This sending of the Eucharist was accompanied by the words *ite missa est,* "go, it (Holy Communion) is sent," so perplexing to Catholics who never understood the ancient practice. It is tempting to reflect on the effect of many Eucharists, which appear to divide the communion. But the present context neither permits nor requires such a diversion. Here we wish only to underscore two theological facts.

The first fact is the central role of the Eucharist as the sacrament, both the sign and the instrument, of the holy communion that is the Church. The second is the central role of the Eucharist also with respect to the mission of the communion-Church. It is to communion, both ecclesial and Eucharistic, that the people of God are called. It is *in* Eucharist that they ritually reveal, make explicit, and celebrate their communion with God, with Christ, and with one another in the Spirit. It is *from* Eucharist that they are regularly sent forth to play their active part in the mission of the communion: "Go now to love and serve the Lord and one another." As the Second Vatican Council so beautifully, and rightfully, put it: the Eucharist "is the summit toward which the activity of the Church is directed; at the same time it is the fountain from which all her power flows" (SC 10), including that power called mission.

The Church embraces all who have been called by God to believe in Christ and who have responded to that call by bonding themselves in initiation to live in communion with Christ and with one another. That communion is a "kind of sacrament" (LG 1), both a sign and an instrument of the Christ and of the kingdom of God which he preaches and serves. It is a sacrament that proclaims, makes real, and celebrates in the world the Christ and the rule of God.[151] As a sacramental communion, the Church is two-tiered. On one level, it is a communion of men and women bonded together by their belief in Jesus whom they confess as the Christ. On another level, it is a communion which is a sacrament in the world of the Christ and of the God he reveals.

The Church is the sacrament of Christ in the world. But Christ is the minister, the servant, the deacon (Mark 10:45) in the world of God and of God's rule. The Church, therefore, empowered by the same Spirit that empowered Jesus, must be the minister, the servant, the deacon of the same God and of the same rule. To repeat once more, without apology: the commitment to Christ in initiation must be followed by an active, Christ-like life in the world. The Church is not for itself; nor is its ministry for itself. The Church is not the presence of God, but the minister of God's presence; it is not absolute grace, but the servant of grace; it is not the kingdom of God, but the servant of the kingdom. It ministers and serves specifically by incarnating in its life in the world the Christ and the God he serves (LG 14). *Gaudium et spes* definitively reversed the Church's centuries-old flight from the world. The Church is *in* the world as "the universal sacrament of salvation" (LG 48); it is *for* the world that is in need of salvation. The Church, in fact, *is* the world in communion with God. The call to be Church is, of necessity, the call to servant life in the world;[152] the acceptance of the call is the acceptance of a servant life in communional *diakonia*.

In the New Testament Churches, ministry is a function of the people-Church. There are individual ministers, a great variety of them, ranging from the apostles, prophets, and teachers of the genuinely Pauline Churches (1 Cor 12:4-12, 28; Rom 12:4-8; Eph 4:11-14), to the overseers *(episkopoi)*, presbyters *(presbyteroi)*, and deacons *(diakonoi)*, of the Deutero-Pauline Letters. The latter triad, as is well known, became the exclusive referent of the term *ministry* in the Roman Empire and, therefore, also in the Roman Catholic Church. How that happened remains unclear, but that it happened and that the exclusivity created a serious misunderstanding of ministry is clear. The ministries of overseers, presbyters, and deacons, ministries though they undoubtedly are, are not simply *the* ministry. That judgment is now so well accepted in the Roman Catholic Church that Vatican II made a substantial change in an important teaching of the Council of Trent. The change is of the greatest import for a theology of ministry and ministers.

Trent had taught that "if anyone says that there is not, by divine ordination in the Catholic Church a hierarchy which is composed of bishops, priests and ministers, let him be anathema" (DS 1776). To bring this teaching into line with the unquestioned, because unquestionable, historical evidence, Vatican II changed it to read, "The divinely established ecclesiastical ministry is exercised on different levels by those who from antiquity *[ab antiquo,* not *ab initio]* have been called bishops, priests and deacons" (LG 28). The replacement of "hierarchy" with "ecclesiastical ministry" was intended to emphasize that it is the ministry of the Church, and not the hierarchical form of that ministry, which is of divine establishment. Acknowledging the historical fact that, from the beginning, ministry in the Church was pluriform, this declaration loosens the exclusive connection of ministry to hierarchy and restores the idea that ministry is a function of the Church, exercised by all those who are called to serve and who actually serve on behalf of the Church.

Hierarchy means sacred or holy origin. The entire Church-communion, therefore, and not only its bishops, presbyters, and deacons, is hierarchical, for its origin is in God, who alone is good and holy (Luke 18:19). It is axiomatic in the Catholic tradition that the sacraments of Christian initiation ritualize incorporation into Christ and into the people which is his body. That incorporation is also the acceptance of the commission or ordination to continue the servant ministry of Christ in the world. Early Christians were instructed that "you are a chosen race, a royal priesthood, a holy nation, God's own people, that you may declare the wonderful deeds of him who called you out of darkness into light" (1 Pet 2:9). *Lumen gentium* gives that instruction its own particular accent. Out of his new people, "Christ the Lord . . . made a kingdom and priests to God his Father" (LG 10). Those priests of the common priesthood are commissioned to "a participation in the saving mission of the Church itself" (LG 33). They are commissioned to servant-priesthood.

Luke opens his account of the ministry of Jesus with a pregnant quotation from Isaiah. "The Spirit of the Lord is upon me. . . . He has sent me to proclaim release to the captives, recovering of sight to the blind and to set at liberty those that are oppressed" (Luke 4:18-19, 43; cf. John 3:16-17; 5:36-37; 6:28-29; 7:29; 8:18; 12:49). Jesus has a strong sense of being called and sent to serve. "If anyone would be first," he explains, "he must be the last of all and the *diakonos*-servant of all" (Mark 9:35; cf. Matt 20:26-27; Luke 22:26-27). To James and John, who seek places of honor, he specifically explains that "whoever would be first among you must be the servant of all. For the Son of Man came not to be served but to serve" (Mark 10:44-45).

The communion-Church, the sacrament of Jesus in the world, can be no more, but certainly no less, than he. Ministry in the Church can be only *diakonia* (service), of God, of the Church, of the world in which both God and Church are embedded. Power in the Church can be only the power of service. Nothing has changed in the Christian ethos since Paul declared love the greatest of charisms (1 Cor 13:13).

The order of loving service continues to outrank any other order in the Church, ordained or not. Like the Christ whose sacrament and body it is, the Church and every believer in it is summoned to be a servant. Whoever is called to ministry in the Church is called to be a servant. And this service comes by incarnating, that is, by embodying and making sacramentally real, the presence-rule in the world of God in Christ and of the Spirit they send to lead the Church into truth, communion, and service.

Ministry Defined

We must now attempt to define the word and the reality that is at the heart of this chapter, namely, ministry. We agree with Cardinal Hume of Westminster, who advised the Synod on the Laity in 1987, that one of the pressing needs in any discussion of ministry today is "greater clarity in the use of the term."[153] In the contemporary Church, *ministry* is used indiscriminately to describe almost anything that Christians do, which cheapens and obscures the reality to which the word refers. When everything is described as ministry, the word becomes meaningless and nothing is distinguishably ministry.

Definitions not only clarify but also, and of necessity, delimit; they include some things and exclude others. With this warning in mind, we define ministry as action done in public, on behalf of the Church, as a result of a charism of service, proclaimed, made explicit, and celebrated in the Church in sacrament, to incarnate in symbol the presence of Christ and of the God whose kingdom he reveals.[154] A clarification of the terms of this definition will clarify also the definition itself.

Ministry is action. But it is intentional action, action as the result of planning, not accident. Christians are initiated, as we have seen, into an active communion of service, not into a passive crowd of spectators. They are called and sent, not to chant a mantric "Lord, Lord," but to do the will of the Father (Matt 7:21; Luke 6:46) in service, "to expend all their energy for the growth of the Church and its continuous sanctification" (LG 33). Aquinas was right, however: *agere sequitur esse,* "action flows from being." To be *Christian* ministry, therefore, action must flow from Christian being, from the belief in and communion with Jesus, the Christ, and with the God he reveals.

In the earliest Christian Churches, such ministry was designated by ordinary words describing Spirit-rooted actions done to spread the good gospel news. These words, *teach, preach, prophesy, serve, recon-*

cile, heal, lead, oversee, and a myriad others, are responsive words. The actions they designate are responses to perceived needs. Ministry is never action for the sake of action; it is always action in response to need. Later in Christian history, such words became institutionalized to designate ministerial offices in the Churches, whether they continued to respond to needs or not. A critical task today in the Church that is diaconal communion is once again discerning needs, "scrutinizing the signs of the times and of interpreting them in the light of the gospel" (GS 4).

Ministry is not only action; it is also action *in public. Public* derives from the Latin *populus,* "people," from which it derives also various nuances. We wish to underscore only two of them. First, acting in an official capacity on behalf of the people, as in *public prosecutor;* second, acting in a way apt to be known by most of the people, as in *made public.* Christian ministry embraces both these meanings. It is action done in public on behalf of the people-Church so that the action can be known by, not only this people, but also the people of the world for whom the Church is called to be a sacrament of unity (LG 1). To paraphrase what we heard Aquinas say about confirmation: it makes a believer fervent in heart and well known (that is, public) by confession. As presbyters are ordained in the sacrament of ordination to perform their office "publicly for men in the name of Christ" (PO 2), so too are all believers ordained in the sacraments of initiation to perform their mission publicly in the name of Christ for the salvation of the world.

Ultimately, what we mean by action in public is well exemplified by what we find from beginning to end in the Acts of the Apostles. There we find a record of the apostles "every day in the temple . . . teaching and preaching Jesus the Christ" (5:42). There also we find Paul in Rome "preaching the kingdom of God and teaching about the Lord Jesus Christ quite openly" (28:31). Paul describes himself as called and sent "to be a minister *[leitourgos]* of Christ Jesus to the Gentiles" (Rom 15:16). The Greek word *leitourgos* designates a public official who performs a *leitourgia* or public office. The fact that this word was appropriated in Christian history to denote only public worship or liturgy obscured its broader, ministerial meaning. Its original meaning underscores the essential nature of Christian ministry as public action.

Ministry is action in public, but not every action in public is ministry. Only that action done on behalf of the communion-Church and for the fulfillment of its mission is Christian ministry. It is now well known and freely acknowledged that neither in the New Testament nor in the apostolic Church is the word *hiereus,* "priest," used to designate any Christian minister. But the priestly element, so much to the fore in Judaism, did not disappear without trace. It was transmuted to express, first, the role of Christ and, then, the role of his body, the people of God. We shall defer treatment of these facts until a later chapter. Here, we are content to assert that Christian ministry necessarily begins in, and flows out from, the communion that is Church in fulfillment of its mission to proclaim in the world "the gospel to every creature" (LG 1; Mark 16:15).

The needs of the Church and of the world are varied, and the communional ministries required to respond to them are, therefore, also varied. Since there are many services required in the Church, there are also required many ministries. Preachers serve by proclaiming the word of God; teachers serve by explaining it; prophets serve by forthtelling it in concrete historical situations. Ministers of all kinds serve by translating the word of God into structures of justice, communion, and peace, and into care for the poor, the unprivileged, the sick, and the imprisoned. Ministers ordained for Christ-like leadership serve by, first, shepherding the people into communion with God and with one another and, then, sending them forth for service. All are servants of the presence, the grace, the word, and the rule of God (see CL 21–22). All ministers of the Church, that is, are essentially gifted to be deacons, whether or not they hold that ordained office.[155] Their prayer should always echo the ancient prayer of Augustine: "not so much placed over you as of service to you."[156]

Sometimes they are deacons who look inward, to serve and to reconcile, to challenge and to send forth, thereby to build up the body of Christ and the people of God *de facto*. Sometimes they are deacons who look outward, to serve and to reconcile, to challenge and to invite men and women into the kingdom of God, thereby to expand the people. But whether they look inward or outward they are deacons, not as isolated individuals, but always as members of, and acting on behalf of, the Christian communion. For Christians, the Church communion, precisely as the sacramental incarnation of Christ, is at the heart of Christian ministry. As we stated at the opening of this chapter, to think of ministry is necessarily to think also of Church.

The word *charisma,* "charism," was introduced into theological terminology by Paul. In its root Greek form, *charis,* it means any free gift. In the theological tradition which derived from Paul, however, even if Paul himself did not hold this meaning,[157] it came to mean specifically a gift of the Holy Spirit that anoints a believer for the service of the people of God. Writing to the Corinthians, Paul enumerates a great variety of such gifts, knowledge, wisdom, faith, power to work wonders, prophecy, healing, teaching, speaking in tongues, discernment and, above all, the "more excellent way" of love (1 Cor 12:8-10, 28, 30; 13:1-13; cf. Rom 12:6-8; Eph 4:11).

There are two important characteristics of charism to be noted. First, it is from the Spirit of God and is given to a person as gift, not as reward for good behavior nor as a result of office. This is the constant teaching of the Church, in agreement with Paul, that "No one can say 'Jesus is Lord' except by the Holy Spirit" (1 Cor 12:3). Second, charism is "for the common good" (1 Cor 12:7), "for the work of ministry, for the building up of the Body of Christ" (Eph 4:12). Because and in so far as the Church is the body of Christ, because and in so far as the Spirit of Christ showers gifts on each member of the body and moves each to communion and service, and because and in so far as Christ himself is present in each gift and in each service, it can be said in truth that Christ fills his body and all things in it with "the power of his resurrection."[158]

Since "charisms are graces of the Holy Spirit that have, directly or indirectly, a usefulness for the ecclesial communion, ordered as they are to the building up of the Church" (CL 24), their recipients have the duty, and therefore also the right, to use them for the good of communion and mission. Such use was well known in the earliest Church-communions. But as ministry in the Church became more and more institutionalized, charismatic ministry was more and more absorbed into hierarchical ministry, eventually vanishing almost entirely.[159] Perhaps that is why John Paul II insinuates an unwarranted distinction between ministries and charisms, as if ministries were not themselves charisms (CL 24). Communional ministries of every kind are, indeed, charisms, gifts freely given by the Spirit of Christ and of God for the upbuilding of Christ's body and God's people.

The behavior of the Spirit of God today, still distributing gifts freely, clarifies what should have always been obvious. Charisms, including the charism of ministry, are not the exclusive possession of ordained ministers. The Second Vatican Council merely acknowledged this fact when it taught that the Spirit "distributes special graces among the faithful of every rank," making them "fit and ready to undertake the various tasks or offices advantageous for the renewal and the upbuilding of the Church"(LG 12). Charism is again rampant in the Church, not only the ecstatic charisms associated with glosso-lalia, but also those more restrained and more important charisms (cf. 1 Cor 14) which named tasks needed for the upbuilding of the Church long before they named offices. Christians always proclaim, make real, and celebrate such gifts in sacraments.

Sacramentality is an essential characteristic of the Catholic tradi-tions. Catholicism reveals, makes explicit, and celebrates in sacra-ment the mysterious presence of the God in whom it steadfastly believes. That is, it marks the points of intersection of the human and the divine with sacrament. It is at those points that charisms are given and ministries arise. The primal sacrament of God, we recall, is the man, Jesus of Nazareth. By being, on one level, a man who, on an-other level, is confessed as the incarnation of God, and by calling into being a communion of believers who, on one level, are men and women and, on another level, are proclaimed as the body of Christ, Jesus set patterns for sacramental realization. The Church follows these patterns in its actions so that, when it acts formally, its actions are not just the actions of men and women but also the actions in the Spirit of Christ and of the God he reveals. As Augustine might say, "when Peter baptizes, Christ baptizes; when Paul baptizes, Christ baptizes; when Judas baptizes, Christ baptizes."[160]

The actions of the Church are sacramental actions. On one level, they appear to be simply human: immersion in water, anointing with oil, a meal with bread and wine, a laying on of hands. On another level, however, they are far from simple. They are symbolic actions, proclaiming, making explicit, and celebrating the presence of God, the Father who creates, the Christ who was dead and who was raised to life, the Spirit who gives gifts fitting believers for ministry in the communion that is the people of God because it is the body of Christ. The sacraments of initiation proclaim, make explicit, and celebrate the charisms of non-ordained ministry on behalf of this people. The sacrament of ordination does the same for the charisms of ordained ministry.

At this point, there arises a problem analogous to the problem with faith discussed in the preceding chapter. There we argued that the word *faith* was theologically ambiguous, referring sometimes to the virtue of faith, other times to the personal act of faith. We argued also that it is the virtue that is gifted in baptism and the act that is necessary to constitute one a believer. In this chapter, we have argued that, in the sacraments of Christian initiation and ordination, the Church proclaims, makes explicit, and celebrates charisms fitting the recipients for ministry in the Church. This argument raises a question. Are all the initiated, then, ministers? Do all automatically have a ministry in the Church? Not quite; at least, not without further specification.

In the sacraments of initiation and of ordination, each participant is fitted by charism for ministry in the Church, and each is called and sent to minister. Pursuing the analogy of our faith discussion, each receives the virtue of ministry. A person becomes an actual minister, however, not in initiation or ordination but in the free response to the call to ministry, in the conscious act of a personal, public ministry. Without that act, every Christian remains a minister only in virtue and in potential. As only an act of personal faith makes a believer, so also only an act of personal ministry makes a minister. Only an action done in public, on behalf of the Church, incarnating in symbol the Christ and the God he reveals, constitutes anyone as a Christian minister.

"Jesus the Christ came into Galilee, preaching the good news of God and saying 'The time is fulfilled and the Kingdom of God is at hand'" (Mark 1:14-15). That kingdom, as we have continually insinuated, is an image for the gracious presence and rule of God in human history, and it is this rule that Jesus serves. For historical men and women, inescapably bound to the earth, the rule of God is ambiguous. Jesus clarifies it by proclaiming it, by making it explicit, and by celebrating it in his words and in his deeds. He serves it, as the theological tradition has always insisted, by incarnating it in the world.

The Church-communion, which claims to be his body, serves in the same way, in its concrete presence, words, and public actions. It clarifies the kingdom by sacramentally incarnating it. Its ministry, always at the point of intersection of the human and the divine, is always a ministry of incarnation, of Christ, of the God he reveals, of the Spirit sent by both. It is to such a ministry of active sacramental incarnation, and not to a passive possibility of ministry, that each and every person who accepts communion in the body of Christ is called. Again paraphrasing Augustine: When Peter ministers, Christ ministers; when Paul ministers, Christ ministers; when the Church that is the sacramental body of Christ ministers, Christ ministers.

Summary

This chapter has been about ministry in the communion called Church. Ministry derives, in the first place, from ritual initiation in the Church and, in the second place, also from ordination, and all who accept initiation in the Church accept also the mission to minister on its behalf. Ministry is action, done in public, on behalf of the Church, which clarifies by incarnating the mysterious presence in the world of Christ and of the God he reveals. With this definition established, we can proceed to ask about that particular group of believers called laity.

Questions for Reflection

1. How do you understand the claim that the resurrection of Jesus was also the birth of the Church? Reflect on the claim that the Church is born too in the sacraments of Christian initiation.

2. Reflect on the words of Pope John Paul II: "Communion gives rise to mission, and mission is accomplished in communion." Do they have implications for you?

3. How do you understand the claim that ministry is a function of everyone in the Church and not only of those who are ordained? In what sense can it be said that every Christian is ordained in the sacraments of initiation?

4. Reflect on that part of the definition of ministry that defines it as action, done in public, as a result of a charism of service.

5. Reflect on that part of the definition that defines ministry as proclaimed, made explicit, and celebrated in sacrament. Are there implications for you?

5

Church-Communion and Laity

The Second Vatican Council perpetuates a common distinction among the members of the communion-Church. The term *laity,* it teaches, refers to "all the faithful except those in holy orders and those in a religious state sanctioned by the church" (LG 31). It is surprising that, thirty years after Yves Congar's plea that laity not be defined negatively ("not-a-cleric"),[161] the only definition of laity that could be offered by a council at which he had such an influence was precisely a negative one. Even more surprising, however, is the fact that the definition would have made no sense in any of the New Testament Churches. In those Churches, there was no such thing as laity or, for that matter, cleric, at least not as we understand the terms today. We shall defer treatment of the latter fact until the next chapter, and here deal only with the fact that there was no laity.

People of God

In the ratification of the covenant in Israel, "all the people answered together and said, 'All that the Lord has spoken we will do'" (Exod 19:8; cf. Exod 24:3; Josh 24:21). *The people* gave their answer to the God who had said to them: "You shall be to me a kingdom of priests and a holy people" (Exod 19:6). When the later Jewish followers of Jesus, Jewish Christians as they are sometimes called,[162] began to reflect on the meaning of their separate movement, they expressed it in terms borrowed from these covenant texts. They perceived themselves as "a chosen race, a royal priesthood, a holy people" (1 Pet 2:9). The self-understanding of both Judaism and

71

Christianity is a corporate, communional understanding, a sense of being a unified people in communion with God and, therefore, also with one another. For both religions everything else depends on and takes its meaning from that one fact of communion.

The ordinary Greek substantive for "people" is *laos,* from which derives the Greek adjective *laikos,* the English adjective *lay,* and the English substantive *laity.* The Old Testament followed the usage in secular literature, using *laos* with two denotations. In a general, more frequent sense, it denoted the whole people of God distinguished from those who were not God's people. In a special, less frequent sense, it denoted the common people distinguished from their priestly and prophetic leaders (Exod 19:24; Jer 26:7).

When the Church came to be described as *laos tou theou,* the people of God (1 Pet 2:10), the first sense of the word was intended. There was no distinction of groups in God's new people. Though there were individuals with special functions, apostles, prophets, teachers (1 Cor 12:28; Rom 12:6-8), presbyters, and overseers (cf. Acts 11:30; 15:2-4; 20:28; 1 Tim 5:1; 4:14; Titus 1:5-7), none of these functions divided the one people. What mattered was being or not being in Christ. Baptismal equality took precedence over any kind of ministerial distinction. It is for this reason that we claimed that, in the earliest Christian Churches, there was no such thing as laity as we understand it today. Gradually, however, beginning in the third century, things changed. *Laos* began to be used in the special sense, distinguishing those in the people who had no special part in the cult from those who did.[163] The latter came to be known as *kleroi,* "clergy," a group not only distinct from, but also more important than, laity. An excursus on clergy will help us better situate laity as it came to be understood in the Western Church.

Clergy

In the Jewish tradition, elders *(zeqenim)* provide service in the communities. The account in Numbers 11:16-17, repeated in a more general way in Deuteronomy 1:9-18, of Moses appointing seventy elders to bear the burden of the people with him formalizes the tradition and validates the leaders as wise bearers of the spirit of Moses and, therefore, of official authority. That this Jewish tradition is continued in the earliest Christian Church in Jerusalem is clear from Acts. *Presbyteroi,* "elders," are mentioned for the first time, offhandedly, as the recipients of the collection brought from Antioch by Saul and Barnabas (11:30). Later, they again welcome this pair to Jerusalem to discuss the question of circumcision (15:2-4), and they gather with James, who clearly presides, to hear Paul's account of his ministry (21:18).

This presbyteral arrangement is not found in Paul's Gentile Churches. There is no reference to presbyters in any genuinely Pauline letter. Paul's concept of ministry was controlled by his concept of Church as the Body of Christ, a Body in which the charismata of the Spirit were given to all, but for different ministries (Rom 12:6-8; 1 Cor 12:4-11; Eph 4:7-12). For Paul, the Spirit had superseded any distinction between priest and people and left it behind. Each and every believer, in Christ and in his Spirit, had a ministry in his charismatic Church, for the Spirit of God had gifted each with a personal charism, and any member could be called upon to exercise any ministry for which she or he was gifted. Some had a regular ministry, which the community recognized and supported. "But the idea of mono-ministry or ministerial autocracy—that is, of all the most important gifts concentrated on one man (even an apostle) or in a select group—is one which Paul dismissed with some ridicule (1 Cor 12:14-27)."[164]

The presbyteral arrangement, however, is found again in the deutero-Pauline communities described in the Pastoral Letters, written toward the end of the New Testament era. Presbyters impose hands on Timothy (1 Tim 4:14); they rule and enjoy special privileges (1 Tim 5:17-19); they are appointed by Titus in every town to "correct what was defective" (Titus 1:5). A presbyter, as seems clear from the evidence, is not just an elder in age, which is what *presbyteros* literally means, but is an elder also in authority, one who has received official office in the people. Timothy and Titus tell us also about another office, that of the *episkopos* or overseer (1 Tim 3:1-7; Titus 1:6-9).

There is a noticeable difference between the references to presbyters and overseers. Presbyters are mentioned always in the plural, overseers always in the singular, as if there are several presbyters in a community but only one overseer. C. Spicq relates the common opinion about the relationship of presbyters and overseer. "The overseer of the Pastorals should be considered as a presbyter enjoying here or there a supreme authority, or better a more particularly defined ministry."[165] *Presbyter* and *overseer* are synonymous terms, and those who are described by either term belong to the same presbyteral college. By the time of the Pastoral Letters, however, in which *overseer (episkopos)* occurs always only in the singular, the episcopal presbyter is emerging from the presbyteral college as a *primus inter pares,*[166] a first among equals, functioning as president, guardian, overseer, and pastor.

From even this briefest outline of the evidence, it should be clear that there is in the New Testament Churches a variety of ministerial structures, from the loosely charismatic structure of prophets and teachers (with very little real distinction between the two) to the more institutionalized structure of presbyters and overseers. The charismatic arrangement disappeared entirely in the second century or, at best, existed only on the fringes of the catholic Church. The institutional structure not only survived, but also became sacralized into a cultic priesthood. It was the development of this priesthood, more specifically the appearance of the notion of *ordo* (order) which accompanied it, that gave rise to the notion of clergy *(kleros)* as a class of believers distinguished from, and more distinguished than, another class called "laity." When that happened, by the middle of the third century, the original unity of the people of God had been shattered and was already on its way to being lost.

In Ignatius, the *episkopos* of Antioch at the opening of the second century, we encounter for the first time a sharply delineated picture of an arrangement in which an *episkopos,* "overseer," is not just a member of a presbyteral college but also its unchallenged head. His letters to the Magnesians and to the Smyrneans indicate similar ministerial arrangements there, with Damas overseeing the Magnesians and Polycarp the Smyrneans.[167] The overseer presides surrounded by his presbyters, who form his council. "No one is to do anything in the church without the *episkopos.* A valid eucharist is one which is either under his presidency or the presidency of a representative appointed by him. . . . It is not right to baptize without the *episkopos,* nor to celebrate the agape without him."[168] The college of presbyters is attuned to its overseer as the strings of a lyre, and conducted by him the whole Church sings as a harmonious chorus to the Father through Jesus Christ.[169] The difference between overseer and presbyter, and the preeminence of the former, could not be clearer. But Ignatius still never calls the overseer "priest," even though it is clear that he alone now ordinarily presides at Eucharist.

If Ignatius is the first in the East to present the overseer as more than just a first among equals, Irenaeus (d. ca. 202) is the first to do so in the West. At the end of the second century, he urges that it is necessary to obey the presbyters who have succession from the apostles and who, together with this episcopal succession, have received the gift of truth.[170] Because he stands in apostolic succession and hands on apostolic tradition, the overseer has preeminent claim to the title of "presbyter." He stands in a line of presbyters who knew the apostles and who received from them the tradition that is still normative in the Church.[171] There is no equivalence between overseers and apostles, for apostles are unique. But overseers are still men of great stature in the community, not because of any special powers they possess, but because they have received the apostolic tradition and the charge to preserve it and because they have been faithful to that charge.[172]

Cyprian, the overseer of the Church at Carthage in the middle of the third century, viewed apostles as the first overseers and the overseers of his day as their direct successors, holding the position in their Churches that the apostles held in theirs. This allowed him to argue to the superiority of the office of overseer in the Church, since "the Lord elected apostles, that is, overseers and leaders, whereas deacons were constituted ministers by the apostles."[173] His position on the primacy of the episcopacy, based on its direct connection to the apostles and, therefore, to the Lord, is not difficult to understand. "You should know that the overseer is in the Church and the Church is in the overseer, and whoever is not with the overseer is not with the Church."[174] Interpreting the Petrine text in Matthew 16:18-19 as applying to the office of overseer,[175] he argues that the episcopal office is the very foundation on which the Church is based. For all the dignity of the overseer, however, he is elected by all the people in communion, overseers, presbyters, and people alike.[176]

Much more important than his legitimation of the monarchical overseer is Cyprian's casting of Christian ministry into Old Testament priestly terms. The one chair founded on the rock, which he interprets to be the overseer, founds not only one Church but also one altar and one priesthood,[177] which is to serve that altar and its sacrifices.[178] Because such priesthood is to serve the altar, priests are to be free from all uncleanness and worldly care and, therefore, like the Levites of the Jewish tradition, are to be supported by the faithful.[179] For Cyprian the *episcopus* (overseer) is undoubtedly *sacerdos* (priest). Presbyters share in his priesthood,[180] and Cyprian explicitly delegates them to preside at Eucharist[181] and penance[182] in his absence.

By sharing in the priesthood of their overseer, presbyters also come to be designated as priests.

With Cyprian, the various roles of members of the people-in-communion are becoming more and more carefully defined. The first undisputed use of the term *layman* occurs in Clement of Alexandria (d. ca. 215).[183] It occurs in the context of the discussion about the place of sexuality in the Christian movement raised by the Encratites, who taught that all the baptized are called to devote themselves to celibacy. Clement's response is that the Apostle Paul "admits that, if his conduct in marriage is beyond reproach, the man of one wife, be he presbyter, deacon or layman, will be saved by begetting children."[184] Only from this moment does the layman emerge as a special category in the people of God and, it should be noted, as an elite, that is, one who was of only one wife, as were presbyters and deacons.

It remained for Cyprian to clarify the relationship of this emerging group, laymen (the term is correct, for it did not include women), to another group emerging in the Church, clerics. Their relationship, as we saw above, was articulated in Old Testament terms. The layman was to receive spiritual assistance from the cleric and, so that the latter could be free from the distractions and cares of profane occupations, he was to provide him with financial assistance. This obligation was probably one of the reasons why women, who can be assumed not to have had financial independence, were not included in the term. When this arrangement solidified, the transition from the original *laos tou theou,* the unified people of God, with distinction of functions but not of status, to a people of God hierarchically divided into clergy and laity was accomplished. Another transition was also accomplished, that from an original unpriestly to a priestly ministry. But we shall defer treatment of that to a subsequent chapter.

One way to describe the transition that Christianity began to undergo in the third century is to say that the original charismatic movement became institutionalized. That institutionalization became solidified when Constantine's Edict of Milan recognized Christianity (313) and, especially, when Theodotius declared it the religion of the empire (381). The Christian religion then took over from the ancient pagan religion the task of safeguarding the empire. Church and state became one. Bernard Cooke comments that "the pattern of ecclesiastical, and more specifically clerical, institutions which in actual historical reality changed drastically during its three centuries of ante-Nicene evolution is now looked upon as *de iure divino.* This puts the divine stamp of approval on that clericalization of the church's faith, theology, liturgy and spirituality."[185] We note here the pattern derived from one Roman word, the use of which contributed greatly to this process.

In the Roman Empire, the word *ordo,* "order" was used with two principal meanings. First, and in general, it designated a class or group in society, the order of scribes, for instance, or the order of librarians or consuls. In this sense, Jerome speaks of "five orders in the Church: bishops, presbyters, deacons, faithful, catechumens."[186] Second, in Rome, *ordo* designated specifically the highest ranking members of the state, namely, the senators. Belonging to the order of senators distinguished one from the mass of the people *(plebs);* it conferred rank and dignity over and above that of the *plebs.* In the municipalities and colonies, this governing dignity was replicated in those who governed, the order of decurions.

Though there is one disputed text in Tertullian that might be construed along the lines of a distinction between clerics *(ordo)* and laity *(plebs),*[187] Latin theology in general did not adopt this terminology quickly. It is not found in the third-century *Apostolic Tradition* or in the writings of Cyprian. Even when it does come into Catholic use, *ordo* refers more simply to ecclesiastical status than to inferior or superior ecclesiastical rank. To belong to the Church at all is to belong to some order. It might be the order of catechumens, penitents, widows, or presbyters. But in every case, *ordo* radically expresses the same theological reality, namely, membership in the Church-communion which is hierarchical, that is, which has its origin in Christ and in his Spirit and which has its final goal in God.[188]

By the fifth century, however, with Christianity firmly established as the religion of the empire, *ordo* increasingly takes on in the Church its second meaning, *ordo* as distinct from *plebs.* It refers either to the entire body of clerics as distinct from the non-clerical members of the Church, or to particular grades within the clerical body: the order of subdeacons, the order of deacons, the order of presbyters, the order of overseers. The stress now is very much on rank and dignity, a fact which can be discerned easily from ecclesiastical language. Pope Innocent I (d. 417) speaks of clerics of "superior and inferior orders,"[189] Leo the Great (d. 461) of clerics of a first, second, third, and fourth order.[190]

This clerical use of *ordo* became so much taken for granted that Gratian was able to assert in the twelfth century that "there are two kinds of Christians," those called "clerics," and those called "lay." Lay people are allowed to possess temporal goods, to marry, to till the earth, to lay their offerings on the altar,[191] but only as a concession to human weakness. It would be better, he implies, that they not do these things; but, since they must, it is allowed. This thinking, which is mirrored in other writings of the time, implicitly denies that those who have received and who make use of such concessions have any active part in sacred things. That belongs only to clerics. The result is that not only are there now two groups of Christians, but two quite unequal groups, clerics following Christ perfectly, laity only imperfectly and needing help from clerics to attain access to God.

The distinction between clergy and laity was greatly enhanced by one legal and two theological developments. The legal development was the treatment accorded to clergy by the civil power. Constantine exempted them from civil and military service, from civil courts and from taxation,[192] exemptions which passed into both the Theodosian and Justinian law codes and, ultimately, into the Catholic traditions. The first theological development was that, in the twelfth-century Latin Church, clergy were required to live a celibate life while non-clerics were allowed to marry. We wish here, not to dwell on this development, but merely to indicate the way it highlighted the distinction and inequality of two groups in the Latin Church. The second theological development, a change in both the theology and the practice of Eucharist which established bishop and priest as men of quasi-magical power, further underscored that inequality.

In the ancient tradition, the Church was known as the true body of Christ *(corpus Christi verum)*. In order to be validly ordained to oversee this body, a man had to be appointed to a pastoral function in and by this body. In the medieval Church the focus shifted from Church to Eucharist, called the mystical body of Christ *(corpus Christi mysticum)*.[193] To be validly ordained to preside over this Eucharistic body, theologians argued, a man needed to be given power over it. This shift of presbyteral focus from pastoral care of a specific Church-communion to sacred power over Eucharist reached its apogee in the Fourth Lateran Council, which taught that "no one can accomplish *[conficere]* this sacrament [Eucharist] except a priest who has been validly and legitimately ordained."[194] Eucharistic ministry now required not only a man appointed by the Church to preside over it, but also a man with the power to accomplish it.

Medieval theology responded to this new focus on Eucharist and on the power required for it with a new distinction of power. There was pastoral power over a Church communion *(potestas iurisdictionis)* and ritual power over Eucharist or Holy Communion *(potestas ordinis)*. A man could have the latter without the former; he could celebrate Eucharist without any connection to a particular ecclesial communion. He could have priestly power without ever exercising any pastoral ministry in a Church. The Council of Chalcedon (451), whose sixth canon forbade ordination to the presbyterate without reference to a particular ecclesial communion, had made that illegal and, indeed, invalid. But once Chalcedon was superseded, a new Church order emerged, one which gave precedence to the communion meal rather than to the communion whose meal it was. It was but a small step then to the private Mass, the celebration of Eucharistic communion with no ecclesial communion present, something that happened especially from the eighth century on.

This change of ecclesial reality and Eucharistic terminology, Gregory Dix comments, enabled priesthood, "which had formerly been the function of all members of the church with the bishop as high priest," to become "a special attribute of the second order of the ministry."[195] The focus on the priestly power of orders as a prerequisite for celebrating Eucharist destroyed the ancient tradition of the entire Church concelebrating Eucharist under the leadership of its overseer-bishop. An ancient *Liber Pontificalis* teaches that "every age concelebrates," young and old alike.[196] Guerricus of Igny still taught at the end of the eleventh century that a priest "does not sacrifice by himself, he does not consecrate by himself, but the whole assembly of believers consecrates and sacrifices with him."[197] Congar has shown beyond any doubt that this is the general position of the Church of the first millennium: the Church communion itself, and not just its *sacerdos* (priest), offer the bread and the wine.[198]

We undertook this excursus on clergy to situate, however briefly, the traditional negative definition of laity repeated by the Second Vatican Council. That we have to insist on such facts is, of course, a sure sign of how far the Church has strayed, not only from its understanding of itself as the people of God in communion, but also from its understanding of the whole people as priest and as, therefore, concelebrating its communion as one. Thirty years after the council, which replaced the vision of a Church organized by the clergy for the laity with the renewed vision of a lay Church (Church as people of God served by the clergy), it continues to be a cause for sadness and frustration that not much has changed. It is time now to discover the council's renewed vision of laity in the communion-Church.

Laity: A Profile

As already noted, the council defines the lay faithful as "all the faithful except those in holy orders and those in a religious state sanctioned by the Church" (LG 30). John Paul II approves the "positive terms" of this definition, and goes on to specify its importance. "Incorporation into Christ through faith and baptism is the source of being a Christian in the mystery of the Church" (CL 9). Faith and baptism, never baptism alone, seal membership in the body of Christ which is the people of God. All believing members of the people, never those baptized who are effectively non-believers,[199] share in the mission and functions of the Christ, who is head of the body. Speaking along these lines in 1980, John Paul II offered a more positive and dynamic definition of the lay faithful. "Laity are by definition disciples and followers of Christ, members of the Church who are present and active in the world's heart so as to administer temporal realities and order them toward God's reign."[200]

The *Code of Canon Law,* published some twenty years after *Lumen gentium*, highlights the notion of a unified people in its definition of "Christ's faithful." They are "those who, since they are incorporated into Christ through baptism, are constituted the people of God . . . they are called, each according to his or her particular condition, to exercise the mission which God entrusted to the Church to fulfill in the world" (can. 204.1). There are still some distinctions acknowledged in the people: some are called clerics and some are called lay people (can. 207.1). But they are distinctions, not between ministers and non-ministers and certainly not between better or worse Christians, but between ministries. For, "flowing from their rebirth in Christ, there is a genuine equality of dignity and action among all of Christ's faithful. Because of this equality, they all contribute, each according to his or her own condition and office, to the building up of the body of Christ" (can. 208). All, in sum, are called to minister.

The council taught that "a secular quality is proper and special to laymen" (LG 31). Paul VI repeated that teaching a decade later, asserting that the Church "has an authentic secular dimension, inherent to her inner nature and mission, which is deeply rooted in the mystery of the Word incarnate and which is realized in different forms through her members."[201] Both the nature and the mission of the Church are rooted in the incarnation, that central Christian doctrine which confesses that God became man in Jesus. In the incarnation, "the gulf between heaven and earth, between God and man, between the supernatural and the natural, between the sacred and the secular . . . has once and for all been overcome so that now we can glimpse heaven on earth, God in man, the supernatural in the natural, the sacred amidst the secular."[202] After, and in the light of, the incarnation, nothing on earth is ever exclusively profane or secular, not even laity or their life in the world.

The secular character at the core of John Paul II's definition of the lay faithful is to be read, he insists, with a *theological* and not just with a sociological meaning. "The term *secular* must be understood in the light of the act of God . . . who has handed over the world to women and men so that they may participate in the work of creation, free creation from the influence of sin and sanctify themselves" (CL 15). Communional service in and for the world, no matter what service it is, is not just *secular* service, in the sense that it falls outside of God's plan of salvation. It is also *salvation* service, in the sense that it is also for the consecration and the salvation of the world. John Paul II returns to this theme again and again.[203] We add only that the secular character of the laity is to be understood also in the light of the incarnation. A theological characteristic of laity is that they live in the world, know the world, value the world, and seek to permeate it with the Spirit of Christ and of the gospel.

To claim that the specific vocation of lay-people is in the secular world and that of clerics is in the world of the sacred, as if sacred and secular were unrelated, as if incarnation had never happened, is loose talk. It is true that lay people live and work and play in the world of everyday reality, that they people the professions and the factories, the schools and the hospitals, the hotels, the fields, and the homes. It is equally true that, in such ordinary social and familial circumstances, they are to incarnate God, Christ, the Spirit, and the ecclesial communion which they call into being, thereby bringing the gospel of reconciliation and salvation to the *saeculum,* the world.

The theological secularity of the lay faithful was, of course, common theological currency long before the council. Already in 1946,

Pius XII described the essential mission of the Church as including the building up of the human community according to Christian principles. The lay faithful, he insisted, "are in the front line of the Church's life; through them, the Church is the vital principle of human society. Consequently, they must have an ever more clear consciousness, not only of belonging to the Church, but of *being* the Church."[204] Yves Congar, "the most prominent ecclesiologist of this century,"[205] and Karl Rahner, "recognized generally today as this century's leading Catholic theologian,"[206] wrote in the same vein in the 1950s.[207] With *Lumen gentium* we wish to highlight something that, in our opinion, they did not.

The laity's theological secularity derives, not from any shortage of clergy, but from "a participation in the saving mission of the Church itself. Through their baptism and confirmation, all are commissioned to that apostolate by the Lord himself" (LG 33). The sacraments of initiation, as we have already noted, not only initiate into Church-communion but also ordain into Church-mission.

The theological secularity which is a distinctive mark of laity is never to be confused with that pagan secularization of which John Paul II frequently complains.[208] *Secularization* names a process in which the material world becomes so exclusively "real" that the life of Christian faith is diminished. When that process goes so far as to extinguish faith, then a person has become a secularized pagan, a baptized non-believer. Such non-believers cannot incarnate for the world the communion-Church which is in the world as a sacrament of communion, of peace, of service, of salvation. Nor can they incarnate the Spirit who calls the world to communion and peace, the Christ who seeks to serve the world by proclaiming to it the liberating word of God, or the God whose word is reconciliation and peace. For they no longer believe any of this.

Secular, on the other hand, as it is used of the lay faithful, identifies a twofold theological quality of Christian believers. They are, first, firmly situated in the secular world where they can, therefore, secondly, incarnate the Church, the Christ, and the Spirit of the God in whom they passionately believe and with whom they intimately commune. For a Christian, to be secular in this sense is a double badge of honor, for it bespeaks commitment both to the world and to the triune God who wills to save it. Such secularity is the distinctive character of the distinctive ministry of lay Christians. It demands deep faith, without which it easily becomes secularization. But until and unless that sad moment of transformation occurs, Christian secularity should never be confused with pagan secularization.

Without a doubt, secularization always poses a serious threat to lay secularity. There is, however, a greater and less obvious threat to authentic Christian secularity today. It is a new flight from the world, the flight of laity who, feeling called to ministry, seek out ministries in and to the Church rather than in and to the world. Imbued with a new-found realization of their call to minister, laity in large numbers are seeking to emulate clerical ministries in the Church rather than to create genuine lay ministries in the world.

The problem with this approach does not lie in the fact that laity seek out ministries for which both they and clergy are certainly competent. It lies, rather, in the fact that they flee the very secular ministries for which *only* lay people, with their location in and knowledge of the world, are truly competent. If lay ministry is ever to become the genuinely secular ministry it can and must be for the salvation of the world, if lay men and women are ever to influence and inspire the world with the spirit of the gospel, laity and clergy alike will have to come to value genuine lay gifts and be on guard against this creeping clericalization of lay ministry. They will also have to learn to collaborate in peaceful communion in the different ministries each holds from the Spirit of God.

Pope John Paul II draws attention to two temptations which the lay faithful "have not always known how to avoid." The first is this clericalization of Christian ministry, the temptation to be so strongly interested in Church services and tasks that some laity "fail to become actively engaged in their responsibilities in the professional, social, cultural and political world." The second is the constant temptation to separate faith from life, to separate "the gospel's acceptance from the actual living of the gospel in various situations in the world" (CL 2).
The Second Vatican Council underscores the double responsibility of priests to "sincerely acknowledge and promote the dignity of the laity and the role which is proper to them in the mission of the Church" (PO 9). To be faithful to this responsibility, they will have to promote the Christian secularity of the laity, on which the salvation of the world depends.

Lay Christians themselves appear to have some difficulty with the description of their vocation as secular, and a consideration of this difficulty will help to clarify just what it might mean in practice. In preparation for the 1987 Synod on the Vocation and Mission of the

Laity, the bishops of the United States entered upon an extensive consultation with laity about their concerns. One of "the most consistent and emphatic" assertions issuing from that consultation was that "church and world should not be divided in our thinking and language."[209] Laity rejected dualism between Church and world, between sacred and secular, between clergy and laity. However much they may be distinguishable in theory, Church and world are not separable in fact; nor are sacred and secular, clergy and laity. The Church is incarnate in the world to be the sacrament of love, hope, reconciliation, forgiveness, peace, justice, transformation, grace, presence, mystery, communion. The sacred is similarly embedded in the secular, seeking to become explicit within it and thereby to sanctify it, to transform it from exclusively secular to also sacred, from exclusively people of the world to also people of God, from exclusively bread and wine to also Eucharist and Holy Communion. The clergy is part of the laity, the *laos,* the people, serving them and proclaiming to them the word of God which calls them to share full responsibility for the Church in the world and the sacred in the secular.

There are tell-tale signs, however, of religious schizophrenia, signs that what is being rejected is not really dualism but just the designation *secular.* While laity say they are opposed to dualistic thinking, when asked to describe how they connect their Christian life and their secular life, "they speak most often of social services and prayer. There is almost never any mention of actions that involve structural change or include political, legislative or economic strategies."[210] Theologically, or theoretically, laity tend toward a unified view and reject dualistic thinking about Church and world. In practice, however, they tend to limit their contributions in the world to recognizably churchy activities, prayer, scripture study, charitable activity, concern for the poor, etc. They are puzzled, therefore, when the Church teaches that "action on behalf of social justice and participation in the transformation of the world appear as a *constitutive* dimension of the preaching of the gospel and of the Church's mission for the redemption of the human race."[211]

Human history contains a long line of dualist heresies about the cosmic battle between good and evil. It runs from Iranian Zoroastrianism (which so influenced both ancient Judaism and early Christianity), to African Manicheeism (against which Augustine struggled), to European Jansenism (condemned in the eighteenth century). Those heresies, with their images of good and evil gods, good and evil spirits, good and evil places and times and people, left the impression that the world was the work of the Evil One rather than of the good God. They became so embedded in the Western Church, even against its own better judgments, that they are not supplanted easily, not even in those who most passionately believe in incarnation.

This is neither a great surprise nor a great disaster. It is simply something for the people-in-communion, laity and clergy alike, to be aware of, one more concrete manifestation of how long it takes for a communion of disciples to learn in practice what it means for them to be Church *in* the world. One more example also, if any more were needed, of the fact that "the church, embracing sinners in her bosom, is at the same time holy and always in need of being purified" (LG 8). The Church that is the communion of the people of God in the world always has to learn that ministry in and to the world is as important as (dare we say even more important than) ministry in and to the Church. Bernier puts it nicely. The "aspect of mission is the most important aspect of ecclesiology, and dwarfs the discussion of the nature and internal structure of the church. The church is and should be structured to better carry out its mission."[212]

Let us illustrate how the ministry of the Church in the world works. Several years ago, two faithful Catholics were moved to a new section in the factory in which they worked. It did not take them long to notice that the twenty-two other men and women in the section made up a very negative group. Their verbal interaction was nonaffirming and destructive, the air was blue with foul language and sexual innuendo, the reading material was the latest pornographic epic. These two simple men noticed also what a relief it was to everyone when they reached the end of the work day. They learned from the factory gossip that the negativity at work spilled over into the home environments. They decided to do something about it.

Dividing the group between them, the two men visited one on one with each person, spending time, listening to personal stories, affirming. Soon the pornography disappeared and the language began to change. The group became more positive and friendships began to form. Finally, after several months, one of the men in the group suggested that maybe they could get together occasionally for breakfast and some prayer. The final outcome was that both work and home became happier places for all the men and women involved.

The beauty of this story of secular ministry is that it is a true story. Two lay faithful, that is, two Christians full of faith, responded to a perceived and dire need in their workplace, and by the simple inter-action of love generated systemic change and set a group of men and women free. When they started to affirm their colleagues, and when their colleagues started to affirm one another, all came alive as indi-viduals in communion, breathing new life into their relationships both at work and at home. That is what it means to say that the spe-cial characteristic of laity is secularity; they contribute to the salva-tion of the world by ministering in the workaday world.

These two baptized believers did ministry by incarnating in the factory the Church that is communion and the Christ who is its head. They had a difficult time understanding that what they did was Chris-tian ministry, every bit as much as what their parish priest did in the ritual of reconciliation was ministry. But it was and it is. Their diffi-culty in understanding derived from the reverse problem to the one we noted above. In their case, theological theory lagged behind minis-terial practice. When it was explained to them that ministry was ac-tion done in public, on behalf of the Church, as a result of a charism of service, proclaimed, made explicit, and celebrated in sacrament, to incarnate in symbol the presence of Christ and of the God whose kingdom he reveals, they had no difficulty understanding that what they did was just that.

There is another story of a simple man with great teaching ability. He teaches auto body mechanics in a state technical college, formally initiating young men and women into the mysteries of unbending fend-ers and rebuilding cars after an accident. Informally, but quite explic-itly, he initiates them also into positive self-images (these are not the most favored children in the land), and into justice toward all, accident victims and insurance companies alike. Because of his skill, both as a teacher and as a motivator, he has become quite famous. He now speaks all over the United States and Canada, teaching teachers how to teach students to repair automobiles and egos and injustice.

Across the length and breadth of the land this man teaches budding auto mechanics not only how to repair automobiles but also how to claim identity as worthwhile people and to deal with other people in justice. By being his very own sensitive, empathetic Christian self, he serves people with all the talent he has, accommodating his service to the special, secular needs of the auto body repair shop. He does not have to be convinced, as did the other two, that what he does is Chris-tian ministry. He sees what he does as action done in public to incarnate the Church and the Christ who is its head. He sees it as the genuine ministry of a layperson in the world.

Summary

This chapter sought, ultimately, to do one thing: to challenge the dualism between laity and clergy in the Church by recovering the ancient vision of the Church as the one, essentially undifferentiated *laos tou theou,* "people of God." This vision, in its turn, inspires another, the vision of an entire Church and its each and every member called and designated to ministry. Tracing the history of the development of the order of clerics does not denigrate or challenge that development, but illustrates that the current order was not always so and, therefore, need not always be so. As for the laity, one must emphasize their essential secularity, in order to challenge and to inspire all of them to assume their rightful ministerial roles in the Church in and to the world.

Questions for Reflection

1. Are you comfortable or uncomfortable with the information that there were no laity and no clergy, as we use the terms today, in the earliest Christian Churches? Can you articulate why you feel that way?

2. What does the term *people of God* mean to you? Could there be today again, do you think, that one people? Do you think that the term *lay* can ever mean more than its present connotation of "less than clergy"? What would be the practical implications of such a renewal?

3. Reflect on the brief history of the development of clerics (clericalism) in the Church. Are you more comfortable with a vision of a lay-centered Church or a clergy-centered Church? Why?

4. Do you feel drawn to a secular ministry or to an ecclesiastical ministry? What real differences do you see between the two?

5. Do you have any stories to share about the secular ministry of lay women and men?

6

Church-Communion and Hierarchy

Preamble

As we indicated briefly in the preceding chapter, the theology and practice of ordained ministry in the Western Church developed in the direction of a priesthood empowered to consecrate Eucharist. That theology and practice, which were not supported in every respect by the theology and practice of the New Testament and the apostolic Church, was solidified by the Scholastics in the thirteenth century and ultimately validated by the Council of Trent in the sixteenth century. The understanding of Trent's teaching in later history hardened the Roman Church's understanding of ministry as exclusively priestly and cultic, so that ministry came to be understood as something done by priests, certainly not by lay people. Against the overall history of the Catholic Church, such a view is a diminution, not only of ministry, but also of priesthood.

The Council of Trent, in Alexandre Ganoczy's words, was "a more or less valid and effective reply to Lutheran and Calvinist questions and challenges. But [history] has also recognized that in the course of the following four centuries a too rigid desire to stick to the letter of the Council has sometimes blocked the progress which ought to have taken place within the structures of the church, in response to new challenges and questions."[213] Trent produced no systematic ecclesiology. Its insistence on the essentially hierarchical nature of ministry, however, in the sense that ministry is something done only by the ordained, produced in the following centuries a matching insistence on the essentially hierarchical nature of Church. It was this hierarchical view, we saw in the opening chapter, that was presented to and rejected by the Second Vatican Council.

Church was imaged, not as the one people of God in communion, but as an institution of power, at the apex of which ruled the pope in union with the college of bishops and at the base of which knelt an obedient people.[214] That model of Church, and of ministry, dominated the ecclesiology of the Roman Catholic Church until the Second Vatican Council, which attempted to supplant it with a communional model more in tune with the ancient tradition of the broad catholic, as distinct from the narrowly Roman Catholic, tradition. The Tridentine model of Church and ministry (Tridentine only in the sense that it was derived from Tridentine principles) was constructed on the notion of the power wielded by one segment of the Church over the other segment. Vatican II attempted to restore an older model in which power-as-service was shared in the one people, both laity and clergy, and in which their communion as disciples of a common Lord was emphasized over their distinction of functions. Though thirty years have passed since its proclamation, the jury is still out on how successful that attempt has been. In this chapter we shall consider ordained ministry as it is presented in the documents of the Second Vatican Council.

Vatican II's Priest

It should be taken as a sign of the complacency of the times that there was no document on priests among the documents proposed for discussion at the Second Vatican Council. The nature and the role of priesthood was assumed to be sufficiently well understood to need no further treatment. That was certainly the assumption for many theological realities in the days of the preparatory commissions. What little the council was to say of priests was located in a short section of the Constitution on the Church. When that document was discussed, however, at the second session in the fall of 1963, there were numerous complaints that what was being said of priests was too skeletal and an equal number of demands that it be given a fuller treatment.

As it was progressively discussed, the document that resulted underwent several revealing title changes, from *De Clericis* (On Clerics) to *De Sacerdotibus* (On Priests) to *De Vita et Ministerio Sacerdotium* (On the Life and Ministry of Priests) to, finally, *De Presbyterorum Ministerio et Vita* (On the Ministry and Life of Presbyters). We call attention here only to the final change, from "On the Life and Ministry of *Priests*" to "On the Ministry and Life of *Presbyters*." The reversal of the terms *life* and *ministry* between the third and fourth titles was of great significance, for by it "the bishops wanted to emphasize that the priesthood is not in the first place a state of life but rather a function, a service, a ministry."[215] The change of wording from *priests* to *presbyters* was of ultimately greater significance, and it offered to the Church a vastly broadened vision of Catholic priesthood.

Both the official title of the document, *De Presbyterorum Ministerio et Vita,* and its opening words, which give it its working title, *Presbyterorum Ordinis,* are to be carefully noted. They are systematically ignored by English translations, which translate them as "Decree on the Ministry and Life of *Priests,*" and "The Order of *Priests.*"[216] This translation ignores the definitive change of title and treats the Latin *presbyter* as if it were synonymous with *sacerdos.* It is not.

Sacerdos, and its Greek equivalent *hiereus,* are cultic terms, which name the one who mediates the holy and offers sacrifice. The English equivalent is *priest.* Though that title is apt for the post-Scholastic minister who focuses on the offering of Eucharistic sacrifice, it is not a title given any Christian minister in the New Testament. As John Robinson notes, with his customary forcefulness, "the unpriestly character of early Christianity must surely have been one of the things to strike an outsider, whether he were Jewish or pagan."[217] The New Testament *presbyteros* is not a priest. He is an elder, which is all *presbyteros* literally means, but specifically an elder who has been given pastoral office in the Church-communion to minister to needs. The progressive, and in the end decisive, change of titles for the document on the Catholic priesthood signals a radical change in theological reality, from a cult-based priesthood mediating the holy to a communion-based presbyterate ministering to needs.

The council leaves no doubt about the priority of that pastoral ministry. "By sacred ordination and by the mission they receive from their bishops, presbyters are promoted to the service of Christ. . . . They share in his ministry of unceasingly building up the Church on earth into the people of God, the body of Christ" (PO 1). The office of presbyter is not restricted to, nor is it focused on, a Eucharistic role. "It is also properly extended to the formation of a genuine Christian communion" (PO 6). This important change of focus and theological reality is missed and obscured by the incorrect rendering of *presbyter* by the English "priest." *Presbyterorum Ordinis* does use *sacerdos,* but only nine times; it more frequently uses *presbyter* to name the minister commonly called "priest." We shall render *pres-*

byter in English by "presbyter" whenever the council's document requires it.

No longer, therefore, does the council view the presbyter as the cultic man. The heart of his spirituality is not the sacrifice of the Mass, as the nineteenth-century school of French spirituality had insisted; rather is it the ministry in and for the communion-body of Christ to which he is elected and for which he is ordained. Nor is the presbyter a man set apart from his people, in the sense that he is segregated from them and set over against them. He is set apart from them only in the sense that he is called to minister to them, to shepherd them into communion with one another and with their Lord. He remains a member of the people, a disciple of the Lord, a brother among brothers (PO 9). He is, of course, unquestionably male, as the contemporary debates about women and priesthood had not yet begun to be seriously aired. An outline, however skeletal, of this presbyter-priest will be helpful.

It is a fact of great theological significance that when the council opened its discussion of ordained priesthood, it drew attention first to the common priesthood of all believers (LG 10). The priestly communion comes before its ministers and the common priesthood of all its members comes before the presbyterate of its ordained ministers. The ordained presbyterate, indeed, emerges from the common priesthood of all believers. Not every member of the Church, however, has the same function in it, for the Lord "established certain ministers among the faithful in order to join them together in one body" (PO 2). These ministers are the presbyters of whom this document speaks. Their ministry is "not confined to the care of the faithful as individuals, but is also properly extended to the formation of a *genuine* Christian communion" (PO 6). The *pastoral* leadership and care of the community, which we emphasized in the preceding chapter, is confirmed by the Church in council to be *the* talent-charism of the ordained presbyterate.

Both Old and New Testaments are clear about the communional nature of Judaism and Christianity. God's self-revelation begins with the election of a holy people, united in their faith that God led them out of Egypt and into a land of milk and honey. From that people emerges yet another holy people, united in their faith that the God of Abraham and Isaac and Jacob raised Jesus from the dead and called them into communion to be the body of Christ and the people of God. The bond that unites the people, however, is not so much their common faith in Jesus as their common communion with him. Much of the activity of the early communion centered on building up the body (Eph 4:12; cf. 1 Cor 14:12; 2 Cor 10:8; 13:10), but that does not mean that it is turned only inward. All are instructed to "do good to all," even if "especially to those who are of the household of the faith" (Gal 6:10).

The council's teaching makes the presbyter specifically responsible for the building up of the body. It makes him responsible also to build a communion that looks, not only inward to itself, but also outward to the larger world. Presbyteral ministry embraces a twofold ministry, a ministry of the word and a ministry of sanctification.[218] "Since no one can be saved who has not first believed, priests, as co-workers with their bishops, have as their primary duty the preaching of the gospel of God to all" (PO 4). No longer is the preaching of the word suspected to be a "Protestant" activity; it is the primary duty of presbyters. By preaching the word presbyters both follow the Lord's command to "go into the whole world and preach the gospel to every creature" (Mark 16:15) and build up the body of Christ that is also the people of God.

Lest the notion of the word that is to be preached be too narrowly interpreted, the council makes clear that it is a twofold word, contained not only in sacred Scripture but also in the celebration of Eucharist. "The faithful receive nourishment from the twofold table of sacred Scripture and the Eucharist" (PO 18). It is from these two tables that presbyters are to nourish their flock and to build up the communion and the body of Christ. Both words are sacred and hierarchical, for both have a sacred origin and are directed to a sacred goal. Each is, therefore, to be Spirit-filled and self-filled, always reflecting not just mechanical competence and official power but also, and primarily, personal faith and unconditional commitment. Presbyters, therefore, are to study the twofold word assiduously, to make every effort to understand and integrate it before it is spoken. Only when the word is integrated can it be proclaimed to hearers convincingly.

"Preaching the word" must be understood in a broad sense. Presbyters fulfill their task of preaching "whether they engage people in conversation and draw them to glorify God, or openly proclaim the mystery of Christ to non-believers, or catechize believers and explain the doctrine of the church to them, or comment on the questions of the time in the light of the mystery of Christ."[219] Commenting on the questions of the time in the light of the word of God is what the

Catholic tradition calls "prophecy." As we demonstrated earlier, prophecy has ancient precedent in the Church, though it long since was absorbed into hierarchical ministry. Presbyters are invited to be prophets again, that is, to speak the word of God in and to contemporary situations. Since prophecy is not exclusively the charism or the task of the ordained, they will have to learn again to listen also to lay prophets and to nurture them. If prophecy is regarded as a form of preaching, presbyters will have to listen to lay prophets preach. That may not be comfortable; prophecy seldom is. It is, however, good ecclesiology.

If presbyters are to proclaim God's word, not just in some abstract fashion but in concrete circumstances, then they need to be as conversant as they can with those circumstances. Since they must preach the gospel to men and women and children of varying levels of education and development and condition, they must cultivate the art of relating to all. They must "learn especially the art of speaking to others in a suitable manner, of listening and communicating patiently and with reverence imbued with love, so that the mystery of Christ living in his Church can be made known."[220] To truly know their sheep, shepherds must live in the sheepfold.

Long before the special option for the poor became politically correct, it was pastorally correct. The Second Vatican Council had proclaimed publicly that the poor were to be a special concern for bishops (CD 12) and for presbyters (PO 6). It cannot be otherwise in a communion that claims to be the body of the Christ who was united to the poor (Matt 25:34-45), and for whom the proclamation of God's word to the poor was an authentic sign of messianic activity (Luke 4:18). The commitment of the Church-communion, and therefore of its presbyter-leaders, to the poor cannot truly be called an *option,* as if it were a choice they could or could not make. It is an option only in the sense that it is a choice that the Church makes. It is also a choice that it *must* make if it wishes to claim to be the sacrament in the world of him who was sent "to preach good news to the poor . . . to set at liberty those who are oppressed" (Luke 4:18).

There remains that other word which is very specifically entrusted to ordained presbyters. Catholic presbyters have not ceased to be persons of the cult, they have ceased only to be exclusively persons of the cult. The Eucharist remains both the source and the apex of their proclamation of the word. It is "the summit toward which the activity of the Church is directed; at the same time it is the fountain from which all her power flows." It is the very heartbeat of the believing communion (SC 10; PO 5). That should not come as a surprise to the Church.

In the Eucharistic concelebration, the people with their leader remember Jesus who was raised from the dead by God, who was made both Lord and Christ (Acts 2:36), who is forever present in their communion, but never more explicitly than when they gather to eat and drink in his memory. Each member of the Church, those of the common priesthood and those of the ordained presbyterate, concelebrates that presence and, precisely by concelebrating it, makes it real, true, and substantial presence. It is the public, ecclesial function of the ordained presbyter, however, acting on behalf of the communion and of Christ, to consecrate and to offer gifts, and it is this liturgical function that essentially distinguishes him from the common priest. It is in this function, above all others, that ordained presbyters share in Christ's ministry "of unceasingly building up the Church on earth into the people of God, the body of Christ and the temple of the Holy Spirit" (PO 1). It is in Eucharist that they, and all who make up Christ's body, can proclaim in thanksgiving *(eucharistia)* and praise *(exomologesis)*[221] their foundational word: "This is my body."

We wish to mention one final element that Vatican II adds to the sketch of the ordained priest. It is an element long ago noted in Augustine's famous dictum: "For you I am a bishop, but with you I am a Christian."[222] The council borrows this idea and paraphrases Augustine's language. Presbyters are presbyters and fathers "in Christ Jesus through the gospel" (1 Cor 4:15). But they are also "brothers among brothers with all those who have been reborn at the baptismal font. They are members of one and the same body of Christ, whose upbuilding is entrusted to all" (PO 9). If presbyters are members of the one body-communion which embraces not only men but also women, then they are brothers not only among brothers but also among sisters. It is time, we believe, for the communion's women members to count.

Ordination into the order of the presbyterate does not nullify prior membership in the people of God. It does not nullify the priesthood shared in common with all. The ordained remain radically members of the people, the *laos*. Though the Church continues to define laity in distinction from clergy, it enjoins upon all presbyters to "sincerely acknowledge and promote the dignity of the laity and the role which is proper to them in the mission of the Church" (PO 9).

The use of the verbs "acknowledge" and "promote" indicates a twofold task. Ordained presbyters, first of all, have to acknowledge the dignity of lay people as members of the body of Christ and the people of God, and they have to realize that dignity is one they share with them. Given the burden of history, that acknowledgement and understanding might not come easily. Thirty years after Vatican II, many lay people are coming to believe that it has not yet happened. But happen it must before both presbyters and laity will be free to carry out in communion their respective tasks in building up the body. And because that building up is both a common goal and a common duty, presbyters are, secondly, to promote the dignity of lay people.

There are many lay people, probably still a majority, who need to hear John Paul II's resounding words. "The lay faithful are given the ability and the responsibility to accept the gospel in faith and to proclaim it in word and deed" (CL 14). There are many who still conceive the Church and ministry in hierarchical categories, in the worst possible meaning of that term, the dualism of clergy and laity, them and us, ministers and non-ministers. There are many who still say of the hierarchy that it is "their church" and "their job to run it." Ordained presbyters have the ministry to call such people, as did the bishops of the United States, to Christian adulthood, holiness, ministry, and service in Church and world.[223] Only when the true identity of the lay person in the Church is understood and accepted by both laity and clergy will both be able to work in communion for the upbuilding of the Church, the people of God, the sacrament of Christ in the world.

Paradoxically, we believe, the true Christian dignity of both laity and clergy will be promoted best by abolishing both terms, at least as terms that separate. Only when all the faithful share their common dignity as members of the one body of Christ and people of God, only when each values the others and communion with them, will each be free to perform his or her ministerial function for the building up of all into the body. Only when all, lay and cleric together, proclaim with one voice "This is *my* body," will that proclamation be really effective.

Vatican II's Bishop

Since at least the thirteenth century, the theology of the sacrament of orders centered on priesthood, the power to offer sacrifice. There was little place for the episcopate. The bishop appeared to be no more than a super-priest. *Lumen gentium* definitively changed the situation when it taught that "by episcopal consecration is conferred the full-ness of the sacrament of orders" (LG 21). This raises two questions. First, in what does the "fullness of the sacrament of orders" conferred by episcopal consecration consist? Second, what is the significance of that fullness for the sacramental Church? Our ecclesiology of com-munion makes the answers to these questions easier than they have traditionally been.

The Church is by nature a mystery, a human reality imbued with the presence of the Trinitarian God. It is, specifically, a mystery of communion, a communion of believers with each other and with their God. That communion, as we have already noted, is essentially Eu-charistic, in the strongest possible sense. Though it is clear from his-tory that the Church makes Eucharist, it is equally clear that Eucharist makes the Church. There is no Church without Eucharist; there is no communion without Eucharist. Here we, first, state and, then, expli-cate the answers to the two questions posed above. The fullness of orders conferred by episcopal consecration is precisely membership in, and communion with, the college of bishops; that collegial com-munion is a sacrament, both a sign and an instrument, of the com-munion that is the Church.

Jesus, the Christ, appointed the Twelve to be with him and to preach in his name the rule of God. Vatican II states that he appointed them "after the manner of a college" (LG 19), and it is to this college of apostles that the "sacred order of bishops" (LG 20; cf. LG 22, 23, 25; CD 3, 4, 6) succeeds. Episcopal consecration establishes a pres-byter, not in a higher priestly power that he posseses in and of him-self, but in communion in the college of bishops. The rite of ordination of a bishop, revised in 1968 "to express more clearly the holy things" it signifies (SC 21), makes the communional nature of episcopacy clear.

The introductory homily speaks of "our brother whom we are about to accept into the *college of bishops.*" The bishop-elect is in-terrogated as to whether he is resolved "to build up the Body of Christ and to remain united to it within the *order of bishops.*" The newly consecrated bishop prays, "Lord God, now that you have raised me to the *order of bishops. . . .*"[224] That ancient maxim, *lex orandi lex cre-dendi,* "the law of prayer is also the law of belief," leaves no doubt. A presbyter is ordained not to the order of *bishop,* but to the order of *bishops.* The fullness of orders, which episcopal ordination confers, is communion in the college of bishops.

Episcopal consecration is not only consecration to membership in the episcopate. It is also ordination to *episkope,* pastoral oversight in "a local Church in which the one, holy, catholic and apostolic Church of Christ is truly present and operative" (CD 11). The local Church, called in ordinary language a diocese, is that portion of the people of God entrusted to a bishop to be pastored into, and safeguarded in, communion "through the gospel and the Eucharist" (CD 11). Episcopal ordination establishes the bishop in such public relationship with a local altar-communion that he is ordained as the ordinary representative of that Church-communion.[225]

Through the gift of the Spirit poured out upon him in ordination, a bishop is "the visible principle and foundation of unity in his local Church. . . . Each individual bishop represents his own Church, but all of them together in union with the Pope represent the entire Church joined in the bond of peace, love and unity" (LG 23). As a good shepherd, he is to pastor the people entrusted to him into, and to safeguard them in, ecclesial communion with Christ and with one another. He is to pastor them into, and to safeguard them in, Eucharistic communion in the communion-meal, where he concelebrates with them and in their name the communion, memorial, and sacrificial meal.[226] Local presbyters, who are "prudent cooperators with the episcopal order" (LG 28), function in this same representative way for a Eucharistic communion, but it is its bishop who publicly guarantees the apostolic communion-Church.

The bishop represents to his Church-communion the universal, apostolic Church of Christ. He represents its apostolic faith, its gospel love, its Christ-rooted reconciliation, its Spirit-gifted communion and peace, so that he may speak for his people in truth, and they may speak with him, the catholic foundational word: "This is my body." He is also to represent his Church to the universal Church, to pastor it into, and to safeguard it in, communion with all those who are in communion with Christ through the Spirit and their bishops in world-wide local Churches. "In and from such individual Churches, there comes into being the one and only catholic [that is, universal] Church" (LG 23). That Church may legitimately be called, therefore, as the Congregation for the Doctrine of the Faith (CDF) calls it, "a communion of churches."[227] In the communion ecclesiology of this book, that means, of course, a communion of communions.[228]

We can distinguish, but not separate, three interrelated communions. There is the communion that is the local Church, united in the episcopacy of its bishop, himself in communion with the college of bishops and its head, the bishop of Rome. There is the communion of communions that is the universal Church, united in the universal episcopacy of the college of bishops and its head. There is the communion that is the college of bishops, united in the apostolic faith, "in the bond of peace, love and unity," and "solicitous for the whole Church" (LG 23; CD 5). No bishop functions as a bishop in the catholic Church apart from these three communions, for he is a member of the episcopal body not only by episcopal consecration but also "by hierarchical communion with the head and members of the body" (LG 22). If a bishop is ever alienated from communion, "he ceases to be an ordained person (no anathematized or excommunicated minister can be regarded as a minister)."[229]

To the extent that the universal "Church of Christ is truly present in all legitimate local congregations of the faithful . . . united with their pastors" (LG 26), the communion that is the local Church and the communion that is the universal Church are, in reality, mirror images. The third communion is the sacrament, both the sign and the instrument, of the other two. As the universal Church is not just the sum of the local Churches and as the local Church is not just a part of the universal Church, so also the college of bishops is not just the sum of all the individual bishops and an individual bishop is not just a part of the college of bishops. The universal Church subsists whole and entire in each local Church; the universal episcopate subsists whole and entire in each local bishop.

These are more than simply two theological facts. They are related facts, in the sense that the communion of local bishops in the college of bishops is the sacrament, the sign and the instrument, of the communion of local Churches in the universal Church. Ordination to the episcopate is a sacrament in the catholic Church, distinct from ordination to the presbyterate, in the sense that a presbyter is ritually introduced to communion in the college of bishops, which is not only the sign of the communion that is the universal Church but is also the means through which that communion is made explicit, maintained, and built up. All of this is inseparably rooted in Eucharist, where the body of Christ subsists whole and entire in each Eucharistic celebration, is made explicit, and is built up.

David Power notes that "safeguarding the unity of the church in the one apostolic tradition, presiding over its essential unity and presiding over its eucharist all go together."[230] Like the Church itself, the *episkope* of a local bishop and the episcopate of the college of bishops are constituted by Eucharist. The consecration of a bishop as "the visible principle and foundation of unity in his particular Church" (LG 23) takes place always in a Eucharistic celebration in that Church. Indeed, the Council of Chalcedon (451) declared absolute ordination, the ordination of a presbyter or bishop without a relationship to a specific Eucharistic community, to be invalid.[231] A bishop's triple representative role, representing Christ to the Church, representing his local Church to the universal Church, and representing the universal Church to his local Church, is publicly made manifest, as is the Church itself as the body of Christ, in the celebration of Eucharist. "Communion between the local churches in the universal church is rooted," the CDF notes, "above all in the eucharist and in the episcopate."[232]

Like the presbyters we have already discussed, Vatican II's bishop is a pastoral person. Finding such a person was the intent of the ancient qualifications for the office. "A bishop must be above reproach, the husband of one wife, temperate, sensible, dignified, hospitable, an apt teacher, no drunkard, not violent but gentle, not quarrelsome, no lover of money. He must manage his own household well, keeping his children submissive and respectful" (1 Tim 3:2-4; cf. Titus 1:5-8). That there are qualifications in that early list which are no longer sought in bishops is evident, which is probably why *Christus Dominus* ignores this reference entirely. We do not wish in this book, however, to deal with the discrepancies, in particular the discrepancy between the ancient requirement that a bishop be the husband of one wife and the modern requirement of celibacy. That would take us too far from our focus. We wish only to insist that a bishop has not ceased to be a pastoral person. The council does not retreat from that.

The tone of *Christus Dominus* is thoroughly pastoral, especially compared to its many thoroughly legal predecessors. In exercising his office of father and pastor, a bishop is to be "in the midst of his people as one who serves." He is to be "a true father who excels in the spirit of love and solicitude for all." He is to gather and mold his whole family "in the communion of love" (CD 16). His preeminent duty is "to serve rather than to rule,"[233] *diakonia* rather than dominion. He is "to announce the gospel of Christ to men [and women]" (CD 12; cf. LG 25; PO 4) and to pastor them into communion. That primary pastoral charge, what we call the pastoral presidency of the bishop in a Church-communion, is made manifest in his liturgical presidency in its Eucharistic-communion. Herve Legrand demonstrates that so it always was. Those who preside over the upbuilding of the Church-communion preside also over the sacraments which upbuild it. He calls presidency over the Eucharistic meal, therefore, "the liturgical dimension of a pastoral charge."[234] In our communional language, we say simply that bishops exercise their servant ministry (LG 18, 27; CD 16) within a communion that is essentially both ecclesial and Eucharistic.

Both the episcopate and the presbyterate, as theologically described by Vatican II, are more pastoral charisms for building up the body of Christ and the Church-communion than priestly powers for "making" the body of Christ in Eucharist. This conception is not to be thought of as deriving from the Second Vatican Council, or from some new, twentieth-century theology. Bernard Botte's analysis of the traditional prayers of ordination has shown beyond doubt that it was always so.[235]

The Bishop of Rome

We shall follow *Lumen gentium* in dealing with the specific ministry of the bishop of Rome in the context of a treatment of the ministry of the episcopal college. The bishop of Rome, commonly called the pope, is not a super-bishop. Beyond episcopal ordination, he receives no sacrament and no ordination placing him above and beyond the episcopal college. He is not beyond the episcopal college; he is a member of it, even as its head. His ministry is a specific form of the sacramental ministry common to all bishops, a local ministry to the Church of Rome and a universal ministry to the catholic Church of Churches. He represents to the Church of Rome the apostolic faith and communion of the catholic Church; he represents to the catholic Church the faith and communion of the Church of Rome. He accepts, as does every bishop ordained into the episcopal college, the *sollicitudo omnium ecclesiarum,* the care of all the local Churches (CD 3). As the historic head of the episcopal college, however, he exercises this universal care in a specific way.

The basis for the primacy in the episcopal college of the bishop of Rome is established by Irenaeus in the second century. "We will speak of the largest church, the best known and oldest of all, founded and constituted by the two most glorious apostles Peter and Paul in Rome. . . . It is with this church, because of its powerful pre-eminence *[potentiorem principalitatem],* that every church must agree."[236] The bishop of Rome is preeminent in the episcopal college because the Church of Rome is preeminent in the communion of all the Churches. And the Church of Rome is preeminent because it is founded in the apostles Peter and Paul.

It is not because Peter, however, and still less Paul (cf. Rom 1:7; 15:28; Acts 28:14-16), were the first to evangelize Rome that they are the foundation of that Church. Nor is it because Peter was its first bishop. In the continuation of the text just cited, Irenaeus carefully distinguishes the "apostles" Peter and Paul from the "bishops" of Rome, Linus, Anacletus, and Clement. The foundation of the Church of Rome on the apostles Peter and Paul does not rest on their evangelizing witness. It rests on a more profound witness, that witness *(martyrion)* we commonly name martyrdom. The martyrdom-witness of Peter and Paul in Rome "makes the church of Rome the one which God has marked with the seal of the most powerful and greatest apostolic authenticity." This martyrdom-witness of the leader of the apostolic college confers on the Church of Rome "the quality and the title of first in the apostolic witness. It holds in this way the primacy of the first seat."[237]

The bishop of Rome, the pope, is a member of the episcopal college; he is a bishop among bishops. His honor, as Pope Gregory the Great (d. 604) insisted, is "the honor of the universal Church . . . the firm strength of my brothers." He is not, Gregory further insisted, "the universal pope," for that title refuses to other bishops "what it attributes to me."[238] His honor, in our communional language, derives from the honor of his local Church in the communion of communions that is the universal Church. Since that Church, and therefore that *cathedra* or episcopal throne, is preeminent in the communion of Churches, so also is the bishop who sits on that *cathedra* preeminent in the communion of bishops, first in the responsibility for the communion that is the catholic Church of Christ.

As the bishop of the local Church of Rome, the pope is the vicar of Christ in Rome. He is not, however, "the sole vicar of Christ on earth," as Bonaventure and many who followed him taught,[239] for every bishop in his local Church is a vicar of Christ (LG 21, 27, 37). As the one who sits on the throne of Peter, the pope is also the vicar and "successor of Peter, to whom Christ entrusted the feeding of his sheep and lambs" (CD 2). He occupies the place in the college of bishops that Peter occupied in the college of apostles.

The pope has, therefore, the task of pastoring not only the lambs but also the sheep (John 21:15-17). He has the task of not only preaching the gospel to the faithful in Catholic communion but also strengthening his brother bishops in communion and in the apostolic faith (Luke 22:32), the task of affirming, strengthening, and vindicating them and their episcopal authority (LG 27). The Second Vatican Council declares this primacy to be of "divine institution" (CD 2), cautiously softening the First Vatican Council's stronger claim that it is "by divine right" (DS 3058). The true nature of papal primacy in the Catholic tradition can be discerned by considering a correspondence between the bishops of Germany and Pope Pius IX following the First Vatican Council in 1870.

After the council, in 1872, Chancellor Bismarck sent a telegram to the German bishops, assigning to the bishop of Rome a power above that of local bishops, who "are only instruments of the pope, his servants without proper responsibility." The German bishops protested and replied that, according to the teaching of the Catholic Church, the pope is bishop of Rome, not of another diocese nor another city. By his rank as bishop of Rome, however, "he is at the same time pope, the shepherd and supreme head of the universal Church, head of all the bishops and faithful, and his papal power must be respected and listened to everywhere and always." The bishops concluded that "the decisions of the Vatican Council do not furnish the slightest pretext to claim that the pope has become by them an absolute sovereign." Pius IX, in turn, responded to this episcopal teaching with approbation, declaring that it "gives the pure catholic doctrine, and consequently that of the Holy Council and of this Holy See, completely established and clearly developed by irrefutable arguments."[240]

The Second Vatican Council echoes this communional judgment. "Bishops govern the local churches entrusted to them as vicars and ambassadors of Christ." Their power, "which they personally exercise in Christ's name, is proper, ordinary and immediate." They are not "to be regarded as vicars of the Roman Pontiff, for they exercise an authority which is proper to them" (LG 27), an authority which is not destroyed by the universal authority of the pope. Catholic teaching could not be clearer. A bishop is the most publicly designated representative of Christ in his local Church. He exercises episcopal authority, however, always in communion with the college of bishops and its historic head, the bishop of Rome, for episcopal ordination and grace are always given for communion. Any rupture of communion with the episcopal college or its head is a rupture also of communion in the universal Church.

Because he sits on the *cathedra* of Peter as the bishop of the preeminent Church founded on the martyrdom-witness of Peter, the head of the college of apostles, the bishop of Rome is the head of the college of bishops. As such, and not because he has episcopal power beyond that of any other bishop, he is also the supreme pastor of the universal Church. He is "the visible source and foundation of the communion of the bishops and of the multitude of the faithful" (LG 23); the one who is to pastor all, faithful and pastors alike, and to confirm them in the apostolic faith (LG 25); the one by whom the authority of every local bishop is "affirmed, strengthened and vindicated" (LG 27), not diminished. Because he is the successor of Peter in the local Church of Rome, he is the successor also of the universal charge given to Peter: "feed my lambs . . . feed my sheep" (John 21:15-17). He is the successor, ultimately, to that ancient task and title which Gregory the Great gave himself and Paul VI placed at the head of every document approved by the episcopal college at the Second Vatican Council: "Bishop, *Servant of the Servants of God.*"[241]

This communional theology of the primacy of the bishop of Rome will collide in many minds, as it did in the mind of Chancellor Bismarck, with the presumed dogma of infallibility, and therefore absolute papal power, defined by the First Vatican Council in 1870. We must, therefore, explicate the dogma of infallibility the council actually defined.[242] That the pope is absolutely infallible, with no limitation, is presumed by most Catholics to be the dogma defined by the First Vatican Council. It is not. There was a group of bishops at the council who wanted such a maximalist definition, but they did not get it. The council defined a minimalist version, following the recommendation of the Deputation of the Faith conveyed by Monsignor Gasser. The sentence "the pope is infallible" is incomplete, he argued, "since the pope is infallible only when he defines, in a solemn judgment, for the universal Church, a question of faith or of morals.[243] That recommendation was fully incorporated in the council's definition, which we set out in full and explicate here.

"The Roman Pontiff: (1) when he speaks *ex cathedra*, that is, when, *acting in the office of pastor and teacher of all Christians,* by virtue of his supreme apostolic authority, (2) he *defines doctrine concerning faith or morals to be held by the universal Church,* through the divine assistance promised to him in the person of Saint Peter, (3) *enjoys the infallibility with which the divine redeemer willed his Church to be endowed* in defining doctrine concerning faith or morals" (DS 3074; cf. LG 25). The first two italic phrases specify the exacting conditions under which the pope is defined to be infallible. The third suggests that infallibility is a charism primarily of the Church and situates the infallibility of the pope within that of the entire Church-communion.

According to this definition, the pope is not infallible absolutely, but only under the two specific conditions highlighted above. The pope is infallible only when: (1) he speaks *ex cathedra,* that is, as *Lumen gentium* explains, as the successor of Peter *as* "the supreme pastor and teacher of all the faithful" (LG 25), and therefore as the head of the episcopal college; (2) he proclaims by a definitive act a judgment on faith or morals to be held by the universal Church. If we must speak of papal infallibility (and since it is a dogma of the Catholic Church we must), we are obliged, at the very least, to speak only of the dogma which Vatican I defined and the Church believes and teaches.

We must maintain our focus here. Our question is not papal infallibility in general, but only infallibility in the context of the communional theology of papal primacy we have articulated. Those who continue to conceive of papal infallibility as absolute also imagine that the pope makes an infallible judgment in isolation, not in communion. Such a conception, which ignores the limitations specified in the definition, is theologically naive.

No pope acts alone when making an infallible judgment about apostolic faith. He acts, rather, *ex cathedra Petri,* as the successor of Peter in the pastoring and strengthening of the faith of the universal Church. He acts, therefore, specifically as head of the college of bishops and of the universal Church, for it is only as head of the college of bishops that he is head also of the catholic Church. The apostolic faith of that Church, which every bishop is ordained to preach and to safeguard, has already been defined by the great councils of the early Church, Nicea (325), Constantinople (381), Ephesus (431), and Chalcedon (451), the creeds of which the Catholic communion still confesses. A papal judgment *in accord* with this faith is an infallible judgment, not as a solitary judgment of the supreme pastor of the universal Church, but as a judgment in communion with the centuries-long faith of the Church as it is affirmed, strengthened, and vindicated by the entire college of bishops. A judgment *contrary* to that faith is, by definition, simply not an infallible judgment.

When he makes a judgment about faith or morals to be held by the communion of communions as revelation, and as therefore necessary for salvation, the bishop of Rome, the successor to the chair of Peter, does not act in solitary isolation. He acts as head of and in communion with the episcopal college and in communion, therefore, also with their local Churches. This is apparent in the case of the Marian dogmas, immaculate conception (1854) and assumption (1950), defined by Pius IX and Pius XII, the only two papal judgments for which infallibility is authentically claimed.

Tillard notes that these dogmas "are only the echo of the declaration of Mary *theotokos,"*[244] made by the Council of Ephesus. Even more precisely, they are a communional echo which demonstrates that the pope, seeking to make an infallible judgment within the exacting limitations imposed by the First Vatican Council, stands not alone but within the communion of the episcopal college as its head, and therefore also within the communion that is the catholic Church, the radical infallibility of which he shares. The definition of the First Vatican Council leaves no doubt. When the bishop of Rome, *ex cathedra,* as the successor of Peter as head of the apostolic college, by a definitive act proclaims a judgment on faith and morals to be held by the catholic Church, the infallibility he enjoys is the "infallibility with which the redeemer willed his Church to be endowed in defining doctrine concerning faith or morals" (DS 3074).

In a densely argued essay, Karl Rahner sets forth a similar position. "The bearer of the highest and supreme power in the church is the united episcopate with and under the Pope as its head. . . . There is only one subject endowed with supreme power in the church: the college of bishops assembled under the Pope as its head. But there are two modes in which this supreme college may act: a collegiate act properly so called, and the act of the Pope as the head of the college."[245] It is at this point that the third phrase we underscored earlier in the definition of infallibility comes to the forefront. Infallibility, it implies, is first a property of the universal, catholic Church and only then a property of both the college of bishops and of its head, the bishop of Rome.

"The entire body of the faithful," the Second Vatican Council teaches, "anointed as they are by the Holy One, cannot err in matters of the faith" (LG 12). The communion-Church itself, "from the

bishops to the last member of the laity," enjoys the gift of infallibility from the Spirit of God, when "it shows universal agreement in
matters of faith or morals" (LG 12). The college of bishops enjoys the
gift of infallibility from the same Spirit, "provided that while main-
taining the bond of communion among themselves and with Peter's
successor, and while teaching authentically on a matter of faith or
morals, they concur in a single viewpoint as the one which must be
held definitively" (LG 25). The pope enjoys the gift of infallibility
from the same Spirit, "when he speaks *ex cathedra*, that is, when, acting in the office of pastor and teacher of all Christians . . . he defines
doctrine concerning faith or morals to be held by the universal
Church" (DS 3074).

Authentic Roman Catholic doctrine here is simply stated. Infallibility is not an isolated charism of the bishop of Rome. The universal
Church itself receives the charism of infallibility from the Spirit of
God. As representatives of that Church, each in their different ways,
both the college of bishops and its head are recipients of the same
charism. Just as we are now aware that whether we say "local
Church" or "universal Church" each inescapably implies the other, so
also we must become aware that "whether we say 'Pope' or 'college
of bishops' our conceptions of both these entities must be such that
each implies the other."[246] The gift of infallibility, the assurance that
the Spirit of God will not permit the body of Christ that is the people
of God to be led into error, is as communional a gift as the communion-
Church itself. It is also as sacramental, for the infallibility of both the
college of bishops and of the pope are sacraments, signs and instruments, of the infallibility of the Church.

Ordination as Sacrament

Both bishops and presbyters have long been ordained (from Latin
ordinare, "to designate") to specific office in the Church by a ritual
laying on of hands. The Catholic Church has long included this ritual
of ordination among its solemn sacraments. The definition of *sacrament* has varied through the centuries.[247] We define *sacrament* as "an
external sign which reveals, makes explicit, and celebrates the inner
presence and action of the God who is Grace." The question at issue
in general always is: What grace is revealed, made explicit, and celebrated in this sacrament? The question at issue specifically here is:
What grace is proclaimed, made explicit, and celebrated in the sacra-

ment of ordination? An initial answer can be derived from a traditional way of speaking of the ordained bishop and presbyter: he is a
vicar of Christ *(vicarius Christi),* even another Christ.

The phrase *vicarius Christi* appears first in Tertullian, though he
applied it to the Holy Spirit.[248] Later in the third century, Cyprian, his
fellow North African, applies the image, if not the exact phrase, to the
bishop, who acts in the place of Christ *(in vice Christi).*[249] Presbyters
were spoken of in the same way as early as the end of the fourth century,[250] and thereafter it became a commonly accepted way of speaking of both bishops and priests in the catholic Churches. In papal
documents of the modern era, this view of the role of bishops and
presbyters is dominant, and it is presented in a Eucharistic context
and in function of the power of orders. Priests are the "Redeemer's
legates"; they take the place of God *(Dei vices gerit);* they take the
place of Christ *(personam gerit Domini nostri Jesu Christi).*[251] Vatican II echoes this view, teaching that in the celebration of Eucharist
the priest acts in the name of Christ (LG 10, 21, 28; PO 2, 13).

It is one thing, though, to state that a bishop or presbyter is a vicar
of Christ and acts in the person of Christ, and another thing to ground
that assertion theologically. The traditional approach, itself grounded
in a Scholastic theology which links sacraments to Christ without any
mediation on the part of the Church, has been to make it a function
of the power of orders. In this approach, the representative function
of bishops and presbyters derives from institutional considerations.
By the fact that they have been ordained to the office of presiding at
Eucharist by one who holds the apostolic office of overseeing the
Church, and who stands in an unbroken line of succession going back
to the apostles and, indeed, to Christ himself, they are vicars of
Christ.

This traditional insistence on an almost physical succession of ordination is open to several objections. First, the unbroken succession
which it supposes is historically more than doubtful. Second, it too uni-
laterally ignores the mediation of the people-communion in the process
of ordination, putting too much weight on the sacrament as a source of
power over the Eucharistic body of Christ and no weight whatever on
the pastoral service required to preside over the ecclesial body of
Christ, which we have seen to be the priority of both bishops and presbyters. Third, it totally ignores the presence of Christ in his body (SC
7) and the fact that both this presence and Christ's presence in sacrament is not just objective but also and, more properly, interpersonal,

and therefore has as much to do with interpersonal communion as with sacramental power.

Objective presence is drawn into personal presence only by personal faith. Edward Kilmartin, speaking of Eucharist, states that "without the exercise of faith no sacramental presence of Christ or the passion of Christ is possible."[252] He goes on to insist that considerations of the role and of the importance of personal faith "are germane to the question of the representative role of apostolic office. They point to the conclusion that office directly represents the faith of the church and only to this extent can represent Christ."

Ordination is sacramental in that it proclaims, makes explicit, and celebrates the communion-Church as faithful to the apostolic tradition *and* Christ as the source and guarantor of that faith. The *and* can be and has been misleading, however, especially when it is read disjunctively. We need, therefore, to rephrase in order to underscore what we intend. Ordination is a sacrament in the Church in which believers (we do not say *male* believers) are designated as representatives of Christ in so far as, and to the extent that, they are faithful representatives of the faithful Church. We must explain this assertion.

The Second Vatican Council speaks of several modes of Christ's presence in the Church. He is present "especially in liturgical celebrations"; he is present in Eucharist, "not only in the presence of his minister . . . but especially under the Eucharistic species"; he is present in the sacraments "by his power"; he is present in the proclaimed word; he is present in the praying Church (SC 7). The preparatory schema had sought to establish an order in those presences, from Christ's abiding presence in the Church to his presence in word, prayer, sacrament, and Eucharist. That effort could not win enough votes in the council and the weaker text cited above was agreed on. The stumbling block was the desire of the majority of bishops to give precedence to Christ's presence in the Eucharistic minister *(vicarius Christi)* and in the Eucharistic species *(corpus Christi).*

When God raised Jesus from the dead, his mysterious presence in and for the world was established for all time. To be real presence for us, however, that presence needs to be drawn into personal presence. Though I am objectively present in a football crowd, it cannot be said that for most of the crowd I am personally present. For most of them, indeed, I am not really present at all but really absent. So it is with the post-resurrection presence of Jesus; it needs to be drawn from mysterious presence into personal, and therefore humanly real, presence.

The presence of the risen Christ was drawn into real personal presence initially by the faith of the first believers, who believed in the mighty work of God in raising Jesus from the dead and making him manifest as the Christ. This faith became the faith of the Church, the apostolic faith preserved in both the local Churches and in the universal, catholic Church. Apostolic office is an office of witnessing to, pastoring into, and preserving that apostolic faith in the name of the Church.

Ordination establishes believers directly in an order and a ministry of service; it establishes them as representatives of the servant Church, vicars of the Church. In Jesus, Jean Galot insists correctly, "priesthood has become service, that is, ministry. It is this principle of priestly authority exercised as a service that constitutes the ideal of ministry which the disciples must try to live."[253] It is only to the extent that they are ordained as representative of the servant Church that believers are ordained also as vicars of the Christ, who came "not to be served but to serve" (Mark 10:45; cf. LG 27, 28; CD 16), and who is mysteriously one with the Church. Ordination establishes believers in an order of ministers, either the order of deacons (which we have not dealt with in this book),[254] the order of presbyters, or the order of bishops, who act directly in the name of the Church and, therefore, indirectly in the name of Christ.

There is, as Congar has noted, "a Christian mystery which embraces Christ and his ecclesial body."[255] Because of the communion between Christ and his Church, a communion so important that the Church images it in that most intimate of human communions called marriage,[256] what one does in the Church as vicar of Christ is done and can be done only and to the extent that he does it as vicar of the Church. We have traced, admittedly briefly, because the facts are well known and not disputed, the development from the New Testament ideas of the one high priest, the priestly people, and non-priestly ministries to the priestly ministries of the third century. That development leads to the inescapable conclusion that there developed in the Church, undoubtedly under the prompting of the Spirit of God (John 16:13), a presbyteral and episcopal ministry of witnessing to the apostolic faith and of overseeing other ministries aimed at building up the body of Christ. That ministry is today the ministry of the ordained bishop shared with ordained presbyters.

It is because they have the charisms required for pastoral leadership in the Church *(potestas iurisdictionis)*, the ecclesial body of

Christ, that the Church endows bishops and presbyters also with sacramental power *(potestas ordinis)* over Eucharist, the sacramental body of Christ. Ordination publicly proclaims, makes explicit, and celebrates a double presidency, a ritual authorization to act as a representative servant of the Church and, therefore, also as a representative servant of Christ. This approach to ordained leadership in the Church is clear as far back as the *Apostolic Tradition,* where we find it expressed in the consecration of both bishops and presbyters.

The prayer for the consecration of a bishop prays the Father, who knows all hearts, to grant him "to feed your holy flock, to exercise sovereign priesthood without reproach, to make known incessantly your propitious face, to offer the gifts of your holy church." That for the consecration of a presbyter prays for him to "help and govern your people with a pure heart."[257] To the extent that the expression "vicar of Christ" is appropriate at all, it appears "linked, not to the power to consecrate, but to the charge to build up and to preside over the Church."[258] Episcopal and presbyteral ordination establishes believers as sacraments of the Church united in apostolic faith. In its turn, this Church is the sacrament of the Christ who, in his turn, is the sacrament of God who raised him from the dead and showed him to Peter, the Twelve, James, and Paul (1 Cor 15:5-8).

Ordination, like every other sacrament in the Church, is a sacrament because it reveals, makes explicit, and celebrates a gracious reality far beyond the literal reality of the words and actions which comprise it. Ordinary words and actions proclaim, make explicit, and celebrate in believers the faith of the apostolic Church, which ordains them in those words and actions to be its representatives and, therefore, representatives also of the Christ whose body it is and of the God whose people it is. The words and the actions of the ordination ceremony seek to make clear that the election-ordination is the work not only of the Church, but also of the Holy Spirit of God.

What, then, happens in the sacraments of ordination? The ordaining bishop, representative leader of the local Church to the universal, catholic Church and of the catholic Church to the local Church, lays hands on the individual to be ordained and prays over him the prayer of consecration. For presbyters he prays: "Almighty Father, grant to these servants of yours the dignity of the priesthood. Renew within them the Spirit of holiness. As co-workers with the order of bishops may they be faithful to the ministry that they receive from you, Lord God, and be to others a model of right conduct." For bishops he prays: "So now pour out upon this chosen one that power which is from you, the governing Spirit whom you gave to your beloved Son, Jesus Christ, the Spirit given by him to the holy apostles, who founded the Church in every place to be your temple for the unceasing glory and praise of your name."[259]

The words and the gestures of the ritual are meaningful on several levels. They symbolize: (1) the election, by the apostolic Church and, therefore, also by the Spirit of God, of believers who share the apostolic faith of the Church (absence of this faith nullifies the sacrament); (2) the public verification of the apostolic faith of these believers by the bishop of the local Church who has the office of guaranteeing the faith of that Church; (3) the ordination of these believers to an office of pastoral leadership in the Church,[260] an office in which they are *vicarii ecclesiae,* publicly designated representatives of the Church, both local and universal; (4) the ordination, therefore, of these believers as also *vicarii Christi,* representatives of Christ, so that when they proclaim the gospel, forgive sins, or bless bread and wine, it is the Church and the Christ who proclaim, forgive, or bless; (5) the authoritative revelation of these believers' Spirit-gifted charism for the pastoral task of "building up the communion through preaching, admonition and leadership";[261] (6) the appointment of these believers to represent and to nurture the faith of the communion-Church, an appointment which is to be understood as strengthening rather than severing connection to the body, much as Christ the head is connected to the Church which is his body.[262]

Ordination establishes both the presbyter and the bishop in a *holy order,* but the meaning of that phrase needs careful attention. It can be clarified by reflecting back on what we said earlier about order, namely, that to belong to the Church at all, as catechumen, penitent, believer, deacon, presbyter, or bishop, is to belong to a holy order. The charism of pastoral leadership, which is initially given by the Holy Spirit to a believer in baptism, is proclaimed, made explicit, and celebrated in another sacrament, the sacrament of ordination, in and through which the believer is established in a new order in the Church. It is a *holy* order, not because either the presbyter or the bishop alone is holy, still less because they belong to an order holier than other orders in the people, but simply because it is an order in the people called to holiness (LG 39–42). "Holy order is, in the first instance, neither an office nor a function, but a quality manifested by the entire Church when its behavior imitates the Lord's, when its teaching is faithful to the apostles' message, and when its leaders are trusted exemplars worthy of imitation by all."[263]

The restored recognition of Christian initiation as the ritual source which proclaims, makes explicit, and celebrates the ministerial gifts of the Spirit (LG 10) should not and does not preclude the need for further sacramental order in the Church. The charism of leadership is always authorized and celebrated in ritual, both inside and outside the Church, and that is what happens in ordination. The charism of pastoral leadership possessed by a believer is revealed and made explicit for all to celebrate, and is further enhanced with communional and sacramental authorization.

Because of the presence of the Spirit and the Spirit-gifts of apostolic faith and pastoral leadership, believers are ordained to presbyteral and episcopal ministry in the Church. They are ordained, that is, to action in public, on behalf of the Church, as a result of the charism of servant leadership, to incarnate in symbol the presence of the Christ, of his Spirit, and of the God who sends them both. Those initially ordained to Christian ministry in the sacraments of Christian initiation are now ordained anew and specifically to the Christian ministry of pastoral and liturgical leadership. They are ordained, not to monopolize ministry but to promote and challenge all ministries through their own ministry of exemplary leadership. It is thus that they are to build up the body of Christ which is also the people of God and communion-Church.

Summary

In this chapter, we sought to situate and to deal with the ordained presbyterate and episcopate within the perspective of the model of Church as the communion of the people of God. The ordained presbyterate and the common ecclesial priesthood of the people must be related: the former is a task and a function of pastoral leadership in the people. The ordained episcopate is also related to the communion-Church itself: communion in the college of bishops is a sacrament of the communion of all the local Church-communions in the universal, catholic Church of Christ. Ordination establishes presbyters and bishops as both pastoral leaders of the Church-body of Christ and liturgical leaders of the Eucharist-body of Christ. While the sacraments of initiation establish all believers as members of the people, the sacraments of ordination designate some of them as representative leaders of the people *(vicarii ecclesiae)*. To the extent that they are first members and sacramentally designated leaders of the people, they are also members and representatives of Christ *(vicarii Christi)*. Only because they are first members of the holy order of the people of God can they then be also members of the holy order of the presbyterate or of the episcopate. We challenge the people generally and the clergy specifically to see their original holy unity as the indispensable source of their subsequent and secondary functional differentiation.

Questions for Reflection

1. When the Second Vatican Council wanted to speak of ordained presbyters, it spoke first of the common priesthood of all believers. Why do you think it did so? What implications do you see?

2. How do you understand the terms *holy orders of the Christian people* and *holy orders of the clergy?* Are they in any way meaningful to you? Do they have any implications for you as a member of the Church?

3. Reflect on the relationship between pastoral leadership and liturgical leadership in the Church. What do you believe happens in the sacraments of Christian initiation and ordination? What are the implications for Christian living?

4. Reflect on the term *vicar of Christ*. What are the practical implications for presbyters, for bishops, and for the people of God?

5. What is your personal vision of Church and of ministry?

7

Communion of Communions—
Church of Churches

Preamble

For many in every Christian denomination, the greatest scandal of
Christian history is that the Church, for whose unity Jesus fervently
prayed (John 17:20-23), is so divided. We accept this judgment as
true, but we also call attention to one foundational area in which the
divided Churches are at one. Catholic, Orthodox, and the vast majority of Protestant Christians confess their common faith in "one, holy,
catholic, and apostolic Church." (Though this solemn profession of
faith was first promulgated by the First Council of Constantinople in
381, all the Christian Churches commonly refer to it as the Nicene
Creed.)[264] The contradiction between the common confession of faith
in "one Church" and the divided state of the Christian Churches provides a prime motive for the modern ecumenical movement. It is this
Christian contradiction of communion, and the ecumenical questions
to which it gives rise, that we confront in this chapter.

In the opening chapter, we noted the judgments of John Paul II that
"communion is the very mystery of the Church" (CL 18) and of the
1985 synod that the vision of Church as communion was the most
important teaching of the Second Vatican Council. We noted also the
transition from a pre- to a postconciliar ecclesiology, from a juridical
vision of Church as institution and structure to a theological vision of
it as grace and communion. Communion, we insisted, connotes a
richer reality of grace than mere Church institution and membership.
Our communion is not only with and in an ecclesiastical institution,

but also with God. Though there must be some institutional communion, more important is communion with God in grace. This will be of central importance in this chapter, where we take up again the notion of communion under three separate headings. First, its use in the documents of the Second Vatican Council; second, its use in common ecumenical statements since the council; third, its implications for the longed for and much talked about reality of communion between the Christian Churches.

Communion in the Documents of Vatican II

The Decree on Ecumenism, *Unitatis redintegratio,* uses the word *communion* or an equivalent some forty-three times. That alone is testimony enough to the important place it occupied for the council fathers in ecumenical matters. The document makes two distinctions which are of interest to us in this chapter. The first is between "perfect ecclesiastical communion" and imperfect ecclesiastical communion (UR 4), the second is between ecclesiastical communion (UR 4) and "communion with the Father, the Word and the Spirit" (UR 7).

A first, and very clear, assertion emerges in *Unitatis redintegratio.* Communion with God is not linked exclusively to ecclesiastical communion with any Church, including the Catholic Church. Ecclesiastical communion, whether perfect or imperfect, is not the exclusive way to communion with God. The decree asserts that Orthodox Christians, though not in communion with the Catholic Church, in their celebration of Eucharist "gain access to God the Father through the Son," and enter "into communion with the most holy Trinity" (UR 15). In their celebration of the Lord's Supper, other Christians, who look to Christ "as the source and center of ecclesiastical communion" (UR 20), commemorate the Lord's death and resurrection and profess "life in communion with Christ" (UR 22). Communion with God is not, the council asserts, a gift given exclusively to or through the Catholic Church. It is a gift of God given where and to whom the Spirit of God wills.[265]

We have already noted that Pope Pius XII's encyclical *Mystici Corporis* asserts that the Catholic tradition does not support any separation between the mystical body of Christ and the visible Church. It does not support the concept, suggested by some Protestant theologians, of a perfect, spiritual Church separate from an imperfect, historical Church. This assertion, however, was not what raised theological difficulties with the encyclical. The Pope went further and asserted an exclusive identification between the mystical body and the historical Roman Catholic Church, such that non-Catholic Christians, even those in the state of grace, could not be considered members of Christ's mystical body.[266] Since even Catholic theologians objected that they could not see how Christians graced by Christ and his Spirit could be excluded from Christ's body, the Pope returned to the question in his encyclical *Humani Generis* (1950) and insisted that the mystical body of Christ and the Roman Catholic Church were one and the same.[267]

It is no surprise, then, that the preparatory theological commission for the Second Vatican Council, the secretary of which was Sebastian Tromp, Pius XII's chief collaborator in the writing of *Mystici Corporis*,[268] produced a draft of the constitution on the Church which stated that "the Roman Catholic Church *is* the mystical body of Christ . . . and only the one that is Roman Catholic has the right to be called Church."[269] The criticisms raised against this assertion contributed to the withdrawal of the draft and to the reformulation of a text, *Lumen gentium*, which asserted something quite different. Instead of saying that the mystical body of Christ *is* the Catholic Church, *Lumen gentium* said that it *"subsists* in the Catholic Church" (LG 8). The official explanation given for the change was "so that the expression might better agree with the affirmation about ecclesial elements which are to be found elsewhere."[270] There was no official explanation of the meaning of the crucial word *subsists.*

One thing is certain. The council's explicit decision to reject the copulative *is* was a decision to reject the absolute and exclusive identity between the Church founded by Christ, the body of Christ, the communion of the people of God, and the Roman Catholic Church. Were that not so, there would have been no incentive to change *is* to *subsists in,* and there would have been no resolution to the criticisms of the exclusive identity which contributed to the rejection of the preparatory draft. Most commentators have interpreted the change as a significant opening to the ecclesial reality of other Christian communions, in keeping with the explanation of the preparatory commission adduced above. That still leaves unanswered many questions which, for our purposes here, we reduce to three. What is the significance of the change from *is* to *subsists in* for (1) the Catholic Church, (2) other Christian Churches, and (3) the Church founded by Christ?[271]

First, what is the significance of the change for the Catholic Church? The answer to that question hinges on the meaning assigned to the word *subsists*. Cassell's New Latin Dictionary indicates that the primary meaning of the word *subsistere* is "to continue, to stay, to remain." To say, then, that the Church established by Christ "subsists in the Catholic Church" is to say that it continues to exist in the Catholic Church. This reading is confirmed as correct by two passages in the Decree on Ecumenism.

The unity Christ intended for his Church, the decree first asserts, "subsists in the Catholic Church as something she can never lose" (UR 4). It asserts, secondly, when speaking of Churches separated from the Catholic Church, that the Anglican communion is one "in which some catholic traditions and institutions continue to subsist" (UR 13).[272] This interpretive connection between *Lumen gentium* and *Unitatis redintegratio* follows a principle established by Pope Paul VI when the two documents were promulgated together in 1964. The doctrine on the Church, he decreed, is to be interpreted in the light of the further explanations given in the Decree on Ecumenism.[273] Following this principle, it is correct to assert that the meaning of *subsists* in *Lumen gentium* is that the Church established by Christ continues to exist, though not exclusively, in the historical Catholic Church.

There is a caveat here, to which the council draws attention and which we must heed. The continuity and identity asserted between the Church established by Christ and the modern Catholic Church is a continuity and identity of *means* to communion, not necessarily of communion itself. There is no guarantee that any Catholic congregation is in communion with God simply because it is Catholic. Communion follows not from the access to the means of communion, common faith, common sacraments, common life of disciples, but from the Spirit-filled *use* of the means. The council recognizes this distinction and sadly acknowledges that the Catholic Church falls short. "Although the Catholic Church has been endowed with all divinely revealed truth and with all means of grace, her members fail to live by them with all the fervor they should" (UR 4). The assertion that the Church established by Christ "subsists in the Catholic Church" is not an assertion either of perfect communion between Catholics and God or of perfect non-communion between non-Catholic Christians and God. This brings us to our second question, what is the significance of the change from *is* to *subsists in* for other Christian Churches?

The very title of chapter 3 of *Unitatis redintegratio* provides an immediate answer to our question: "Churches and Ecclesial Communities Separated from the Roman Apostolic See." There can be no doubt that, in the council's view, there are Christian Churches apart from the Catholic Church, and that the Church founded by Christ continues to subsist in those Churches. A clear statement of this fact is made about both the Anglican Church and the Eastern Catholic Churches.

In the Anglican communion "some Catholic traditions and institutions continue to subsist *[subsistere]*" (UR 13). In the Eastern Churches, "there flourish many particular or local Churches; among them, the Patriarchal Churches hold first place; and of these, many glory in taking their origins from the Apostles themselves" (UR 14). This entire chapter would have to be ignored or radically revised were one to suggest that the council was not of the opinion that there were genuine Christian Churches, genuine continuations of the Church founded by Christ, outside the Roman Church.

Paul VI's principle of the mutual clarification of *Lumen gentium* and *Unitatis redintegratio* provides further clarification. The former declares that "the Church recognizes that in many ways she is linked with those who, being baptized, are honored with the name of Christian" (LG 15). It goes on to specify those many ways. "There are many who honor sacred scripture . . . lovingly believe in God the Father Almighty and in Christ, Son of God and Savior . . . are consecrated by baptism, through which they are united to Christ . . . receive other sacraments within *their own Churches and ecclesial communities* . . . rejoice in the episcopate, celebrate the holy Eucharist and cultivate devotion toward the Virgin Mother of God . . . share with us in prayer and other spiritual benefits . . . are joined with us in the Holy Spirit" (LG 15).

The Decree on Ecumenism repeats these shared elements, noting that the communities in which they are present and the Holy Spirit is active are "separated from *full* communion [not from *all* communion] with the Catholic Church" (UR 3). Given such clearly stated positions on both the existence of Christian Churches apart from the Catholic Church and their significance in the process of salvation or communion with God, it is difficult to see how anyone could claim that the council's intention was to declare that there are only elements of Church, and not Church itself, outside the Catholic Church. That, however, is what the Congregation for the Doctrine of the Faith

(CDF), has officially claimed, and we shall conclude this subsection by examining that claim.

In March 1985, the CDF issued a "Notification" on a book by Father Leonardo Boff, *Church: Charism and Power.* In that book, Boff wrote that the Catholic Church "is the Church of Christ inasmuch as through it the Church of Christ is present in the world." He added, however, citing *Lumen gentium* 8 in his support, that the Catholic Church "cannot claim an exclusive identity with the Church of Christ because the Church may also be present in other Christian churches."[274] The CDF responded that this claim was "a thesis exactly contrary to the authentic meaning of the conciliar text," and added this explanation. "The council, rather, had chosen the word *subsistit* precisely to clarify that there exists only one 'subsistence' of the true Church, while outside of its visible structures there exist only elements of the Church itself."[275] It added that the Decree on Ecumenism (UR 3–4) expresses the same doctrine.

The Congregation for the Doctrine of the Faith is an important teaching office of the Church, and it is proper for it to interpret conciliar documents. Those interpretations, however, must be supported by the obvious meanings of the passages themselves and by the mind of their writers to be truly authentic. In its interpretation of *subsists,* this is clearly not the case. The CDF's interpretation means two things: "1) it is *only* in the Catholic Church that the Church of Christ can be said to 'subsist', and 2) it subsists in the Catholic Church in so exclusive a way that outside of her limits there can be found *only elements* of Church."[276] It is difficult to see how the exclusivity which is the core of the CDF's interpretation corresponds to the approved conciliar statements.

Lumen gentium certainly does not say explicitly, nor does it implicitly suggest, that the Church of Christ subsists *only* in the Catholic Church. In fact, it implies the exact opposite. While it acknowledges that the Church established by Christ subsists in the Catholic Church, it immediately adds that "many elements of sanctification and truth can be found outside her visible structure" (LG 8). It specifies explicitly that among those elements are sacraments received "within [other] Churches or ecclesial communities" (LG 15). Chapter 3 of *Unitatis redintegratio,* as previously noted, is entitled without qualification "Churches and Ecclesial Communities Separated from the Roman Apostolic See."[277] Among those Churches, the Eastern Churches are said to hold a "special position," as local, almost sister,

Churches of the Roman Church (UR 14). There is absolutely no suggestion that, in these apostolic Churches not in full ecclesiastical communion with the Catholic Church, there are *only* elements of Church.

The CDF's interpretation of the crucial word *subsists* is simply not supported by the conciliar documents it purports to interpret. The Church of Christ continues to be found in near-fullness in the Catholic Church, though it confesses the need to "incessantly pursue the path of penance and renewal" (LG 8). It is found also in varying degrees of fullness in many Churches and ecclesial communities not in perfect communion with the Catholic Church. It is not correct, Vatican II definitively taught, to state that the Catholic Church *is* the body of Christ to the exclusion of all other Christian communities. That is the answer to the first two questions posed in this section. There remains only the third one. What is the significance of the change from *is* to *subsists in* for the universal Church founded by Christ?

We could resolve this question quickly by accepting the judgments of two great French theologians, Louis Bouyer and Yves Congar. Commenting on "the preeminent scandal" of the continuing separation of the Orthodox and Catholic Churches, Bouyer declares that, "though dreadfully tempted by the spirit of division, they remain one church, in fact and in right, despite contrary appearances."[278] Congar agrees, declaring forthrightly that, despite the obvious imperfect communion between them, "the Catholic Church of the West and the Orthodox Church of the East have never ceased to be one church."[279] The task of the theologian, however, is never as simple as citing theological answers. The validity of those answers must be demonstrated. That demonstration is the explicit task of the final part of this section.

Congar's judgment is advanced in an extended commentary on a significant passage of the papal bull *Anno Ineunte,* personally sent by Pope Paul VI to Patriarch Athenagoras on 25 July 1967. After rejoicing in the rediscovery by the two Churches of their character as "sister Churches," the Pope hopes "that we can bring to its fullness and perfection the communion existing between us, which is already so rich."[280] On 17 October 1969, the Pope sent a telegram to Athenagoras repeating his hopes for "the reestablishment of the two sister Churches in their full communion."[281] This character as sister Churches, and the communion necessarily flowing from it, is founded on having a common Father in Christ, a common baptism, a common priesthood, a common Eucharist, and, perhaps above all, a common apostolic succession. It is supported by what we have heard the De-cree on Ecumenism say of the Eastern Churches.

Although some of these Churches are separated from the Catholic Church, "they possess true sacraments, above all—by apostolic suc-cession—the priesthood and the Eucharist, whereby they are still joined to us in a very close relationship" (UR 15). The Catholic Church desires that "full communion" be restored between the East-ern Churches and itself (UR 14). It thanks God that many of these Churches "are already living in full communion" with it (those that are named Uniate Churches), and declares that the entire heritage of these Churches, their spirituality and liturgy, their discipline and the-ology, "belongs to the full catholic and apostolic character of the Church" (UR 17).

The language is unequivocal. The Eastern Churches, Orthodox as well as Uniate, are recognized as particular or local Churches in the one Church of Christ. This notion of the local Church is, as we saw in chapter 1, a common one in *Lumen gentium*. The Church of Christ is said to be "truly present in all legitimate local congregations of the faithful which, united with their pastors, are themselves called Churches in the New Testament" (LG 26). A bishop is said to be "the visible principle and foundation of unity in his particular Church, fashioned after the model of the universal Church. In and from such individual Churches there comes into being the one and only Catholic Church" (LG 23; cf. CD 11). The notion of the local Churches within the universal Church is a common notion, in both the East and West. It is common also in the New Testament literature.

Paul frequently uses both *church* in the singular and *churches* in the plural. He addresses his First Letter to the Corinthians "to the church of God which is at Corinth" (1:2), his Letter to the Galatians "to the churches of Galatia" (1:2), both his Letters to the Thessaloni-ans "to the church of the Thessalonians" (1 Thess 1:1; 2 Thess 1:1). He writes to the Romans of the church that is in the house of Prisca and Aquila (16:5) and tells them that "all the churches of Christ greet you" (16:16). He writes to the Corinthians that "the churches of Asia send greetings. Aquila and Prisca, together with the church in their house, send you hearty greetings in the Lord" (1 Cor 16:19). He sends greetings "to Nympha and the church in her house" (Col 4:15). He writes of "all the churches of the Gentiles" (Rom 16:4), "all the churches of Christ" (Rom 16:16), "the churches of God" (1 Cor 11:16; 2 Thess 1:4).

A question arises: how can all those Churches be one Church? Francis Sullivan suggests the two obvious possibilities. Either there was a series of independent Churches who united themselves together into one Church, or a single Church which then developed and spread by multiplying local congregations in different places, while still consciously remaining one Church.[282] There is no evidence anywhere to support the first hypothesis. There is strong evidence to support the second.

Perhaps the most striking evidence is in the Letter to the Galatians. Paul speaks freely of "the churches of Galatia" (1:2) and "the churches of Christ in Judea" (1:22), but he also advances his most telling judgment about the unity of all those apparently separate Churches. "As many of you as were baptized into Christ have put on Christ. There is neither Jew nor Greek, there is neither slave nor free, there is neither male nor female; for you are all one person in Christ Jesus" (3:27-28). That argument is reinforced by the argument against the divisive factions in the Corinthian Church. There, some said "I belong to Paul," others "I belong to Apollos," "I belong to Cephas," even "I belong to Christ" (1:12). Paul's answer to such claims is a classic and definitive no to the foundational question: "Is Christ divided?" (1:13). Christ is not divided, and "no other foundation can anyone lay than that which is laid, which is Jesus Christ" (3:11).

The argument is repeated and reinforced in the Letter to the Ephesians, where the many peoples and the many Churches are said to be one people, one household and temple of God "built upon the foundation of the apostles and prophets, Christ Jesus himself being the cornerstone in whom the whole structure is joined together" (2:20). That unity is further emphasized in the image of the Church as the body of Christ, so common throughout the Letter to the Ephesians (1:22-23; 2:14-16; 3:6; 4:4-16; 5:22-30), and on which we reflected in our opening chapter. In Ephesians, too, is the definitive reason why there is and can be only one, all-embracing Christian Church. "There is one body and one Spirit . . . one Lord, one faith, one baptism, one God and Father of us all" (4:4-6).

This judgment affirms the unity of the Church of Christ and sets forth, at least, some of the reality that founds that unity. The Letter to the Galatians offers evidence of an early threat to that unity. The Judaizers demanded of Gentile converts to the Church of Christ observance of circumcision and the ritual prescriptions of the Mosaic Law.

Paul had not required this of Galatian converts but, as he says, false brethren "slipped in to spy out our freedom which we have in Christ Jesus that they might bring us into bondage" (2:4). Paul thunders against them as he opens his letter.

"I am astonished that you are so quickly deserting him who called you in the grace of Christ and turning to a different gospel" (1:6). There is no gospel, he insists, other than the one he preached and the Galatians accepted, a fact confirmed by "James and Cephas and John, who were reputed to be pillars" of the church (2:9). Paul went to Jerusalem to consult them on the matter of circumcision, bringing with him his uncircumcised convert Titus. Titus "was not compelled to be circumcised" (2:3) and they extended to Paul "the right hand of communion, that we should go to the Gentiles and they to the circumcised" (2:9). To receive the "hand of communion" from the original apostles was crucial for Paul, for it accomplished two things. It demonstrated to him and to his converts that they had the same faith as the old Jewish converts. It was that same faith, undivided by their diverse practices, that joined them all in the communion of the one Church of Christ.

The ancient historian Eusebius of Caesarea provides us with the details of continuing communion in diversity in the early Church. The question of the date of Easter is a case in point. The Churches of Asia celebrated Easter on the fourteenth day of the month of Nisan, a date which did not always fall on a Sunday. From that traditional practice, they took their name, the Quartodecimans. After several Church councils considered the question and ruled that Easter was properly celebrated on Sunday, Victor, the bishop of Rome (c. 190), threatened to excommunicate the Quartodecimans if they did not fall in line with the Sunday celebration. Many bishops, including the great Irenaeus of Lyons, wrote to dissuade him from this course of action. Irenaeus stressed the apostolic origin of the Quartodeciman practice and pointed out to Victor that his predecessors had long respected this practice and had maintained communion with the Quartodecimans in spite of it. Victor never moved on his threat of excommunication.[283]

The Quartodeciman discussion continues in the Church down to our day.[284] In an appendix to its Constitution on the Liturgy, the Second Vatican Council acknowledged "the importance of the wishes expressed by many concerning the assignment of the feast of Easter to a fixed Sunday." It declared that it "would not object if the feast of Easter were assigned to a particular Sunday of the Gregorian calendar,

provided that those whom it may concern give their consent, especially the brethren who are not in communion with the Apostolic See."[285]

Easter is the bedrock event of Christianity (1 Cor 15:14), the event without which there is no Christian movement, no communion in Christ, no Church of Christ. Unanimity in its celebration would be a powerful sign of communion in the one faith. Yet the Catholic Church remembers, and reveres, Irenaeus's argument about the apostolicity of the two traditions of celebrating Easter. Thus we point out and underscore the firmest Catholic tradition that within the communion of the one faith a diversity of customs has always been, and continues to be, legitimate.

Communion in an Ecumenical Context

Ecumenical documents since the Second Vatican Council converge on situating communion as a function of both baptism and Eucharist. The seminal document of the World Council of Churches, *Baptism, Eucharist and Ministry (BEM),* expresses the ecclesial meaning of baptism as incorporation into the body of Christ, declaring that "through baptism, Christians are brought into union with Christ, with each other and with the church of every time and place."[286] The Roman Catholic Church has criticized this document on several grounds,[287] but never on this. The Church of Christ, of which the baptized are made members and with which they are called to be in communion, transcends each and every one of the historical Churches. In theological language, a person is baptized into not only some local Church but simultaneously into the universal Church of Christ, which comes into being in and from the local Churches, *in et ex ecclesiis* (LG 23). This is the basic reason why *BEM* recommends, and the Churches accept, the practice of not rebaptizing a Christian previously baptized in another Christian tradition.

Traditional sacramental theology defines sacrament as "an outward sign instituted by Christ to give grace."[288] Baptism specifically proclaims, makes explicit, and celebrates both the death and the resurrection of Jesus and the new life in Christ to which the baptized are called (Rom 6:4; Col 2:13-14; *BEM* 2.A.3). That new life is communion, not only communion with one another in the Church, but also and especially communion in the life of the Father, the Son, and the Holy Spirit, in whose name baptism is celebrated. That communion with God is *the* grace of baptism in which every other grace is rooted. Baptism is truly a sacrament of initiation, for it initiates the baptized into the grace of communion. It is this communion with God which grounds the fact that the Spirit-filled actions of Christians "can truly engender a life of grace, and can be rightly described as capable of providing access to the communion of salvation" (UR 3). This access is available to all Christians, not only to those in full ecclesiastical communion with the Roman Catholic Church.

There is another Christian sacrament of initiation: Eucharist. *BEM* says, as we have maintained throughout this book, that "it is in the eucharist that the communion of God's people is fully manifested" (2.D.19). The 1976 Moscow Statement, the outcome of the consultation between the Orthodox and the Anglican Churches, expresses the same point more directly and beautifully. "The church celebrating eucharist becomes fully itself, that is, *koinonia,* fellowship, communion."[289] Both documents provide clear echoes of *Unitatis redintegratio.* Eucharist, it declares, is a wonderful sacrament "by which the communion of the Church is both signified and brought about" (UR 2). The grace sacramentally given in Eucharist, as in baptism, is communion, both with God in Christ and with the Church of Christ subsisting in a local Christian Church. The Church, both local and universal, as we have frequently said, is essentially Eucharistic.

Though our two benchmarks, communion with the triune God and ecclesiastical communion, are in historical reality not separable, they are always distinguishable. They should never be dissolved one into the other. Citing with evident approval Paul's judgment in Galatians that all the baptized are "one in Christ" (Gal 3:28), the Decree on Ecumenism proceeds to insist that "it is the Holy Spirit, dwelling in those who believe . . . who brings about that marvelous communion of the faithful" (UR 2). This marvelous communion is the result, not of membership in some historical Church, though that too flows from baptism, but of the grace-full indwelling presence of the Trinity in the baptized. It is communion with God which founds ecclesiastical communion, not the other way round.

Ecclesiastical communion, however, is not to be in any way discounted, for, in a Church which is mystery and sacrament, communion with the transcendent, triune God is concretized and made visible in sacramental relationships. The sacraments confessed without debate by all the Christian traditions are baptism and Eucharist. The baptismal relationship to an external ecclesiastical institution objectifies and makes visible the relationship of internal communion with God in Christ. The Eucharistic relationship objectifies and makes visible the related communion to that God and to the Church in which Eucharist is celebrated.

It is of particular significance in this context that the Roman Catholic Church, which does not recognize the validity of a Eucharistic celebration in any ecclesial community which does not have proper apostolic succession, does recognize that such Eucharists "commemorate the Lord's death and resurrection" and signify "life in communion with Christ" (UR 22). It confesses, that is, the grace-filled and, therefore, the salvific character of such Eucharistic celebrations. Though their validity and efficacy as a way to signify and bring about ecclesiastical communion is called into doubt, no doubt is cast on their validity and efficacy as a way of both signifying and bringing about communion with God.

There are deep implications here for any Church that believes that divine communion is both the goal and the source of any and all ecclesiastical communion. It remains for those implications to be drawn out explicitly for the scandal of divided Christendom to be healed and, more importantly, for Jesus' prayer for communion to bear final fruit. "That they may all be one; even as thou, Father, art in me, and I in thee, that they also may be in us; that the world may believe that thou hast sent me" (John 17:21).

An earlier discussion is of great importance here. According to *Lumen gentium*, a bishop is "the steward of the grace of the supreme priesthood, especially in the Eucharist . . . by which the Church constantly lives and grows." "This Church of Christ," the council adds, "is truly present in all legitimate congregations of the faithful which, united with their pastors, are themselves called Churches in the New Testament" (LG 26). Any discussion of communion in the Church of Christ begins with these local communions gathered with their bishop in Eucharistic communion, for the one Church of Christ is objectified in these local altar communions (cf. LG 26), themselves objectified and made visible in their bishops.[290] Full ecclesiastical communion in any historical Christian Church is the full communion of these local communions. We discover here an analogy for the full communion of the historical Churches.

The idea we appeal to is the ancient one of "communion of communions." There are certain prerequisites. First, each communion would acknowledge and rejoice in its own communion, and that of the others, with the God they confess as Father, Son, and Holy Spirit. Second, each communion would accept the others' baptism, and would admit to Eucharistic communion the members of every other communion confessing Eucharist as a commemoration of the Lord's death and resurrection and as a means both to signify and to bring about life in communion with Christ and the God he reveals (UR 22). Third, such intercommunion would imply that each communion confesses that the others hold all the essentials of the Christian faith, but would not imply that any of them accepts, or needs to accept, all the theological opinions, ritual practices, or institutional structures of any other.[291]

Those who continue to conceive of ecumenism in exclusively Roman terms, as a return to full ecclesiastical communion with the Roman Catholic Church,[292] will have problems with our suggestion. Both they and we have two immediate tasks, which we will face in the following and concluding section. The first is to be clear about what the Catholic Church was saying ecclesiologically in and through the Second Vatican Council. The second is to clarify the implications of what it was saying.

The Church of Christ and the Churches

The first task is easy, following from what we have said about *Lumen gentium*'s transition from *is* to *subsists in*. The Catholic Church was saying in that transition that, despite the teaching of both *Mystici Corporis* and *Humani generis,* the Church and body of Christ was not identical to the Roman Catholic Church. The Church of Christ does continue to be embodied in the Catholic Church, but in a way that does not exclude its embodiment also in other Christian Churches. The Church of Christ continues to exist substantially in the Roman Catholic Church, but in an "inclusivist" not an "exclusivist" way,[293] in a way that includes its substantial embodiment also in other Christian traditions (LG 8).

We highlight here another facet of Vatican II's assertion about the relationship between the Church established by Christ and the Roman Catholic Church. Though the latter is a continuing substantial embodiment of the Church of Christ, it is far from being a perfect embodiment. It is an *ecclesia semper reformanda,* a Church always in need of reformation and purification, a Church pursuing a "path of penance and renewal," a pilgrim Church waiting to be "revealed in total splendor" (LG 8). The Roman Catholic Church, the council conceded, is an imperfect and perfectible realization of the Church of Christ, as are other Christian communities. The degree of imperfection may differ in the different Churches, but there is, the council asserts, a degree of imperfection of realization of the universal Church of Christ in each and every historical local Church.

We confront our second task through two distinctions. The first is variously described as the distinction between the inner and outer elements of the Church, between the hierarchical institution and the body of Christ, between the human and the divine. *Lumen gentium* warns us that "the society furnished with hierarchical agencies and the mystical body of Christ are not to be considered as two realities, nor are the visible assembly and the spiritual community." They form, rather, "one interlocked reality which is comprised of a divine and a human element" (LG 8). We confess that one reality; indeed, we have dealt with it as an interlocked sacramental reality in chapter 3. We insist here only that, though the divine and the human are not separable in the Church, they are distinct, not identical and, therefore, never to be identified.

Catholic ecclesiology prior to the Second Vatican Council tended to concentrate very narrowly on the external, visible institution, overlooking the internal, spiritual communion. It was, we recall, a preparatory document that did just that which was rejected in 1962 and replaced by *Lumen gentium* in 1964. Congar has described the transition from the preparatory document to the approved document as a transition from the priority of "organizational structures and hierarchical positions" to "the priority and even the primacy of the ontology of grace."[294] We describe it as the transition from a juridical vision that sees the Church as institutional and structural to a theological vision that sees it as mystery and communion.

Exclusive focus on hierarchical institution allowed the claim that the Roman Catholic Church and the body of Christ were coextensive to stand. Taking seriously, as *Lumen gentium* does, the dimension of mystery and communion and grace, does not permit such a claim to stand. The body of Christ, the mystery of communion and peace between Christ and those who believe in him and the God he reveals, does not coincide with the institution of the Roman Catholic Church. There is a real, if imperfect, communion between all those who share the grace of God. In terms of the benchmark categories operating in this chapter, there can be communion with God without ecclesiastical

communion, perfect or imperfect, with any particular Church institution. Where there is this communion of believers with God in Christ
through the Spirit, there is also, and necessarily, communion between
these believers, however imperfect it may be.

We note here again that the continuity and identity asserted between the Church established by Christ and the Roman Catholic
Church is a continuity and identity of *means* to communion, not necessarily of communion itself. Communion follows not from access to
the means of communion, but from use of the means. There is no
guarantee that any Catholic congregation or individual is in communion with God, and with one another, simply because they are
Catholic. There is no guarantee that any non-Catholic congregation or
individual is not in communion with God, and with one another,
simply because they are non-Catholic. There may be, indeed, fuller
bonds of communion between two grace-filled Christians of different
Christian Churches than between two members of the same ecclesiastical institution not living a grace-filled life.

Mystici Corporis declares that of the two dimensions of communion, the spiritual and the institutional, the former is far and away
(omnino) the more important.[295] *Lumen gentium* agrees, declaring that
"the communal structure of the Church serves Christ's Spirit, who
vivifies it" (LG 8). Given this theological fact, it simply cannot be
presumed that the Church of Christ is better realized in the Roman
Catholic Church than in any other. Institutional Roman Catholics
who lack the life of grace and the Spirit are, at best, in only imperfect
communion with the Church of Christ.

Those Christians, on the other hand, who are not in ecclesiastical
communion with the Roman Catholic Church, but who live a life of
grace in the Spirit, are in a most important way in communion with
the Church of Christ and with Roman Catholics who are also in communion with it. They can never be declared strangers to Christ and to
God, to grace and to the Spirit, to sanctification and salvation. From
the more important perspective of the unchanging structures of grace,
rather than from the changing structures of institution, Gregory
Baum's assertion is beyond debate. *"Concretely* and *actually* the
Church of Christ may be realized less, equally, or even more in a
church separated from Rome than in a church in communion with
Rome."[296]

Summary

In this chapter, from the basis of the operational category of communion, we confronted theologically the divisions which scandalously rend the Church established by Christ, and the ecumenical movement which seeks to heal those divisions. Following the Second Vatican Council, communion should be considered under two benchmark headings, communion with God and communion with an ecclesiastical institution. One must understand the teaching of the Vatican Council that the Church established by Christ "subsists in the Catholic Church" (LG 8), and that there is a sisterly communion between the Catholic Church and the Orthodox Church. Finally, recent ecumenical statements about the sacraments of baptism and Eucharist lead us to propose a communion of communions model for the Church of Christ. Our hope in this chapter was not so much to solve all ecumenical problems as to consider and offer possible solutions to the foundational one, the divisions which keep Christian Churches from communion with one another.

Questions for Reflection

1. How do you distinguish and relate communion with God and communion with an ecclesiastical institution? In your judgment, is it a legitimate distinction?

2. Reflect on the implications for a Roman Catholic theology of Church of the Second Vatican Council's teaching that the Church established by Christ "subsists in the Catholic Church"? In your judgment, is it possible to claim that a Catholic or a Lutheran is in communion with God just by being in communion with the Catholic or the Lutheran Church?

3. How do you understand the claim of the Congregation for the Doctrine of the Faith that Vatican II's teaching that the Church established by Christ "subsists in the Catholic Church" means that there is only one embodiment of the Church of Christ among the historical Churches? In your judgment, is such a claim in accord with the conciliar texts?

4. On what basis can it be argued that "the Catholic Church of the West and the Orthodox Church of the East have never ceased to be one Church"? In your judgment, does diversity of practice compromise communion?

5. How do you evaluate our suggestion for the healing of Christian divisions according to a model of communion of communions? Do you see any theological problems with it?

8

Communion and Spirituality

Spirituality

Spirituality is a misunderstood word because the word from which it is derived, the English *spirit,* is misunderstood. Jean Danielou identifies the source of the problem. When we say that God is a spirit, he asks, are we speaking Greek or Hebrew? "If we are speaking Greek, we are saying that God is immaterial. If we are speaking Hebrew, we are saying that God is a wind-storm and an irresistible force. This is why, when we speak of spirituality, a great deal is ambiguous. Does spirituality mean becoming immaterial or does it mean being animated by the Holy Spirit?"[297] The attentive reader of this book will have no doubt that, when we say *spirit,* we are speaking Hebrew. When we say *spirituality,* we are also speaking Hebrew. We are saying with Hebrew Paul life "in the Spirit" (Rom 7:6; 8:9; 14:17; 1 Cor 14:2; Phil 2:1; Col 1:8). We are saying with Karl Rahner life from and in and toward God.[298] Believers live spiritual lives when they realize, in faith and hope and love, the divine life that indwells both them and the world in which they live, and when they respond to the indwelling God in the ordinariness of their daily lives.

There is another source of confusion in the Christian use of *spirituality.* It is regularly accompanied by a modifier, *Franciscan,* for instance, or *Jesuit,* or *lay.* This practice raises two questions. Are there many spiritualities in the abiding Spirit, and are there specific differences among these spiritualities? An ecclesiology of communion, the approach to Church as a gathering of believers in communion in the one Spirit, clarifies the theological fact that, despite many modifiers, there is only one Christian spirituality. The modified spiritualities are, in Hans Urs von Balthasar's words, "special spiritualities." They arise from the variety of ways God is revealed to different groups in the communion, and from the fact that the communion then receives and celebrates these various revelations as the word of God. That word received *objectively,* von Balthasar argues, is theology; received *subjectively* it is spirituality.[299]

Christian spirituality is radically *one.* As there is only "one Lord, one faith, one baptism, one God and Father of us all" (Eph 4:5-6), so also there is only one spirituality, one life from and in and toward God. There are, however, a variety of ways in which individuals and groups accept and respond to that one life, given their different depths of faith, their different religious experiences, and their different needs brought to the word of God in Christ. When we speak of a variety of spiritualities, we are speaking not of specifically different spiritualities but only of the different ways of embracing and living the one life of God in Christ through the Spirit.

The Second Vatican Council clarifies the meaning of that one spiritual life. It is a life defined by a mission, namely, to consecrate the world in the ordinary activities of ordinary life. *Lumen gentium* names these ordinary activities of spiritual men and women: "their ordinary married and family life, their daily labor, their mental and physical relaxation, if carried out in the Spirit, and even the hardships of life if patiently borne." All these activities, in all their ordinariness, become spiritual sacrifices offered to the Father, and through them believers "consecrate the world itself to God" (LG 34), *ad maiorem dei gloriam,* "for the greater glory of God," as Jesuit spirituality proclaims. The consecration of the world accomplished in the ordinariness of life, though a difficult task, is not an extraordinary one. In a Church that is communion, it is a communional concern, specifying a communional dimension of Christian spirituality. The apostolic task of consecrating the world to the greater glory of God is accomplished not by individuals in isolation, but by believers in communion with one another and with the triune God, who dwells within and waits to be revealed in their world.

The sacraments of Christian initiation provide the starting point for describing an apostolic spirituality. The sacrament of baptism ritualizes believers' acceptance of the gift of God in Christ through the Spirit and their gift of themselves in return. It marks their ritual entrance into the mystery of the life of God in Christ and into the communion-Church that is the body of Christ. Baptism, however, is not only the ritual entrance into the life of God and of grace, it is also the root for any subsequent flowering of that life. It is intimately connected to the sacrament of confirmation, sometimes called the sacrament of the Christian apostolate. It hardly seems necessary to state the further connection of both baptism and confirmation to apostolic spirituality. Among the symbolic actions performed in both baptism and confirmation is an anointing with oil. The Gregorian prayer for the consecration of this oil gives insight into the meaning of these anointings. "Confirm this creature, chrism . . . in order that, when the corruption of the first birth shall have been swallowed up, the pure perfume of a life pleasing to you may yield fragrance in each one's temple, after the infusion of the *sanctifying force of anointing*" (emphasis added). The sacramental water reveals the forgiveness of sins, the swallowing up of the corruption deriving from the first, biological birth by the second, ritual birth in Christ and his Spirit. The sacramental oil reveals other meanings.

A brief excursus on the meaning of the oil used in sacramental actions is necessary at this point. The economic history of the biblical lands shows that oil, grain, and wine were its most important agricultural products, so much so that when Deuteronomy enumerates the blessings of God, it specifies this trio (7:13). Enoch teaches that the tree of life in the center of Paradise was an olive tree (*2 Enoch* 8:5, Rec. A and B) and rabbinical teaching insists that the olive leaf which the dove brought back to Noah as the first sign of the new world and the new life after the great flood (Gen 8:11) came from this tree of life.[300] Oil, so vital in the economic life of Israel, took on in its symbolic life the meaning of life from and with God. Enhanced with such symbolic meaning, oil is an obvious candidate for use in ritual actions, like Christian initiation, which emphasize God-given and God-directed life.

Anointing reveals to the initiates, and to the assembled communion, that the new life in communion is to be a life in Christ, a holy life, guaranteed by the Spirit received in the water, who is not only a Holy Spirit but also and necessarily a holifying (or sanctifying) Spirit. The symbolic water and oil do not mean that the Spirit of God was not given in baptism but only in confirmation. Rather do they mean that the life of the Spirit initiated in the water is to be a life of holiness, a life of spiritual sacrifices in ordinary life, guaranteed by the Spirit of God, who is at once a Spirit of life and a Spirit of holiness. As Jesus was designated *Christos* by the Holy Spirit in his Jordan baptism, so too are believers designated *christos* by the same Spirit in their initiation. The external anointings done by the representatives of the local Church proclaim, make explicit, and celebrate this internal fact.[301]

This view of the essential relationship of baptism and confirmation, though articulated in somewhat different language, is not unlike the view of Thomas Aquinas. Aquinas does not doubt that confirmation is given, as the very name implies, "to confirm what was previously given,"[302] including the Holy Spirit.[303] There is some completion of baptism in confirmation, but this must be carefully explained. Confirmation signifies a gift of *well-being*, not simply of *being*.[304] This well-being is compared to the situation of the apostles after Pentecost. Before Pentecost, they had already received the gift of the Spirit for their own life in the Spirit; at Pentecost, they were renewed in the same Spirit and driven to proclaim that life to others.[305] Similarly, at baptism, believers receive the gift of the Spirit for their own Spirit-filled lives and, at confirmation, they are renewed in the Spirit for the public proclamation of that life to others.

Aquinas locates the sacramental effectiveness of confirmation, not in the conferral of an absent Spirit, but in the strength given by a present Spirit to live a Christ-like life. We recall Latreille's cogent summary. "The person confirmed is deputed to a spiritual combat, which is distinguished from the spiritual combat of the baptized person as an external combat is distinguished from an internal combat, or as a public testimony is distinguished from a private."[306] Confirmation is not, as some contemporary interpreters would have us believe, the sacrament of adult age, for chronological age has nothing to do with it. It is the sacrament of perfect age, that age when Christians not only say they are possessed by the Spirit of God in Christ, but also live Spirit-filled lives. This returns any discussion of baptism and confirmation, and of the one Christian spirituality they ritualize, to the simplicity of the gospel: "Not everyone who says to me 'Lord, Lord,' shall enter the kingdom of heaven, but he who does the will of my Father who is in heaven" (Matt 7:21). The spirituality demanded of those who have been anointed by the Spirit of Christ into the communion-body of Christ is a spirituality of apostolic deeds to be done that confirmation proclaims, makes explicit, and celebrates as the perfection of the life gifted by the Spirit in baptism.

The communion ritually achieved in baptism and confirmation, sacraments which may be celebrated only once, is made manifest and made to grow time and time again in the celebration of the Eucharist. The Congregation for the Doctrine of the Faith expresses the situation correctly when it states that the communion that is the Church of Christ "is rooted not only in the same faith and the common baptism, but above all in the eucharist and the episcopate."[307] An extended line of commentators explains why that is so.

Paul's words are well known. "Because there is one bread, we who are many are one body, for we all partake of the one bread" (1 Cor 10:17). Not so well known, but equally apposite, are the words of Augustine: the Eucharist is the sacrament "through which the Church is made in the present age."[308] Vatican II is no less convinced. "Truly partaking of the body of the Lord in the breaking of the Eucharistic bread, we are taken up into communion with him and with one another" (LG 7). As we have stated several times throughout this book, the communion-Church is essentially Eucharistic. So also is the one apostolic spirituality which its members are called to live. Initiation into both the Church and its spirituality is ritually achieved not only in baptism and confirmation but also, and especially, in Eucharist.

Cosmology as Christian Secularity

For a full and adequate understanding of Christian spirituality, we need to ask how the new life of the Spirit is nourished and sustained. How can Christian believers continue to accept the theological facts of their anointing by the Holy Spirit and their apostolic calling for the consecration of the world? We name three ways. First, as we have just explained, they must participate in the rich sacramental life in the communion of Christ's body, especially that communion celebrated in Eucharist. Second, they must continually challenge themselves and be challenged by reflection on the word of God in Scripture and on its impact for the world in which they live. Third, they must discover and appreciate the goodness of the world created by God. Since we take the first and second ways to be self-evident for the nourishment of and challenge to spiritual growth, and therefore to require no extended explanation, we shall concentrate here on the third way: the world as the principal locus of life from and toward God.

Traditionally, the ambivalent Christian struggle against dualist systems which see creation as a war between good and evil, spirit and matter, have created tensions between Christian believers and the world. The world was and is regarded by many, along with the flesh and the devil, as something that potentially leads away from God. Today both the Church and its members are challenged not to separate themselves from the world, but to be both *in* and *for* the world.

We recall here an earlier discussion from chapter 5. "A secular quality is proper and special to lay persons" (LG 31). John Paul II explicated that teaching in his definition of the lay faithful, "disciples and followers of Christ, members of the Church who are present and active in the world's heart so as to administer temporal realities and order them toward God's reign." The secular quality special to lay persons, he insisted, must be read in a theological perspective and not in a sociological one. The term *secular* is to be understood in the light of the act of God "who has handed the world over to women and men so that they may participate in the work of creation, free creation from the influence of sin and sanctify themselves" (CL 15). We added then, and we add again now without apology, that the secular character of lay persons is to be understood also in the light of the incarnation.

The great Russian physicist and social activist, Andrei Sakharov, articulated the root of all his activities in his speech accepting the 1975 Nobel Peace Prize. "We should not minimize our sacred endeavors in this world . . . we must make good the demands of reason and create a life worthy of ourselves and of the goals we only dimly perceive."[309] Believers who are in Christ and who are anointed by his Spirit agree. They live in the world, know the world, value the God-gifted goodness of the world, and seek to permeate the world with the gospel Spirit of forgiveness, reconciliation, communion, and peace. Embracing Joel's and Peter's image of the messianic age as the age when "I shall pour out my Spirit upon all flesh" (Joel 2:28; Acts 2:17), they embrace "all flesh" on which the Spirit is poured and see themselves as communionally sharing in the messianic restoration of "all flesh" in this Spirit. They do this, not "to make good the demands of reason" but to make good their theological root in the God who creates all things, who saves them, and who recreates anew to life.

Lumen gentium declares the Church to be a great sacrament: a sacrament "of the unity of all mankind" (LG 1; SC 26) and "of salvation" (LG 48; AG 5). To be faithful to this task, to be not only the example in the world but also the sacrament, the sign and the instrument, in the world of salvation, forgiveness, reconciliation, communion, and peace, the Church cannot flee the world and its needs. As "the faithful herald of the gospel message of salvation in Jesus Christ, it belongs in the heart of the world."[310] This statement is but an echo of *Apostolicam actuositatem,* the document on the apostolate of the laity. Christ's redemptive work, and therefore the Church's sacramental redemptive work, involves the renewal of the temporal order. "The mission of the Church is not only to bring to people the message and grace of Christ, but also to penetrate and perfect the temporal sphere with the spirit of the gospel. . . . In fulfilling this mission of the Church the laity therefore exercise their apostolate both in the Church and in the world, in both the spiritual and the temporal orders" (AA 5).

In the council's judgment, the world is not a place to be avoided; it is to be embraced and brought to God. The council's message to the Church is clear: believers in communion with one another and with Christ through his Spirit are to be engaged in the world, to contribute to its development, and to root in it Christ and the God he makes known. It is this task that defines the apostolic spirituality to which the Church and its members in communion are called. No longer is matter believed to be necessarily at war with spirit. In the incarnation, as Dermot Lane notes, "the gulf between heaven and earth, between God and humans, between the supernatural and the natural, between the sacred and the secular . . . has once and for all been overcome, so that now we can glimpse heaven on earth, the supernatural in the natural, the sacred amidst the secular."[311] After the incarnation, nothing is exclusively secular, not even the world. The Church and the world are not opposites; the Church *is* the world in communion with the indwelling God and with the women and men who confess God's presence.

Communional ecclesiology, then, points to a new relationship between the Christian and the world. It retrieves an ancient and radical answer to the question: "What is the world?" The world is the good creation of the good God of Christ. Neither Vatican II, of course, nor the communion-Church for which it speaks, "sold out" to the world as we experience it. The Church continues to be called, and to respond to the call, to oppose the forces of evil that continue to plague the human spirit. Whole areas of life, or better of nonlife, violence, hatred, racism, sexism, selfishness, injustice, oppression, and other forms of evil, are not from the Spirit of communion and peace but from the spirit of darkness opposed to Christ and to Christ's people. An apostolic spirituality which embraces the world that God created good is never to be interpreted as embracing and canonizing also the evil that corrupts that good world.

The perennial conflict between the world as created good by God and the world as corrupted by evil keeps in focus an important theological fact for the Church in communion, the fact that it is not by human effort alone, not simply by horizontal communion, that the world will reach fulfillment. Human effort alone goes only so far; fulfillment is, ultimately, a gift of God's Spirit, a gift of vertical communion. Still, the world possesses its own goodness, which for Christians is rooted in and clarified by the incarnation of God. To discover God's presence in the world, and to clarify this presence for those who do not have eyes to see it, is to discover and to clarify a radically new relationship between the gospel of God in Christ through the Spirit and human historical circumstance.

Anthropology as Christian Secularity

In historical reality touched by the presence of Christ, the human person is central. The world is no more than the sphere in which people live their lives and believers carry out their communional mission. Vatican II states this in other words. "Faith throws a new light on everything, manifests God's desire for man's total vocation, and thus directs the mind to solutions which are fully human" (GS 11). It asks more searchingly: "What does the Church think of man? What recommendations seem needful for the upbuilding of contemporary society? What is the ultimate significance of human activity throughout the world? From the answers it will be increasingly clear that the people of God and the human race in whose midst it lives render service to each other" (GS 11).

Congar indicates some implications of the relationship between the world and the Church. The world is not set against the Church, in opposition to it; rather are they in profound and mutual interrelationship. "The world and history furnish the church with the matter for her own life and the conditions . . . for the carrying out of her mission." It is not simply a matter of the Church adapting to the times. "It is a question of assuming in Christ the matter of earthly history."[312] Despite, therefore, the supernatural character of the Church's vocation to the world, an ultimately otherworldly stance is rejected. Communional and apostolic spirituality responds to the needs of human history and of the concrete situation of the world, and draws the world into communion, reconciliation, and peace.

Gaudium et spes throws interesting light on the relationship between the Church and the world. It uses sparingly the image of the messianic people of God so prominent in *Lumen gentium*. It does this to repudiate any suggestion of a people somehow separated from, and privileged over, other people in the world. Instead, the council notes that "the communion of Christians realizes that it is truly and intimately linked with the human race and its history" (GS 1). And again, "the Church, at once a visible assembly and a spiritual communion, goes forward together with humanity and experiences the earthly lot of the world; she is like a leaven and a kind of soul for human society" (GS 40). The communion that is Church is not separate from the world; it is an intimate part of the world, of humankind and of human history. It is also called and challenged to be a leaven at the heart of that world and its people.

The Christian theological perspectives of creation, incarnation, sacrament, and grace throw positive light upon the world, and underscore God's call to his people to be in service to the world. The consecration of the world, bringing it to Christ and Christ to it, is the primary call and challenge to the believer in communion, who is to be in and for the world under the gracious promptings of the Holy Spirit.

Spirit-Rooted Spirituality

Lumen gentium underscores the presence and action of the Holy Spirit in the Church. The spirituality we present here is not a Pelagian spirituality deriving from believers' unaided action. It is, rather, a graced spirituality, deriving from the Spirit of God gracing every member of the communion. "By these gifts he makes them fit and ready to undertake the various tasks or offices advantageous for the renewal and upbuilding of the Church" (LG 12) and, therefore, also of the world. "The Holy Spirit was sent on the day of Pentecost that he might forever sanctify the church. . . . He is the Spirit of life. . . . [He] guides the church into the fullness of truth and gives her a unity of communion and service. . . . He makes the Church grow, perpetually renews her and leads her to perfect union with her spouse" (LG 4). This central role of the Holy Spirit in ecclesial, and therefore in secular, life has long been a belief of the Orthodox Churches. The Second Vatican Council was a first step in a rediscovery of that role by the Western Church.

Our presentation of the Church as a Spirit-graced communion is in line with the pneumatology, that is, the theology of the Spirit, proposed by Heribert Mühlen. Mühlen's fundamental thesis stands contrary to a thesis that has been traditional in Roman Catholic theology since Johann Adam Möhler in the nineteenth century. The Church can no longer be conceived, Mühlen argues, exclusively as a continuation of the incarnation of the Son of God. It is to be conceived also as the incarnation of the Holy Spirit according to the theological formula, at once Trinitarian and Christological, one person in many persons, the Holy Spirit in Christ and in the Church. In his important encyclical on the Holy Spirit, John Paul II states explicitly that the Church is the sacrament, the sign and the instrument, of the presence and action of both Christ and the Spirit. "All of this happens in a sacramental way," he explains, "through the power of the Holy Spirit who, drawing from the wealth of Christ's redemption, constantly gives life."[313]

Mühlen derives the concept of one mystical person *(una mystica persona)* from Augustine, who spoke of the "total Christ" as a communion of many persons having its source of unity in the Holy Spirit.[314] Pius XII embraced Augustine's total Christ in *Mystici Corporis,* and taught that the uncreated Spirit of God is the life-giving principle, the soul, of the total Christ, the mystical body, the Church.[315] The concept of one person in many persons has its roots in the biblical concept of corporate personality.[316] In the Old Testament, the focus is on the whole elect people. Individuals, such as Abraham, Moses, and David, find their importance not only as leaders but also as representatives of the entire people. This corporate notion underlies also the presentation of Jesus in the New Testament. It is only in corporate personality that one man can truly "give his life as a ransom for many" (Mark 10:45), or meaningfully say "as you did it to one of the least of my brethren, you did it to me" (Matt 25:31-40). For Mühlen, and for us, the Church in the Spirit is one total person, one great *I,* made up of one original ego, Christ, and many other egos, the believers who comprise it.[317]

Mühlen's pneumatology has ramifications for a communion-ecclesiology. The Church is anointed, as was Jesus, by the Holy Spirit. The one baptismal anointing of Jesus is matched by the many baptismal anointings of those who believe in him, and their formation into one mystical person.[318] Through their anointing, both Jesus and the communion of believers are designated (or "ordained") to God's work of sanctification and salvation in the world. Each takes on an apostolic task in salvation history. Peter explains to the Gentile Cornelius that "God anointed Jesus with the Holy Spirit" and that "he went about doing good and healing all who were oppressed by the devil, for God was with him" (Acts 10:38). Jesus' anointing, Peter argues, grounds his apostolic activity, and Luke agrees. "The Spirit of the Lord is upon me, because he has anointed me to preach good news to the poor" (4:18-21). The anointing of Jesus symbolizes his reception and acceptance of a mission from God. It makes him *christos,* Christ, the anointed one for others, the bearer of the Spirit.

The apostolic mission symbolized in the anointing of Jesus is symbolized also in the anointing of believers as *christos* and Christians. To the extent that the communion-Church shares in the mission of Jesus through the anointing of the Spirit, it can be said that the Church results from the Spirit. It can be said also that the Church is now, as Jesus was once, the bearer of the Spirit. Paul tells the Corinthians that "it is God who establishes us with you in Christ, and has commissioned us" (2 Cor 1:21). John explains to his Church that "the anointing which you received from him abides in you" (1 John 1:27). The anointing of the Christian is a commission to apostolic mission sealed by the Holy Spirit. Both the anointing and the commission abide in believers and in their communion as charisms for others.

The relation of believers to the anointing of Jesus places us squarely in the context of the great mysteries of Christianity: Trinity, incarnation, and grace. The anointing of Jesus is a mystery of grace, and of grace that is uniquely the Son's; for neither the Father nor the Holy Spirit appears in human form. With *Mystici Corporis,* which situates Christ as not only the head of the Church but also its sustainer and hypostasis, we can speak of two hypostatic unions. In the first, one human being is created by the hypostatic communion of the human and the divine in Jesus; in the second, one mystical person is created by the hypostatic communion of believers in Christ. The first is the result of the Son being sent by the Father for the salvation of the world; the second is the result of the Spirit being sent by the Son for its consecration.[319]

Sanctification names an action in which God chooses something for himself; *consecration* names an action in which something is set apart for God. The Spirit's anointing is at once sanctifying and consecrating. It sanctifies those anointed and consecrates their every action for God. In the case of Christ, sanctification results in the communion of the human and the divine in his person. His consecration results in a life lived everywhere and always for God and, therefore, for the salvation and consecration of the world. In the case of the Christian, sanctification results in the communion of believers with God and, therefore, with one another in the Church that is God's people. Their consecration results in a life in Christ through the Spirit, a life we have called a spiritual life, which results in the consecration of the world. The Church is in the world to be the sacrament, not only of Christ, but also of the Spirit, who sanctifies and consecrates both the Church and the world.

This model of the Church as "one person in many persons" is used by the Second Vatican Council, which draws an analogy between the mission of the second and third persons of the Trinity. "Just as the assumed nature [Christ's human nature] inseparably united to the divine Word serves him as a living instrument of salvation, so, in a similar way, does the communal structure of the Church serve Christ's Spirit, who vivifies it by way of building up the body" (LG 8). There is need for precision here, lest we conclude too much.

Classical Christology teaches that the second person of the Trinity, the Son, is consubstantial with us because he is personally (or, in Greek, *hypostatically*) united to a human nature like ours. He makes that human nature, therefore, unerringly holy. Classical pneumatology, on the other hand, teaches that the Spirit is not consubstantial with us because he is not personally united to a nature like ours. The Spirit is united to us in communion, and he makes us holy, therefore, not by divine pressure but by divinely respecting our free cooperation. Long human history demonstrates the sad fact that we frequently withhold that cooperation. The communion-Church in history, therefore, as the council does not shrink from confessing, is made up of sinners, "at the same time holy and always in need of being purified" (LG 8). It is, none the less, still the historical manifestation, the sign and the instrument, the sacrament of the Spirit of Christ.[320] As a sacrament of the Spirit, it is necessarily engaged in the consecration of the world.

Spirituality of the Ordinary

Monasticism, with its perceived tendency to flee the world, is no longer the ideal of an ecclesial spiritual life. The Church that is the sacrament in the world of Christ, the person in whom the divine and the human intersect, is challenged to be in the world the corporate person in whom the divine and the human continue to intersect. It is challenged to bring God to the world and to bring the world to God. It faces the task of developing a suitable program for the consecration and sanctification of the world, for a humanism which is Christ- and Spirit-centered and yet truly human and of this world. The challenge is to develop new forms of spirituality to extend and deepen the rule of God in the world. Thirty years ago, Congar submitted three signs of the quest for new actualizations of holiness, signs which have only been enhanced in the intervening years.

The first sign is the realization that religion in Christ and in his Spirit is not a water-tight compartment of life, the obligation of which can be met through Sunday Eucharist and other eccelesiastical actions. That perspective was dealt a death blow in the 1930's by the theology of Catholic Action, the message of which was clear. "Put Christ back into the whole of your life; don't be Christians only on Sundays; the faith is not an overcoat, to be hung up in the cloakroom of office or factory; it is a total quality which must inform the whole personality and its integral life."[321] Daily life is the stuff out of which authentic saints are made, living in and ordering the world according to the gospel of Christ.

The second sign is the deepening sense of the secular character of the Church as well as of the world (LG 30), and the creative probing of that secularity, such as we have sought to do. In this context, the spiritual life, life from and toward God, is nourished by a human life flowing from and toward communion with God and with our brothers and sisters. God is sought on earth as much as in heaven.

The third sign is that the saints who are held up in our day for the edification of the communion-Church achieve holiness in the ordinary circumstances of everyday life in the world, not in a flight from the world. Mother Teresa of Calcutta comes to mind as a translucent example of such holiness, which penetrates deeply into a spiritually impoverished world and reveals in it the love of God. Reflecting on the effect she had on countless people as a result of one appearance on BBC television, Malcolm Muggeridge seeks to explain. "Here was the answer. Just get on the screen a face shining and overflowing with Christian love; someone for whom the world is nothing and the service of Christ everything; someone reborn out of servitude to the ego and the flesh and into the glorious liberty of the children of God."[322] Mother Teresa's transparent spiritual life, her life from and toward

God, is the same "demonstration of the Spirit and of power, that your faith might rest not in the wisdom of men but in the power of God" (1 Cor 2:4-5) that the Church-communion and each of its members is called to for the consecration and salvation of the world.

In traditional spirituality, Christians were encouraged to be in the world as strangers. That approach fostered a deep opposition between the Church and its faithful, on the one hand, and a world hostile to its life of communional faith, hope, and love, on the other. To really live the Christian faith, it was supposed, withdrawal from the world and its attractions, its infamous "works and pomps," was demanded. In our times, the Catholic Church has reversed this approach and has invited its members to seek their sanctification through committed involvement in the sanctification of the world. Though Christian believers *are* pilgrims in this passing world, they are called and challenged to work for its betterment (GS 43).

Jesus prayed for his immediate disciples, and surely also for the generations that would follow them. "I do not pray that you take them out of the world, but that you keep them from the evil one" (John 17:15). God's first word to the first humans was just as definite about their location and function in the world: "Be fruitful and multiply and fill the earth and subdue it" (Gen 1:28). When God created *'ad'am*, God created her and him free, free to reject or to accept the divine will (DS 373–97). God first creates in the world a people in his image and then delivers the salvation of the world into their hands. A proper characteristic of an ecclesial spirituality in the world is obedience to God's will in whatever state of life believers find themselves. Jesus' "not what I will but what you will" (Mark 14:36) and Mary's "let it be done to me according to your word" (Luke 1:38) still stand as models of the free and sanctifying yielding of the believer to the rule of God.

Vocation, God's call to an individual believer, has both a narrow and a broad sense. In its narrow sense, *vocation* is the call of an individual believer to a particular life or function in the Church. In this sense, we speak of a vocation to the single life, the married life, the religious life, or the priestly life. In its broad sense, *vocation* denotes simply the doing of God's will. In this broader meaning, Christians in communion are invited to discern and to respond to their role in God's plan for the world in Christ through the Spirit. As the body of the Christ who declared himself to have come "not to be served but to serve" (Mark 10:45), they cannot discern their responsibility for the world in any terms other than *diakonia* ("service"). Christians may be pilgrims in the world, but they are not tourists. They are called to serve the salvation of God's present creation even as they pass through it to a future life.

Every age has its "master words" defining its relationship to Christ and his Spirit. "The mind of the middle ages answered to 'unity' and 'order'; during the first third of the sixteenth century, everybody was stirred by the 'gospel' and 'Christian freedom'; the eighteenth century was all for 'reason,' 'nature' and the sublime."[323] We suggest for our generation the master words *communion, commitment, responsibility, service.* These are more than mere vocabulary, for they express the deepest reality of the Church and of the Christian today. They may be challenging words, connoting difficult meanings for the majority of contemporary Christians, many of whom grew up in a tradition in which the master words were exclusively hierarchical. But they are words, and realities, that must be learned if the communion-Church is ever to be effective in fulfilling its Spirit-given mission in the world.

Under the Sign of the Cross

We set apart, as a fitting way to conclude this chapter and this book, two major Christian master words, *Love* and *the Cross.* Christian love, the inseparable love of God and of neighbor, grounds Christian action and contemplation and, indeed, the whole Christian life. In the Christian scheme of things, which is essentially communional or corporate, to love one's neighbor is to love God and to love God is to love one's neighbor. The concern for the consecration of the world we talked of is, and has to be, worked out in the light of Jesus' command: "You shall love the Lord your God with all your heart. . . . You shall love your neighbor as yourself" (Mark 12:30-31).

Though we, and the gospel, speak here of two commandments, in reality there is only one. There are no other commandments greater than this one-in-two. Paul has no doubt. "The commandments . . . are summed up in this sentence, 'you shall love your neighbor as yourself' . . . love is the fulfilling of the law" (Rom 13:9-10). John puts it concretely. "If any man says 'I love God' and hates his brother, he is a liar; for he who does not love his brother whom he has seen cannot love God whom he has not seen" (1 John 4:20). Matthew, as we have seen, makes the practical love of neighbor the basis for the great, final judgment (Matt 25:31-46).

Rahner explains that love of neighbor is not just one good act among many. It is the whole of the moral life, the very basis and essence of morality, without which there is no Christian morality. Under the gracious Spirit of God, love of neighbor becomes a saving act of the love of God. This neighbor-love is more than obedience to a gospel commandment; it is not done just for the sake of God, so that another human becomes only the material for the love of God. "Love of neighbor is the *primary act of love of God* . . . he who does not love the brother whom he sees, cannot love God whom he does not see. He can only love God whom he does not see by *loving his visible brother*."[324]

The Jewish mystic Martin Buber sums up this dimension of both Jewish and Christian teaching in a story. A man, filled with a great passion for God, abandoned the world of created things and wandered about in the great emptiness until he came to the gate of Mystery, where he knocked. "Someone within called out: 'What do you want?' 'I have proclaimed thy praise to the ears of mortal men and women but they were deaf to it. So now I come to thee, so that thou thyself mayest hear me and answer.' 'Turn back,' called the voice from within, 'there is no one to listen to you here. I have sunk my hearing in the deafness of mortal men and women.' "[325] The moral is clear: salvation is given in the genuine love of neighbor, for "he who loves his neighbor has fulfilled the law" (Rom 13:8).

Finally, a communional spirituality that brings to the world the life-giving word of God stands wholly under the sign of Christ's cross. The alternate yes and no that believers must say to the world, yes to God present in the world, no to everything that denies that presence, requires a turning away from ego-centrism to other-centrism. They require the denial of the self and the taking up of the cross (Mark 8:34). "There is never any serious spiritual life," Congar notes, "without a purification of faith, hope and love, the virtues by which we cleave to God, in order that it might be *to God* that we cleave, in himself and for himself."[326] This judgment is but a particular reflection of the universal place of the cross in the Christian life. "If I do not go away," Jesus explained to his disciples, "the Counselor will not come to you" (John 16:7). That going away, they came to understand, was his death, which was followed, they also came to understand, by his resurrection and the sending of the Spirit (1 Pet 3:18; Rom 1:1-4). Resurrection, and the Spirit-Counselor-Advocate, always come not only after but also at the price of the cross.

Paul's paradox still states this mystery best. It may stand as summary of, and conclusion to, everything we have said in this book about the Church as communion with our brothers and sisters and with the Trinitarian God. "When I am weak, then I am strong" (2 Cor 12:9-10). Here Paul does not praise powerlessness as such. He merely rejoices in the fact that, when wounded believers share the cross of Christ, they just as surely share the power and the glory and the Spirit of his resurrection.

Summary

In this chapter, on the foundation of the communional ecclesiology presented in this book, we considered the Christian spiritual life as life from and with the Trinitarian God. This life is radically one, despite the variety of ways in which it is modified; it is defined by the mission of consecrating and sanctifying the world that God created good, and is therefore apostolic. It is also essentially secular, as the Second Vatican Council and recent popes have cogently explained, not in the sense that believers are to acquiesce in the many evils that continue to bedevil our world, but in the sense that God has handed the world over to Christians "so that they may participate in the work of creation, free creation from the influence of sin and sanctify themselves" (CL 15). The master words for Christian spirituality in the modern age are *communion with, commitment to, involvement in, responsibility for,* and above all *service to* God in the world and to the world in God. Such spirituality is rooted in the Holy Spirit of God who distributes gifts to all believers to fit them to "seek the kingdom of God by engaging in temporal affairs and by ordering them according to the plan of God" (LG 31). It is rooted also, and of necessity, in the great one-in-two commandment of communion: "You shall love the Lord your God with all your heart . . . you shall love your neighbor as yourself" (Mark 12:30-31). It stands, therefore, also under the sign of Christ's Cross.

Questions for Reflection

1. How do you understand the assertion that the spiritual life is life from and in and with God, and that it is essentially apostolic?

2. Reflect on the theology behind the idea of *Christian secularity.* How does this idea relate to the central theological idea of incarnation?

3. Two images were used in this chapter for the situation of the Church-communion in the world, the image of the Church as a leaven at the heart of the world and the image of the Church as sacrament of communion and of peace. What is your understanding of these images and of how they might be realized in action?

4. Reflect on Mühlen's theological formula that describes the Holy Spirit as "one person in many persons." How does this formula relate to the communion-Church?

5. Recall two well-known gospel sayings. The first is the great commandment: "You shall love the Lord your God with all your heart . . . you shall love your neighbor as yourself" (Mark 12:30-31). The second is the basis of final judgment: "As you did it [not] to one of the least of these my brethren, you did it [not] to me" (Matt 25:40, 45). Reflect on how these two sayings relate to the things discussed in this chapter.

Selected English Bibliography

Baptism, Eucharist and Ministry. Geneva: World Council of Churches, 1982.

Baum, Gregory. *Compassion and Solidarity: The Church for Others.* New York: Paulist, 1990.

Boff, Leonardo. *Church, Charism and Power: Liberation Theology and the Institutional Church.* New York: Crossroad, 1988.

_____. *Ecclesiogenesis: Base Communities Reinvent the Church.* Maryknoll: Orbis, 1986.

Bouyer, Louis. *The Church of God: Body of Christ and Temple of the Holy Spirit.* Chicago: Franciscan Herald, 1982.

Brown, Raymond E. *Antioch and Rome: New Testament Cradles of Catholic Christianity.* New York: Paulist, 1983.

_____. *The Churches the Apostles Left Behind.* New York: Paulist, 1984.

_____. *The Community of the Beloved Disciple.* New York: Paulist, 1979.

_____. *Priest and Bishop: Biblical Reflections.* New York: Paulist, 1970.

Buber, Martin. *The Kingship of God.* New York: Harper and Row, 1967.

Butler, Basil Christopher. *The Theology of Vatican II.* Westminster: Christian Classics, 1981.

Called and Gifted: Reflections of the American Bishops Commemorating the Fifteenth Anniversary of the Issuance of the Decree on the Apostolate of the Laity. Washington: National Conference of Catholic Bishops, 1980.

Carlen, Claudia, ed. *The Papal Encyclicals 1939–1958.* Wilmington, Del.: McGrath, 1981.

Carmody, Denise L. and John T. Carmody. *Bonded in Christ's Love: An Introduction to Ecclesiology.* New York: Paulist, 1986.

The Church as Communion. Entire issue of *The Jurist* 1976.

The Church Local and Universal. Geneva: World Council of Churches, 1990.

Congar, Yves M. J. *Diversity and Communion.* Mystic, Conn.: Twenty-Third Publications, 1984.

_____. *I Believe in the Holy Spirit.* 3 vols. London: Chapman, 1983.

_____. *Lay People in the Church: A Study for a Theology of Laity.* Westminster: Newman, 1959.

_____. *The Mystery of the Church.* Baltimore: Helicon, 1965.

_____. *The Word and the Spirit.* London: Chapman, 1986.

Cooke, Bernard. *Ministry to Word and Sacraments.* Philadelphia: Fortress, 1976.

Cwiekowski, Frederick J. *The Beginnings of the Church.* New York: Paulist, 1988.

Doyle, Dennis M. *The Church Emerging from Vatican II: A Popular Approach to Contemporary Catholicism.* Mystic, Conn.: Twenty-Third Publications, 1992.

Dulles, Avery. *A Church to Believe In.* New York: Crossroad, 1982.

_____. *Models of the Church.* New York: Doubleday, 1974.

_____. *The Resilient Church.* New York: Doubleday, 1977.

Dulles, Avery and Patrick Granfield. *The Church: A Bibliography.* Wilmington, Del.: Michael Glazier, 1985.

Dunn, James D. G. *Unity and Diversity in the New Testament.* London: SCM, 1981.

Fahey, Michael A., ed. *Catholic Perspectives on Baptism, Eucharist and Ministry.* Lanham: University Press of America, 1986.

Galot, Jean. *Theology of the Priesthood.* San Francisco: Ignatius Press, 1984.

Halton, Thomas. *The Church.* Wilmington, Del.: Michael Glazier, 1985.

Hamer, Jerome. *The Church Is a Communion.* New York: Sheed and Ward, 1964.

Harrington, Daniel J. *God's People in Christ: New Testament Perspectives on the Church and Judaism.* Philadelphia: Fortress, 1980.

Kasper, Walter. *Theology and Church.* New York: Crossroad, 1989.

Kloppenberg, Bonaventure. *The Ecclesiology of Vatican II.* Chicago: Franciscan Herald, 1970.

Kress, Robert. *The Church: Communion, Sacrament, Communication.* New York: Paulist, 1985.

Lash, Nicholas and Joseph Rhymer, eds. *The Christian Priesthood.* London: Darton, Longman, Todd, 1970.

Lawler, Michael G. *Symbol and Sacrament: A Contemporary Sacramental Theology.* New York: Paulist, 1987.

_____. *A Theology of Ministry.* Kansas City: Sheed and Ward, 1990.

Lohfink, Gerhard. *Jesus and Community: The Social Dimension of Christian Faith.* Philadelphia: Fortress, 1982.

Lubac, Henri de. *Catholicism: A Study of Dogma in Relation to the Corporate Destiny of Mankind.* New York: Longman's, 1950.

_____. *The Splendour of the Church.* London: Sheed and Ward, 1979.

Meyendorff, John. *Catholicity and the Church.* New York: St. Vladimir's Press, 1983.

Meyer, Harding and Lukas Vischer, eds. *Growth in Agreement: Reports and Agreed Statements of Ecumenical Conversations.* New York: Paulist, 1984.

Miller, John H., ed. *Vatican II: An Interfaith Appraisal.* Notre Dame: University of Notre Dame Press, 1966.

Moltmann, Jürgen, *The Spirit of Life: A Universal Affirmation.* Minneapolis: Fortress, 1992.

_____. *Theology of Hope.* New York: Harper and Row, 1967.

Montague, George T. *The Holy Spirit: Growth of a Biblical Tradition.* New York: Paulist, 1976.

O'Gara, Margaret. *Triumph in Defeat: Infallibility, Vatican I and the French Minority Bishops.* Washington: Catholic University of America Press, 1988.

O'Meara, Thomas F. *Theology of Ministry*. New York: Paulist, 1983.

Osborne, Kenan B. *Priesthood: A History of the Ordained Ministry in the Roman Catholic Church*. New York: Paulist, 1988.

Rahner, Karl. *The Church after the Council*. New York: Herder,1966.

____. *The Shape of the Church to Come*. New York: Seabury, 1974.

____. *Theological Investigations*. Vols. 2, 5, 6, 10, 12, 14, 17, and 20. New York: Crossroad, 1963–1968.

Richard, Lucien, ed. *Vatican II: The Unfinished Agenda*. New York: Paulist, 1987.

Schillebeeckx, Edward. *The Church with a Human Face*. New York: Crossroad, 1985.

____. *The Mission of the Church*. New York: Seabury, 1973.

Schmaus, Michael. *The Church as Sacrament*. Kansas City: Sheed and Ward, 1975.

Stransky, Thomas F. and John B. Sheerin, eds. *Doing Truth in Charity. Ecumenical Documents I*. New York: Paulist, 1982.

Sobrino, Jon. *The True Church and the Poor*. Maryknoll: Orbis, 1984.

Sullivan, Francis A. *The Church We Believe In*. New York: Paulist, 1988.

____. *Magisterium: Teaching Authority in the Catholic Church*. New York: Paulist, 1983.

Tillard, Jean-Marie R. *Church of Churches: The Ecclesiology of Communion*. Collegeville, Minn.: The Liturgical Press, 1992.

Viviano, Benedict T. *The Kingdom of God in History*. Wilmington, Del.: Michael Glazier, 1988.

Zizioulas, John D. *Being as Communion: Studies in Personhood and the Church*. New York: St. Vladimir's Press, 1985.

Endnotes

[1]Walter Kasper, *Theology and Church* (New York: Crossroad, 1989) 1.

[2]See *Mysterium Ecclesiae* 5; *AAS* 65 (1973) 402–04.

[3]*AAS* 54 (1962) 792; cf. GS 62.

[4]*AAS* 56 (1964) 621.

[5]Yves M. J. Congar, *I Believe in the Holy Spirit* (London: Chapman, 1983) 2:5.

[6]Thomas Aquinas, ST 2–2.1.9.ad 5. See also Albert the Great, *In III Sent.,* d.25, q.2, a.2; the Catechism of the Council of Trent, in Henri de Lubac, *La Foi chrétienne. Essai sur la structure du Symbole des Apotres* (Paris: Aubier, 1969) 169, n. 5; Berard L. Marthaler, *The Creed* (Mystic, Conn.: Twenty-Third Publications, 1987) 307.

[7]See Michael G. Lawler, *Symbol and Sacrament: A Contemporary Sacramental Theology* (New York: Paulist, 1987) 134–36.

[8]Juan Alfaro, "Faith," *Sacramentum Mundi: An Encyclopedia of Theology* (New York: Herder, 1968) 2:315.

[9]Kasper, *Theology and Church*, 8.

[10]Walter M. Abbott, ed., *The Documents of Vatican II* (London: Chapman, 1966) 3–4.

[11]International Theological Commission, *Theses on the Relationship Between the Ecclesiastical Magisterium and Theology* (Washington: United States Catholic Conference, 1977) 6.

[12]Gerard Philips, *L'Église et son mystere au IIe Concile du Vatican* (Paris: Desclee, 1966) 1:7, 59 and 2:24, 54, 159.

[13]See its final report, "The Church, in the Word of God, Celebrates the Mysteries of Christ," 2.C.1.

[14]*Catholic International* 3 (1992) 761, n. 1.

[15]Jerome Hamer, *The Church Is a Communion* (New York: Sheed and Ward, 1965); see also Yves Congar, *Divided Christendom. A Catholic Study of the Problem of Reunion*, trans. M. Bousfield (London: Bles, 1939); Henri

de Lubac, *Catholicism: A Study of Dogma in Relation to the Corporate Destiny of Mankind*, trans. L. Sheppard (New York: Longman's, Green, and Co., 1950); Marie Joseph Le Gouillou, *Mission et unité. Les exigences de la communion* (Paris: Desclee, 1960); Gustave Martelet, *Les idées maîtresses de Vatican II* (Paris: Desclee, 1966).

[16]Yves Congar, "The People of God," John H. Miller, ed., *Vatican II: An Interfaith Appraisal* (Notre Dame: University of Notre Dame Press, 1966) 199.

[17]Edward Schillebeeckx, *L'Église du Christ et l'homme d'aujourd'hui selon Vatican II* (Paris: Mappus, 1965).

[18]Augustine, *In Joannis Evangelium Tractatus VI* 1.7: PL 35:1428.

[19]Cf. Didymus, *In Psalmos* 71.5: PG 39:1465.

[20]Edward Schillebeeckx, *Jesus: An Experiment in Christology*, trans. Hubert Hoskins (New York: Seabury, 1979) 438.

[21]It is worthy of note that the New Testament speaks of *ekklesia*-Church only after the resurrection, and to designate those men and women who believe in the resurrection of Jesus. *Ekklesia* is inseparably linked to the death-resurrection of Jesus. See W. G. Kümmel, "Kirchenbegriff und Geschichtbewusstein in der Urgemeinde und bei Jesus," *Symbolae Biblicae Upsalienses* 1 (Zürich: Max Niehans, 1943).

[22]Cf. *Theophile d'Antioche: Trois Livres a Autolychus*, trans. J. Sender (Paris: Cerf, 1948) 1.12.85; Rufinus, *Comment. in Symb. Apost.*: PL 21:345; Augustine, *De Vita Christiana*: PL 40:1033; *Enarr. in Ps XXVI*: PL 36:200; Jerome, *Comment. in Ps 104*: *Corpus Christianorum, Series Latina* 72:230.

[23]Congar, *I Believe in the Holy Spirit*, 3:5; Jürgen Moltmann, *The Spirit of Life: A Universal Affirmation* (Minneapolis: Fortress, 1992) 1.

[24]See *Catholic International* 3 (September 1992) 767.

[25]John D. Zizioulas, *Being as Communion* (New York: Saint Vladimir's Seminary Press, 1985) 140.

[26]See Augustine, *Confessions* 1.1: PL 32:661.

[27]*Acta Synodalia* 2/1:455.

[28]*AAS* 55 (1963) 848.

[29]*The Tablet* (7 November 1987) 1203.

[30]Kasper, *Theology and Church*, 151.

[31]Pier Cesare Bori, *Koinonia: l'idea della communione nell' ecclesiologia recente et nel Nuovo Testamento* (Brescia: Paideia, 1972) 107–19.

[32]See Bori, *Koinonia,* 33–38.

[33]See Abbott, *The Documents of Vatican II*, 99.

[34]Hamer, *The Church Is a Communion*, 175. Emphasis in original.

[35]Moltmann, *The Spirit of Life*, 118.

[36]See, for instance, Mannes D. Koster, *Ekklesiologie im Werden* (Paderborn: Schoning, 1940), who argues that *people of God* is the best image of the Church.

[37]Robert Kress, *The Church: Communion, Sacrament, Communication* (New York: Paulist, 1985) 66.

[38]Karl Rahner, "Membership of the Church According to the Teaching of Pius XII's Encyclical '*Mystici Corporis*,' " *Theological Investigations,* vol. 2 (Baltimore: Helicon, 1967) 83.

[39]Yves M. J. Congar, "The People of God," *Vatican II: An Interfaith Appraisal,* ed. Miller, 199.

[40]Neils Dahl, *Des Volk Gottes* (Oslo: Dybwad, 1941) 278.

[41]Here we abstract completely from the disputed questions as to which letter(s) the Apostle Paul actually wrote. It makes no difference to any thesis in this book.

[42]Heinrich Schlier, "Leib Christi," *Lexicon für Theologie und Kirche,* ed. Joseph Hofer and Karl Rahner (Freiburg: Herder, 1957–1965) 6:908.

[43]See Jean-Marie R. Tillard, *Church of Churches: The Ecclesiology of Communion* (Collegeville, Minn.: The Liturgical Press, 1992) 37–38.

[44]*Catholic International* 3 (1992) 764, n. 11.

[45]John Paul II, "Address to the Roman Curia," *AAS* 83 (1981) 745–47.

[46]See "The Church: Local and Universal," a study commissioned and received by the Joint Working Group between the Roman Catholic Church and the World Council of Churches (Geneva: World Council of Churches, 1990).

[47]Jean Jacques von Allmen, "L'Église locale parmi les autres églises locales," *Irenikon* 43 (1970) 512.

[48]Lucien Cerfaux, "Les images symboliques de l'église dans le Nouveau Testament," *Vatican II: Textes et Commentaires* (Paris: Cerf, 1967) 256.

[49]Bernard Cooke, "Synoptic Presentation of the Eucharist as Covenant Sacrifice," *Theological Studies* 21 (1960) 25; see also X. Leon-Dufour, "Prenez! Ceci est mon corps pour vous," *Nouvelle Revue Théologique* 104 (1982) 225–27.

[50]Augustine, *Enarr.in Pss.56* 1: PL 36:662; compare *Sermo 341*: PL 39: 1499–1500; *Sermo 455*: PL 38:265; *Enarr.in Pss.60* 2–3: PL 36:724.

[51]We are fully aware of the contrived nature of the word *communional*. We select it deliberately over *communal* to provoke reflection on, first, the word and, then, the dynamic reality of the Church which is communion.

[52]See Zizioulas, *Being as Communion,* 209–14.

[53]Miller, *Vatican II,* 200.

[54]Zizioulas, *Being as Communion,* 140.

[55]Karl Rahner, "Current Problems in Christology," *Theological Investigations*, vol. 1 (London: Darton, Longman and Todd, 1965) 150.

[56]Bernard, *De Consid.* 5.11.24: PL 182:802; *Sermo 88 de Diversis* 1: PL 183:706; *In Die Pent.Sermo 1* 1: PL 183:323.

[57]Thomas Aquinas, *Comment.in Romanos*, cap.1, lectio 6, *Opera Omnia* (Roma: Fiaccadori, 1860) 13:15.

[58]Thomas Aquinas, *In III Sent.* d.25, q.1, a.1, qa.1, obj.4; also ST 2–2.1.6.

[59]George T. Montague, *The Holy Spirit: Growth of a Biblical Tradition* (New York: Paulist, 1976) 268.

[60]Michael Schmaus, "Holy Spirit," *Encyclopedia of Theology: The Concise Sacramentum Mundi,* ed. Karl Rahner (New York: Seabury, 1975) 642.

[61]C. Perrot, "Prophètes et prophétisme dans le Nouveau Testament," *Lumière et Vie* (November–December 1973) 29–30.

[62]*Didache* 11, *The Fathers of the Church. The Apostolic Fathers* (Washington: Catholic University of America Press, 1962) 181.

[63]*The Martyrdom of Saint Polycarp* 16, ibid., 159.

[64]Justin Martyr, *Dialogus Cum Tryphone* 82: PG 6:670.

[65]Irenaeus, *Adv.Haereses* 5.6.1: PG 7:1137.

[66]Origen, *Contra Celsum* 7.11: PG 11:1435.

[67]Cited in Eusebius, *Historia Eccles.* 5.17: PG 20:474.

[68]Avery Dulles, "The Succession of Prophets in the Church," *Concilium* 34 (New York: Paulist, 1968) 56.

[69]John Henry Newman, *Discourses to Mixed Congregations* (London, 1886) 279; Charles Journet, *The Church of the Word Incarnate*, vol. 1 (New York, 1955) 132–41.

[70]Yves M. J. Congar, *The Word and the Spirit* (San Francisco: Harper and Row, 1986) 68.

[71]Benedict T. Viviano, *The Kingdom of God in History* (Wilmington, Del.: Michael Glazier, 1988) 13.

[72]Martin Buber, *The Kingship of God* (New York: Harper and Row, 1967) 58. Cf. L. Kohler, *Old Testament Theology*, trans. A. S. Todd (Philadelphia: Fortress, 1953) 30. "The one fundamental statement in the theology of the Old Testament is this: God is the ruling Lord."

[73]C. H. Dodd, *The Parables of the Kingdom* (London: Collins, 1967) 29–61.

[74]J. Weiss, *Jesus' Proclamation of the Kingdom of God* (Philadelphia: Fortress, 1971).

[75]See Rudolph Schnackenburg, *God's Rule and Kingdom* (New York: Herder, 1963) 61.

[76]Edward Schillebeeckx, *God the Future of Man* (London: Sheed and Ward, 1977) 156.

[77]Jürgen Moltmann, *Theology of Hope* (New York: Harper and Row, 1967) 326–38.

[78]Novatian, *De Trin.* 29: PL 3:944.

[79]Pope Paul VI, *AAS* 55 (1963) 848.

[80]See Emile de Backer, "Tertullian," *Pour l'histoire du mot sacramentum,* ed. J. de Ghellinck (Louvain: Spicilegium Sacrum Lovaniensis, 1924) 145–46.

[81]Tertullian, *De Spectaculis* 24: PL 1:655–56; *De Baptismo* 1: PL 1:1197; *De Idolatria* 6: PL 1:668; *De Corona* 11: PL 2:91; *De Jejuniis* 10: PL 2:966–68; *Adv. Marcionem* 1.14:PL 2:262.

[82]Tertullian, *Adv. Marcionem* 4.34: PL 2:442; *De Pudicitia* 10: PL 2:1000; *De Corona* 3: PL 2:79.

[83]Peter Lombard, *Liber Sententiarum* 4, dist.1, cap.4. See Lawler, *Symbol and Sacrament*, 29–34.

[84]Karl Rahner, "History of the World and Salvation History," *Theological Investigations* 5 (London: Darton, Longman and Todd, 1966) 98.

[85]Aquinas, ST 3.60.1.

[86]Ibid., 3.60.2.

[87]Ibid., 3.62.3; cf. 3.62.1. ad1.

[88]Ibid., 3.60.1.

[89]Kasper, *Theology and Church*, 115.

[90]See Avery Dulles, *Models of the Church* (New York: Doubleday, 1974).

[91]Otto Semmelroth, "The Integral Idea of the Church," J. Feiner, ed., *Theology Today. Renewal in Dogma,* trans. P. White and R. Kelly (Milwaukee: Bruce, 1964) 137.

[92]Robert Bellarmine, *Controversiae*, 2, lib.3, cap.2.

[93]John F. Clarkson et al., *The Church Teaches* (St. Louis: Herder, 1961) 93.

[94]See the speech of Bishop Emile de Smedt, *Acta Concilii Vaticani II*, vol. 1, part 4 (Roma: Typis Polyglottis Vaticani, 1971) 142–44.

[95]Paul Tillich, *Systematic Theology*, vol. 3 (Chicago: University of Chicago Press, 1967) 162–72.

[96]*AAS* 35 (1943) 199–200.

[97]Abbott, *The Documents of Vatican II*, 99.

[98]Peter Lombard, *Liber Sententiarum*, 4, dist.1, c.4.

[99]"Huius iustificationis causae sunt . . . instrumentalis item sacramentum baptismi, quod est 'sacramentum fidei' *sine qua* nulli umquam contigit iustificatio."

[100]It is not without significance that, when Leo XIII enthroned Scholasticism as the official Roman Catholic way to do philosophy and theology, it was not the Scholasticism of the post-Reformation centuries he lauded but that of the thirteenth.

[101]See George Worgul, *From Magic to Metaphor: A Validation of the Christian Sacraments* (New York: Paulist, 1980).

[102]Piet Fransen, "Sacraments: Signs of Faith," *Readings in Sacramental Theology*, ed. C. Stephen Sullivan (Englewood Cliffs, N.J.: Prentice Hall, 1964) 62. Emphasis in original.

[103]Edward Schillebeeckx, *Christ the Sacrament of the Encounter with God* (New York: Sheed and Ward, 1966) 83.

[104]Thomas Aquinas, *In IV Sent.* d.15, q.1., a.3, sol.3 ad 2; d.6, q.1, a.3, sol.2; d.4, q.3, a.3, qc.4, obj.1.

[105]Ibid., d.6, q.1, a.3, sol.1; cf. ST 3.68.8.

[106]Louis Villette, *Foi et Sacrement: de Saint Thomas à Karl Barth* (Paris: Bloud et Gay, 1964) 40.

[107]Fransen, "Sacraments: Signs of Faith," 63.

[108]Cf. Colman O'Neill, "The Role of the Recipient and Sacramental Signification," *The Thomist* 21 (1958) 257–301; 508–40.

[109]Ibid., 275–76. Emphasis in original.

[110]Obvious difficulties with such an approach arise in the baptism of infants. But the baptism of adults, not the baptism of infants, is the paradigm for sacramental baptism. The baptism of infants is an exception to a general rule. For one solution to such difficulties, see ibid., 276–96.

[111]Aquinas, ST 3.49.3. ad 1.

[112]See "Propositions on the Doctrine of Christian Marriage," 2, 3, *Contemporary Perspectives on Christian Marriage,* ed. Richard Malone and John R. Connery (Chicago: Loyola University Press, 1984) 15, 19–21.

[113]See Augustine, *Epist.98* 5: PL 33:362. See also Aquinas, ST 3.68.9; "Baptism for Children," *The Rites of the Catholic Church* (New York: Pueblo Publishing, 1976) 188; Jean Charles Didier, *Faut-il baptiser les enfants?* (Paris: Cerf, 1967).

[114]Schillebeeckx, *Jesus,* 438.

[115]Jean-Marie R. Tillard, "Sacramental Questions: The Intentions of Minister and Recipient," *Concilium* 31 (1967) 130.

[116]Gustave Martelet, "Sixteen Christological Theses on the Sacrament of Marriage," Malone and Connery, *Contemporary Perspectives on Christian Marriage,* 279.

[117]Juan Alfaro, "Faith," *Sacramentum Mundi: An Encyclopedia of Theology* (New York: Herder, 1968) 2:315.

[118]Ladislas Örsy, "Faith, Sacrament, Contract and Christian Marriage: Disputed Questions," *Theological Studies* 43 (1982) 385.

[119]Tillard, "Sacramental Questions," 130.

[120]Susan Wood, "The Marriage of Baptized Non-Believers: Faith, Contract and Sacrament," *Theological Studies* 48 (1987) 294.

[121]Aquinas, ST 1–2.59.1.

[122]Ibid., 1–2.49.1.

[123]Ibid., 1–2.49.3.

[124]Ibid., 3.69.4.

[125]Aquinas, *In IV Sent.* d.6, q.1, a.3, ad 5: "Faith directs intention, and without [faith] intention cannot be right."

[126]*The Rites of the Catholic Church* (New York: Pueblo Publishing, 1976) 310.

[127]Semmelroth, "The Integral Idea of the Church," 137.

[128]Leonardo Boff, *Church: Charism and Power* (New York: Crossroad, 1988) 78.

[129]Henri de Lubac, *Meditations sur l'Église* (Paris: Aubier, 1953) 175. Cf. Schillebeeckx, *Christ the Sacrament.*

[130]Augustine, *Epist. 187*: PL 33:845.

[131]Semmelroth, "The Integral Idea of the Church," 139.

[132]Contemporary Roman Catholic theology has specified the traditional sacrament of holy orders as three separate sacraments, diaconate, priesthood, and episcopacy. That means that there are now *nine* officially recognized sacramental paradigms.

[133]Kress, *The Church*, 62.

[134]See Lawler, *Symbol and Sacrament*, 32.

[135]Walter Kasper, "Wort und Sakrament," *Glaube und Geschichte* (Mainz: Grunewald, 1970) 309.

[136]Karl Rahner, *The Church and the Sacraments* (New York: Herder, 1963) 41–74. See also Schillebeeckx, *Christ the Sacrament*; Lubac, *Catholicism*, 291.

[137]Francis A. Sullivan, *The Church We Believe In: One, Holy, Catholic and Apostolic* (New York: Paulist, 1988) 9.

[138]Thomas F. O'Meara, *Theology of Ministry* (New York: Paulist, 1983) 15.

[139]Donal Dawe, *Jesus: The Death and Resurrection of God* (Atlanta: John Knox, 1985).

[140]Alfred Loisy, *L'Évangile et l'Église* (Paris, 1902) 111.

[141]See Arnold Van Gennep, *The Rites of Passage* (London: Routledge and Kegan Paul, 1960).

[142]Cyril, *Catechesis XX, Mystagogica*, 3: PG 33:1079.

[143]Paul Bernier, *Ministry in the Church: A Historical and Pastoral Approach* (Mystic, Conn.: Twenty-Third Publications, 1992) 204.

[144]Cyprian, *De Zelo et Livore* 12: PL 4:646.

[145]Aquinas, *In IV Sent.* d.7, q.7, a.2, qc.2.

[146]Ibid., a.2.

[147]Aquinas, ST 3.84.4. ad 2.

[148]Jean Latreille, "L'adulte chrétienne, ou l'effet du sacrement du confirmation chez Saint Thomas d'Aquin," *Revue Thomiste* 58 (1957) 20.

[149]Ignatius, *Ad Philadelph.* 4, *The Fathers of the Church*, vol. 1 (Washington: Catholic University of America Press, 1962) 114.

[150]Gregory Dix, *The Shape of the Liturgy* (London: Dacre, 1945) 21.

[151]See Lawler, *Symbol and Sacrament*, passim.

[152]See Patrick McCaslin and Michael G. Lawler, *Sacrament of Service: A Vision of the Permanent Diaconate Today* (New York: Paulist, 1986); John F. Booty, *The Servant Church: Diaconal Ministry and the Episcopal Church* (Wilton, Conn.: Morehouse-Barlow, 1982).

[153]See *Origins*, 5 November 1987, 380.

[154]Cf. O'Meara, *Theology of Ministry*, 136.

[155]See McCaslin and Lawler, *Sacrament of Service*.

[156]Augustine, *Sermo 340* 1: PL 38:1484.

[157]See Enrique Nardoni, "Charism in the Early Church since Rudolph Sohm: An Ecumenical Challenge," *Theological Studies* 53 (1992) 168.

[158]Ernst Käsemann, "Ministry and Community in the New Testament," *Essays on New Testament Themes*, trans. W. J. Montague (Naperville, Ill.: Allenson, 1964) 74.

[159]See Edward Schillebeeckx, *Ministry: Leadership in the Community of Jesus Christ* (New York: Crossroad, 1981) 24.

[160]Augustine, *In Joannis Evangelium* 6.1.7: PL 35:1428.

[161]See Yves Congar, *Lay People in the Church: A Study for a Theology of Laity* (Westminster: Newman Press, 1959) 1–21.

[162]Jean Danielou, *A History of Early Christian Doctrine. The Theology of Jewish Christianity* (Philadelphia: Westminster, 1964).

[163]Ignace de la Potterie, "L'Origine et le sens primitif du mot 'laic,'" *Nouvelle Revue Théologique* 80 (1958) 840–53.

[164]James D. G. Dunn, *Unity and Diversity in the New Testament* (Philadelphia: Westminster, 1977) 114.

[165]C. Spicq, *Les Épîtres Pastorales*, 1 (Paris: Gabalda, 1969) 73. See also J. Crowe, *The Acts* (Wilmington, Del.: Michael Glazier, 1979) 156; Schillebeeckx, *Ministry*, 18, 146.

[166]See Spicq, *Les Épîtres Pastorales*, 71.

[167]See Ignatius, *Epist. ad Magnesios* 2: PG 5:758; *Epist. ad Smyrneos* 8–9: PG 5:714; *Epist. ad Polycarpum*: PG 5:718.

[168]Ignatius, *Epist. ad Smyrneos* 8: PG 5:714.

[169]Ignatius, *Epist. ad Ephesios* 4: PG 5:714.

[170]Irenaeus, *Adv. Haereses*, 4.26.3–4: PG 7:1053.

[171]Ibid., 3.3: PG 7:848–54.

[172]Cf. David Power, *Ministers of Christ and His Church* (London: Chapman, 1969) 45.

[173]Cyprian, *Epist. LXV* 3: PL 4:396.

[174]Cyprian, *Epist. LXIX* 8: PL 4:406.

[175]Cyprian, *Epist. XXVII* 1: PL 4:298.

[176]Cyprian, *Epist. LXVII* 4–5, *Saint Cyprien: Correspondence*, ed. Louis Bayard (Paris: Belles Lettres, 1925) 229–31; see also Patrick Granfield, "Episcopal Election in Cyprian: Clerical and Lay Participation," *Theological Studies* 37 (1976) 41–52.

[177]Cyprian, *Epist. LIX* 5: PL 4:336.

[178]Cyprian, *Epist. LXVI* 1: PL 4:398; also *Epist. LXVII, Saint Cyprien*, 228.

[179]Cyprian, *Epist. 1* 1, *Saint Cyprien*, 2.

[180]Cyprian, *Epist. LXI* 3, ibid., 195.

[181]Cyprian, *Epist. XII* 1, ibid., 33; *Epist. V* 2, ibid., 13.

[182]Cyprian, *Epist. XVIII* 2, ibid., 51.

[183]There is an earlier use of the word *laikos,* in Clement of Rome's Letter to the Corinthians. But it is not clear that the word has the connotation which will be given it later by Clement of Alexandria and succeeding generations. See Alexandre Faivre, "The Laity in the First Centuries: Issues Revealed by

Historical Research," *Lumen Vitae* 42 (1987) 132. See also his *Les Laïques aux origines de l'Église* (Paris: Centurion, 1984) 13–57.

[184]Clement, *Stromatum* 3.12: PG 8:1191.

[185]Bernard Cooke, *Ministry to Word and Sacraments* (Philadelphia: Fortress, 1980) 557.

[186]Jerome, *Comment. in Isaiam Prophetam* 5.19: PL 24:185.

[187]Tertullian, *De Exhortatione Castitatis* 7: PL 2:922.

[188]See Nathan Mitchell, *Mission and Ministry: History and Theology of the Sacrament of Order* (Wilmington, Del.: Michael Glazier, 1982) 207–15; also Pierre Van Beneden, *Aux origines d'une terminologie sacramentelle: ordo, ordinare, ordinatio* (Louvain: Spicilegium Sacrum Lovaniense, 1974).

[189]Innocent I, *Epist. II* 3.5: PL 20:472.

[190]Leo I, *Epist. XIV* 4: PL 54:672–73.

[191]Gratian, *Decretum* 2, Causa 12, q.1, c.7.

[192]See Jacques Gaudemet, *L'Église dans l'Empire Romain* (Paris, 1958) 176–79.

[193]See Henri de Lubac, *Corpus Mysticum: l'eucharistie et l'église au Moyen Age* (Paris: Aubier, 1949).

[194]MAN 22:982.

[195]Dix, *The Shape of the Liturgy*, 34.

[196]See L. Duchesne, ed., *Vita Zephyrini*, 1:139, cited in Schillebeeckx, *Ministry*, 152, n. 44.

[197]Guerricus, *De Purificatione B. Mariae Sermo* 5: PL 185:87.

[198]Yves Congar, "L'ecclésia ou communauté chrétienne, sujet integrale de l'action liturgique," *La Liturgie d'apres Vatican II* (Paris, 1967) 241–82; see also B. Botte, "Note historique sur la concelebration dans l'église ancienne," *La Maison Dieu* 35 (1953) 9–23; R. Raes, "La concelebration eucharistique dans les rites orientaux," ibid., 24–47.

[199]See "Propositions on the Doctrine of Christian Marriage," 2, 3, *Contemporary Perspectives on Christian Marriage,* ed. Malone and Connery, 15, 19–21.

[200]John Paul II, "Communion, Participation, Evangelization," *Origins* 10 (1980) 135. He repeated the idea of a Church "in the heart of the world" in his address to the bishops of Scotland in October 1992. See "Specialis Filia Romanae Ecclesiae," *Catholic International* 4 (1993) 5. See also LG 31 and CL 15.

[201]*AAS* 64 (1972) 208.

[202]Dermot Lane, *The Reality of Jesus* (New York: Paulist, 1975) 137.

[203]See, for example, John Paul II, "Unity in the Church's Mission with Diversity in Apostolates," *L'Osservatore Romano* 723, n. 8, 22 February 1982, 6; "On Liberation Theology," *Origins* 8 (1979) 600; "The Church in Rural Africa," *Origins* 10 (1980) 23; "Specialis Filia Romanae Ecclesiae," *Catholic International* 4 (1993) 5.

[204]*AAS* 38 (1946) 149.

[205]Richard P. McBrien, *Catholicism* (San Francisco: Harper and Row, 1981) 662.

[206]Ibid., 56.

[207]Congar, *Lay People in the Church*, 1–21; Karl Rahner, "L'Apostolat de Laïcs," *Nouvelle Revue Théologique* 78 (1956) 3–32.

[208]See, for instance, CL 4; also his "Address to the Bishops of Switzerland" and his "Address to the Priests of Switzerland," *AAS* 71 (1985) 56, 64, 67.

[209]Robert Kinast, "Laity View Their Roles in Church and World," *Origins* 17 (1987) 95–99.

[210]Ibid., 96.

[211]*AAS* 63 (1971) 924.

[212]Bernier, *Ministry in the Church*, 204

[213]Alexandre Ganoczy, "'Splendors and Miseries' of the Tridentine Doctrine of Ministries," *Concilium* 10 (1972) 75.

[214]See Dulles, *Models of the Church*.

[215]Daniel Donovan, *What Are They Saying about the Ministerial Priesthood?* (New York: Paulist, 1972) 3.

[216]See Abbott, *The Documents of Vatican II*, 532 , and *Vatican Council II: The Conciliar and Post-Conciliar Documents*, ed. Austin Flannery (New York: Costello, 1975) 863.

[217]John A. T. Robinson, "Christianity's 'No' to Priesthood," *The Christian Priesthood*, ed. N. Lash and J. Rhymer (London: Darton, Longman and Todd, 1970) 4. See also Raymond E. Brown, *Priest and Bishop: Biblical Reflections* (London: Chapman, 1971); Kenan B. Osborne, *Priesthood: A History of the Ordained Ministry in the Roman Catholic Church* (New York: Paulist, 1988) 40–85; Edward Schillebeeckx, *Ministry: A Case for Change* (New York: Crossroad, 1981).

[218]"Ratio Fundamentalis," *AAS* 62 (1970) 330.

[219]Ibid., 330.

[220]Ibid., 357.

[221]See J. P. Audet, "Literary Forms and Contents of a Normal *Eucharistia* in the First Century," *Studia Evangelica: Papers Presented to the International Congress on the Four Gospels in 1957* (Berlin, 1959) 643–44.

[222]Augustine, *Sermo 340* 1: PL 3:1483.

[223]*Called and Gifted: Reflections of the American Bishops Commemorating the Fifteenth Anniversary of the Issuance of the Decree on the Apostolate of the Laity* (Washington: NCCB, 1980).

[224]See *The Rites of the Catholic Church as Revised by the Second Vatican Ecumenical Council* (New York: Pueblo Publishing, 1980) 2:90–99.

[225]See Zizioulas, *Being as Communion*, 214–25.

[226]See Lawler, *Symbol and Sacrament*, 230, 129–42.

[227]"Some Aspects of the Church," 2.8.

[228]See Jean-Marie R. Tillard, *Church of Churches: The Ecclesiology of Communion* (Collegeville, Minn.: The Liturgical Press, 1992) 29–33.

[229]Zizioulas, *Being as Communion*, 233.

[230]David Power, "The Basis for Official Ministry in the Church," *Official Ministry in a New Age*, ed. James Provost (Washington: Canon Law Society of America, 1981) 66.

[231]See Lawler, *Symbol and Sacrament*, 229.

[232]"Some Aspects of the Church Understood as Communion," 3:11.

[233]*The Rites*, 91.

[234]Herve Legrand, "The Presidency of the Eucharist According to the Ancient Tradition," *Worship* 53 (1979) 428, 435. Cf. Susan Wood, "The Sacramentality of Episcopal Consecration," *Theological Studies* 51 (1990) 479–96.

[235]Bernard Botte, "L'Ordre d'apres les prieres d'ordination," *Études sur le sacrement de l'ordre*, ed. J. Guyot (Paris: Cerf, 1957) 13–25; "Caractère collegial du presbyterat et de l'episcopat," ibid., 97–124; "Collegial Character of the Priesthood and the Episcopate," *Concilium* 4 (New York: Paulist, 1965) 177–83. See also Joseph Lecuyer, *Études sur la collegialité episcopale* (Le Puy: Mappus, 1964) 57–79.

[236]Irenaeus, *Adv.Haer.* 3.3: PG 7:848–49; cf. Tertullian, *De Praescript.* 36: PL 2:49.

[237]Tillard, *Church of Churches*, 286.

[238]Gregory the Great, *Epist.VIII* 3: PL 77:933.

[239]See Bonaventure, *Prima Controversia Generalis* 3; *De Ecclesia Militante* cap.2; and *Controversia V* cap.4.

[240]See O. Rousseau, "La vraie valeur de l'episcopat dans l'église, d'apres d'importants documents de 1875," *Irenikon* 29 (1956) 121–42, 143–50.

[241]See Gregory the Great, *Letters*, book 13.1: PL 77:1253.

[242]See Hans Küng, *Infallible? An Inquiry* (New York: Doubleday, 1971); Gustave Thils, *L'infaillibilité pontificale: sources, conditions, limites* (Gembloux: Duculot, 1969); Francis A. Sullivan, *Magisterium: Teaching Authority in the Catholic Church* (New York: Paulist, 1983); Margaret O'Gara, *Triumph in Defeat: Infallibility, Vatican I and the French Minority Bishops* (Washington: Catholic University of America Press, 1988).

[243]MAN 52:1213.

[244]Tillard, *Church of Churches*, 282.

[245]Karl Rahner, "On the Relationship Between the Pope and the College of Bishops," *Theological Investigations* 10 (New York: Crossroad, 1977) 55.

[246]Ibid., 63.

[247]See Lawler, *Symbol and Sacrament,* 29–34.

[248]Tertullian, *Adv. Valentinianos* 16: PL 2:569; *De Praescript. Adv. Haer.* 13: PL 2:26; ibid., 2: PL 2:40; *De Virginibus Velandis* 1: PL 2:889.

[249]Cyprian, *Epist. 63* 14, *Saint Cyprien: Correspondence*, 209; *Epist. 59*,

ibid., 174. For the contributions of both Tertullian and Cyprian, see Michele Maccarone, *Vicarius Christi: Storia del Titolo Papale* (Roma: Lateranum, 1952) 26–35.

[250]See Edward J. Kilmartin, "Apostolic Office: Sacrament of Christ," *Theological Studies* 36 (1975) 246.

[251]Pius XII, *Mediator Dei, AAS* 39 (1947) 538–39, 553–56; *Mystici Corporis, AAS* 35 (1943) 232–33; Paul VI, *Mysterium Fidei, AAS* 57 (1965) 761–63.

[252]Kilmartin, "Apostolic Office," 225.

[253]Jean Galot, *Theology of the Priesthood* (San Francisco: Ignatius Press, 1984) 45. Cf. Edward Schillebeeckx, *The Church with a Human Face* (New York: Crossroad, 1985) 85–89; Cooke, *Ministry,* 343–48; O'Meara, *Theology of Ministry* (New York: Paulist, 1983) 32–33.

[254]See McCaslin and Lawler, *Sacrament of Service.*

[255]See his preface to Bernard D. Marliangeas, *Cles pour une théologie du Ministère: in persona Christi, in persona Ecclesiae* (Paris: Beauchesne, 1978) 6. The entire work should be consulted for the question here under discussion, namely, *vicarius Christi-vicarius ecclesiae.*

[256]See Michael G. Lawler, *Secular Marriage, Christian Sacrament* (Mystic, Conn.: Twenty-Third Publications, 1985).

[257]Botte, *La Tradition Apostolique*, 45, 57.

[258]Marliangeas, *Cles pour une théologie du Ministère*, 14.

[259]Apostolic Constitution *Pontificalis Romani, AAS* 60 (1968) 373.

[260]See Edward J. Kilmartin, "Ministère et ordination dans l'église chrétienne primitive," *La Maison Dieu* 138 (1979) 49–92.

[261]Schillebeeckx, *Ministry*, 30.

[262]Cf. *Ratio Fundamentalis, AAS* 62 (1970) 329. "Every priest is taken from the people of God and constituted for this same people. But although priests, in virtue of the sacrament of orders, carry out the task of both father and teacher, nevertheless with all the Christian faithful, they are disciples of the Lord. . . . They are brothers among brothers, as members of one and the same body of Christ." See also Yves Congar, "Ministères et structuration de l'église," *La Maison Dieu* 102 (1970) 7–20, and "La hierarchie comme service selon le Nouveau Testament et les documents de la tradition," *L'episcopat et l'église universelle* (Paris: Cerf, 1962) 67–100.

[263]Mitchell, *Mission and Ministry*, 302.

[264]See Sullivan, *The Church We Believe In,* 213, for an attempted reconciliation of this fact.

[265]In this chapter, we focus exclusively on the various Christian communions. To maintain our focus, we prescind entirely from any consideration of the gifts of God outside these communions.

[266]*AAS* 35 (1943) 202.

[267]*AAS* 42 (1950) 571.

[268]We vividly recall Tromp saying frequently in an ecclesiology class "as I said in *my* encyclical."

[269]*Acta Synodalia Concilii Vaticani Secundi* (Roma, 1970) 1.4.15. Emphasis added.

[270]*Acta Synodalia*, 3.1.177.

[271]See Sullivan, *The Church We Believe In*, 25.

[272]It is noteworthy that, in these two texts, the Latin *subsistere* is rendered variously by the English "dwell" and "exist," both of which obscure the connection between these two texts and the crucial one in LG 8. See Abbott, *The Documents of Vatican II*, 23, 348, 356.

[273]*AAS* 56 (1964) 1012–13.

[274]We cite from the English translation, *Church: Charism and Power* (New York: Crossroad, 1988) 75.

[275]*AAS* 77 (1985) 758–59.

[276]Sullivan, *The Church We Believe In*, 29.

[277]See the explanation of these terms in Abbott, *The Documents of Vatican II*, 355. "Implicit in the use of these terms . . . is the idea that the more a church has of the structures of the Catholic Church, the more it approaches the ideal of the church. On this institutional scale of measurement, some are more properly called churches than others, and the Decree regards Eastern Churches as practically sister Churches of the Roman Catholic Church. Another reason, of course, for the expression 'ecclesial communities' . . . is that some Christian bodies do not wish to be called 'church.'"

[278]Louis Bouyer, *The Church of God: Body of Christ and Temple of the Holy Spirit*, trans. Charles Underhill Quinn (Chicago: Franciscan Herald Press, 1982) 512.

[279]Yves Congar, *Diversity and Communion*, trans. John Bowden (Mystic, Conn.: Twenty-Third Publications, 1985) 94.

[280]*AAS* 59 (1967) 853.

[281]See Congar, *Diversity and Communion*, 202, n. 12.

[282]Sullivan, *The Church We Believe In*, 35.

[283]Eusebius, *Historia Ecclesiastica* 5.23–25: PG 20: 490–510.

[284]See Congar, *Diversity and Communion*, 17–18.

[285]Abbott, *The Documents of Vatican II*, 177.

[286]*Baptism, Eucharist and Ministry* (Geneva: World Council of Churches, 1982) 2.D.6.

[287]See "Baptism, Eucharist and Ministry: An Appraisal," *Origins* 17 (1987) 402–06.

[288]*The New Baltimore Catechism* (New York: Benziger, 1953) 137.

[289]See Harding Meyer and Lukas Vischer, eds., *Growth in Agreement: Reports and Agreed Statements of Ecumenical Conversations* (New York: Paulist, 1984) 45.

[290]See Susan Wood, "The Sacramentality of Episcopal Consecration," *Theo-*

logical Studies 51 (1990) 479–96.

²⁹¹Those who are skilled in ecumenical matters will, no doubt, recognize the resemblance of our suggestion to that of the Bonn Agreement between the Anglican and the Old Catholic communions in 1931. See Meyer and Vischer, *Growth in Agreement*, 37.

²⁹²This approach has recently been dubbed "Romanity" by Geoffrey Wainwright. See his response to the Congregation for the Doctrine of the Faith's letter on "The Church as Communion," *Catholic International* 3 (1992) 770.

²⁹³See Avery Dulles, "The Church, The Churches, and the Catholic Church," *Theological Studies* 33 (1972) 199–234.

²⁹⁴Yves Congar, "The People of God," Miller, *Vatican II: An Interfaith Appraisal*, 199.

²⁹⁵*AAS* 35 (1943) 223.

²⁹⁶Gregory Baum, "The Ecclesial Reality of the Other Churches," *Concilium* 4 (New York: Paulist, 1965) 82.

²⁹⁷Cited from Congar, *I Believe in the Holy Spirit,* 1:4.

²⁹⁸Karl Rahner, *Spiritual Exercises,* trans. Kenneth Baker (New York: Herder, 1965).

²⁹⁹Hans Urs von Balthasar, "The One Spirituality of the Church," *Theology Digest* 10 (1962) 189.

³⁰⁰*Gen.Rabba* 33.20c.30.

³⁰¹See Origen, *Comment.in Joannem VI:* PG 11:111D; Methodius, *Convivium Decem Virginum* 8.8: PG 12:83; Eusebius, *De Eccles. Theologia* 3.15: PG 15:515; Tertullian, *De Bap.* 6: PL 1:1207.

³⁰²Aquinas, ST 3.72.7. ad 2.

³⁰³Ibid., 3.84.4. ad 2.

³⁰⁴Aquinas, *In IV Sent.* d.7, q.1, a.1, qa.2 ad 1.

³⁰⁵Ibid., d.7, q.7, a.2, qa.2.

³⁰⁶Latreille, "L'adulte chrétienne," 20.

³⁰⁷"The Church as Communion," *Catholic International* 3 (1992) 764.

³⁰⁸Augustine, *Contra Faustum* 12.20: PL 42:265.

³⁰⁹Andrei Sakharov, *Memoirs* (New York: Vintage Books, 1992) xiii.

³¹⁰John Paul II, "Specialis Filia Romanae Ecclesiae," *Catholic International* 4 (1993) 5.

³¹¹Lane, *The Reality of Jesus*, 137.

³¹²Yves M. J. Congar, "God's People on Man's Journey," *Proceedings of the Third World Congress for the Lay Apostolate* , vol. 1 (Rome: Committee for International Congresses, 1967) 113.

³¹³*AAS* 78 (1986) 891. See 891–94.

³¹⁴Heribert Mühlen, *Una Mystica Persona: la Chiesa come il mistero dello Spirito Santo in Christo e nei cristiani: una persona in molte persone* (Roma: Citta Nuova, 1968) 27. See Augustine, *Enarr.in Pss.17* 51: PL 36:154; *Enarr.in Pss.90* 11: PL 37:1159; *In Joannis Evangel.* 21.8: PL 35:1568.

[315]*AAS* 35 (1943) 220.

[316]H. Wheeler Robinson, *Corporate Personality in Ancient Israel* (Philadelphia: Fortress, 1980).

[317]Mühlen, *Una Mystica Persona*, 164–67, 170–76.

[318]Ibid., 300–07, 404–38.

[319]Ibid., 307–16.

[320]Ibid., 511–41.

[321]Congar, *Lay People in the Church*, 394.

[322]Malcolm Muggeridge, *Something Beautiful for God* (London: Fontana, 1971) 31–32.

[323]Congar, *Lay People in the Church*, 414.

[324]Karl Rahner, "The Unity of the Love of God and Love of Neighbor," *Theology Digest* 15 (1967) 93.

[325]Cited in Moltmann, *The Spirit of Life*, 250–51.

[326]Congar, *Lay People in the Church*, 426. Emphasis in original.

Index